Ronnie L Littlejohn is Professor of Philosophy and Director of the Center for Asian Studies at Belmont University, Nashville. He is the author of many articles in the field of Chinese and comparative philosophy, and also of a collection of essays on the Daoist classic *Liezi*, as well as previous works on ethics and theology.

'Littlejohn organizes his introduction around the central metaphor of a spreading kudzu vine, whose roots, trunk, stalks, branches, and leaves grow beneath, in, around, and over the vast and complex terrain of Chinese culture. He does a marvellous job exploring the origins, developments, and transformations of Daoism by guiding readers through canonical texts, across historical contexts, and around expressions of Daoism in fine art, popular symbols, literature, ritual, and other forms of material culture. The result is a masterful and comprehensive introduction to this protean, venerable, and vital tradition that will engage and enlighten novices and experts alike and delight anyone interested in Chinese religion, philosophy, or culture.' – *Philip J Ivanhoe, Reader-Professor of Philosophy, City University of Hong Kong*

'A marvellously detailed and highly readable history of Daoist religion and culture. The book also presents a wealth of information on how Daoism has shaped Chinese philosophy, politics and art throughout the centuries. A must-read for anyone who wants a fuller appreciation of Chinese history, and highly recommended for introductory classes on Chinese religions.' – *James Miller, Associate Professor of Chinese Religions, Queen's University, Ontario, Canada*

Daoism: An Introduction
Ronnie L Littlejohn
HB: 978 1 84511 638 5
PB: 978 1 84511 639 2

Jainism: An Introduction
Jeffery D Long
HB: 978 1 84511 625 5
PB: 978 1 84511 626 2

Islam: An Introduction
Catharina Raudvere
HB: 978 1 84885 083 5
PB: 978 1 84885 084 2

Zoroastrianism: An Introduction
Jenny Rose
HB: 978 1 84885 087 3
PB: 978 1 84885 088 0

Daoism

An Introduction

by

Ronnie L Littlejohn

I.B. TAURIS

LONDON · NEW YORK

Published in 2009 by I.B. Tauris & Co Ltd
6 Salem Road, London W2 4BU
175 Fifth Avenue, New York NY 10010
www.ibtauris.com

Distributed in the United States and Canada Exclusively by Palgrave Macmillan
175 Fifth Avenue, New York NY 10010

I.B. Tauris Introductions to Religion

ISBN: 978 1 84511 638 5 (HB)
ISBN: 978 1 84511 639 2 (PB)

A full CIP record for this book is available from the British Library
A full CIP record is available from the Library of Congress

Library of Congress Catalog Card Number: available

Designed and Typeset by 4word Ltd, Bristol, UK
Printed and bound in India by Thomson Press (India) Limited

Contents

Implements of Daoist Masters' Ritual Craft

Important Daoist sites in China

MONGOLIA

The Great Wall

Hengsha

Yellow River
(Huang He)

Fen River

Chang'an
(Xi' an)

Songshan

Louguantai ▲

Luoyang

▲ Huashan

Zhongnanshan

C H I N A

(Crane Call)
▲ Hemingshan

Chengdu ●

Yangzi River
(Chang jiang) ● Chongqing

Tsangpo

Brahmapura

I N D I A

Irrawaddy

Bangladesh

Pearl River
(Xi jiang)

Scale 1: 15 000 000

150   0   150   300   600 km.

VIETNAM

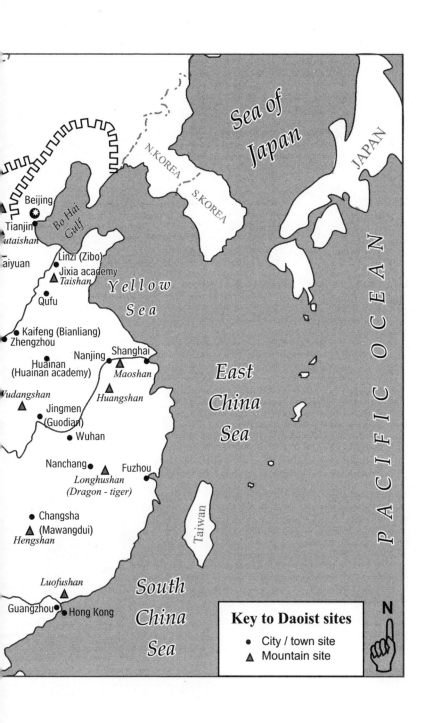

For my beloved sons, Jeff and Jeremy
my two Mo-ye swords

Introduction and Acknowledgements

The time is right for a broad overview of the history of Daoism in English. I.B.Tauris and my editor, Alex Wright, are to be commended for having the vision to commission a work of that sort. This book represents a next step in the explosion of scholarship about Daoism. It is made possible by the fact that we are positioned now to bring many strands of Daoist history together and follow the permutations of the great vine of Daoism as it has grown for over 2,000 years.

Since the mid-1990s we have had available two highly recognized introductions to Daoism in English: Kristofer Schipper's *The Taoist Body* (1994) and Isabelle Robinet's *Taoism: Growth of a Religion* (1997). However, for all its merits, Schipper's work does not put the reader down into the Daoist canon (authoritative collection) of texts with the sort of specificity that is needed, and Robinet's otherwise splendid work draws to a conclusion in the Yuan dynasty. I have tried to build on these two works, but I have attempted more. During the years since the publication of these two works, there has been an exponential growth in scholarly writing about Daoism, field research in Daoist practices and translation of Daoist texts. I believe that this present volume is a much more robust survey of the history of Daoist teaching and practice because it makes use of this wide range of new scholarship.

With the year 2000 publication of the indispensable two-volume collection of essays *Daoism Handbook*, edited by Livia Kohn, we have available to us a number of scholarly papers that treat crucial topics in Daoism rather exhaustively, based on our present stage of available materials. Each essay covers the history, texts, worldview and practices related to the topic, and I have used these essays as major sources for the current volume. Additionally, in 2007, the first of the two volumes of the massive *Encyclopedia of Taoism* (2007), edited by Fabrizio Pregadio, became available. This work provides both short essays and brief entries on an assortment of facts and data related to

Daoism. When completed, there will be over 1,700 entries and the present work is indebted to many of these.

Recently James Miller published *Daoism: A Short Introduction* (2003), making use of some of the best of the burgeoning scholarship on Daoism. From one point of view the strength of this brief work is that it groups the introduction to Daoism on a topical rather than historical frame (it has only a brief historical survey of five pages). However, this may also be seen as the weakness of the work, and the book you are about to read is an historical introduction to Daoism. Hans-Georg Moeller's *Daoism Explained: From the Dream of the Butterfly to the Fishnet Allegory* (2004) is a study of several of the principal analogies and themes of Daoist classical texts, with many provocative and inviting interpretations about the connection between these ideas and Western Continental philosophy. However, it was not a part of Moeller's intention to write a broad overview of Daoism, and thus both the present volume and Moeller's book can be used with profit. A recent work that does make an effort to connect its readers to the history of Daoist teaching and practice is Russell Kirkland's *Taoism: The Enduring Tradition* (2004). Although a fine work, the present book is unlike Kirkland's in its more explicit connections to Chinese cultural history, its extensive use of the Daoist canon of texts, and its intentional use of material culture (art, literature, archaeology) to contextualize and aid in the interpretation of Daoism's spread and development.

In writing this work, I have tried to distinguish it from those mentioned above by exploiting not only the availability of new English translations of texts from the Daoist canon but also the greater availability of these texts in Chinese. Here I must give credit to scholars such as Stephen Bokenkamp for his *Early Daoist Scriptures* (1997), D.C. Lau and Roger Ames for their *Yuan Dao: Tracing Dao to Its Source* (1998), Harold Roth for his *Original Tao: Inward Training (Nei-yeh) and the Foundations of Taoist Mysticism* (1999), Livia Kohn for her translations of Daoist texts on morality in *Cosmos and Community: The Ethical Dimension of Daoism* (2004), and again to Roth who will soon deliver a full translation of the *Master of Huainan*. An important aid in writing this book is the edited companion to the entire Daoist canon done by Schipper and Franciscus Verellen in 2004. A team of scholars assisted them in providing excellent overviews of the contents of virtually every work under the title *The Taoist Canon: A Historical*

Companion to the Daozang 2 vols, plus index. A substantial additional resource for doing a history of Daoism can also be found in Louis Komjathy's *Title Index to Daoist Collections* (2003). At the principal website for Daoist scholars known as *Daoist Studies*, Komjathy is also supervising the uploading of PDF facsimiles of the Chinese texts of the entire canon, with about 300 already available.

As for the connection between these new realities and my own work, my situation is not unlike that of the disciples you will read about in this book. I, too, have moved from teacher to teacher, learning from one and being sent to another to gain something more and something different. Nonetheless, perhaps because I am aware of the wide terrain of Daoist studies, I realize keenly that there will be many times throughout the reading of this work when scholars will feel I have been too superficial, or they will argue with me over this or that generalization. Since Daoism is so vast, other readers will wonder why I could have left out this figure or that text. Even so, my hope is that readers will find a great deal that is new or at least gathered in one place for the first time. My intention has been to make a study of this great tradition accessible, rewarding and interesting.

I owe tremendous gratitude to a great number of scholars and friends who have educated me, corrected me and inspired me in ways that gave me the confidence to undertake this project. Among these I include Roger Ames, Ned Davis, Jeff Dippmann, Norman Girardot, Jonathan Herman, Terry Kleeman, Livia Kohn, Louis Komjathy, Michael LaFargue, James Miller, Henry Rosemont, Jr, Hal Roth, Yong Huang and Robin Wang. I also want to express my appreciation to my colleagues in the Daoist Studies Group of the American Academy of Religion; the Association of Chinese Philosophers in America; the Society for the Study of Chinese Religions; the Society for Asian and Comparative Philosophy; and the working group Southeast Early Chinese Roundtable.

To a few friends I wish to express heartfelt thanks for reading portions of the text and offering many insightful suggestions. First, I want to thank Jeanie Reynolds for assisting me in the editing of the manuscript. She saved me from many errors. Next, I am grateful to P.J. Ivanhoe, my friend and teacher, who reminds me whenever I work with him that 'the outward appearance of great virtue (孔德) comes forth from the Dao alone'. To Erin Cline, my partner in field research with Daoist lineages in Fujian Province, thank you for reminding me often that the world is a spiritual vessel (神器). Finally, to Li Qingjun, my friend and teacher, thank you for always reminding me that the space between Heaven and Earth is inexhaustible in its possibilities for joy.

Preliminary Considerations and Conventions

For readers who have no experience with Chinese names and words I have included a quick pronunciation guide, which may be of some help. It is based on the pinyin system of Romanization of Chinese characters that I have used. Throughout the work, I translate most terms and titles into English. As is the general practice of I.B.Tauris, I have made all titles italic, including *Daodejing* 道德經 and *Zhuangzi* 莊子. I have indexed the English title from the text with its pinyin Romanization and the Chinese characters in the Glossary of Titles. I italicize key Chinese terms in the text, putting them in parentheses and in the Glossary of Names and Terms, where I have alphabetized the pinyin and provided the Chinese characters. I only rarely interrupt the text with characters, and when I do so it is in order to make a point of emphasis. Names of important Daoist masters and key people in Chinese culture and history are not italicized, but they appear in the Glossary of Names and Terms along with the Chinese characters that correspond to them.

The Glossary of Titles first gives the italic English title as it is in the text, followed by the number of the work in the Daoist canon in parentheses, the title in italicized pinyin Romanization, and then the Chinese characters. For example: *Code of Nuqing for Controlling Ghosts* (DZ 790) (*Nuqing guilu* 女青鬼律). I follow the accepted scholarly convention for capitalization in the pinyin titles of Chinese texts. Notice in the example above that 'guilu' is not capitalized. For the work number from the Daoist canon, I follow this convention: DZ (*Daozang* canon from the Ming period following Kristofer Schipper and Franciscus Verellen 2004), CT (*Concordance du Tao Tsang* after Kristofer Schipper 1975), or HY (*Combined Indices to the Authors and Titles of Books in Two Collections of Taoist Literature*, Harvard-Yenching Institute Sinological Index Series). Regrettably few of the works in the Daoist canon have been translated into English. Accordingly,

I use those translations that are available and made my own when needed.

The conventions I follow in the treatment of a few very important terms require some explanation because in speaking of Chinese thought in a Western language we use a terminology whose usefulness is severely limited.[1] I realize that not everyone will agree with the way I have handled these terms, but I believe that I have not done them damage and that knowing why I have chosen to treat them as I have will, at least, make the book easier to use. My view is that it is best if readers learn to incorporate certain terms into their own way of talking by watching how and when Daoists employ them, what other concepts are in the context and thereby learn to use them accordingly. Accordingly, I do not translate *dao* (sometimes rendered 'the Way' or 'the Dao'). *Dao* is not 'God' or 'Being itself'. Neither is it a substitute for 'the process of reality'. The *Daodejing*, arguably the most important classical text of Daoism, explicitly cautions against naming *dao*, which I take to mean something like 'Do not substitute another term for it!' I think it is preferable to look at the situations and contexts in which *dao* is used and thereby gather its meaning.

I also leave untranslated the concept of *qi* 氣, which is sometimes rendered into English as 'breath', 'pneuma' or 'spirit'. *Qi* is used in a variety of ways to talk about the energy of existence, but it is neither altogether immaterial nor completely material. It has internal dynamic correlational forces called *yin* 陰 and *yang* 陽 and coalesces into some combination of the Five Phases. I leave *yin* and *yang* untranslated, and when I refer to the Five Phases I mean the Chinese concept of *wu-xing* (五行: wood, metal, fire, water and earth). In their concrescence, these Five Phases of *qi* form all the things of which reality is composed, and each thing is constantly morphing into a new form, whether in our sensory range or not.

De 德, like *dao*, is another excellent example of a concept that has no single usage in its natural language home and is thus very difficult to reduce to an equivalent term in another target language such as English. It has most often been rendered as 'virtue' or 'power'. Typically, it is used to talk about the powerful charisma of an extraordinary person, but it is not delimited to a person's moral character. I do not translate *de*. Furthermore, *wu-wei* 無為 is made up of two Chinese characters, but when these occur together they form a single concept used for a sort of conduct fundamental to Daoism. When these two Chinese characters are doing the work of this single concept, I hyphenate them to indicate they are joined. This is different from a literal translation of each character separately, which would be *wu* = 'no' and *wei* = 'action' (i.e., 'no action' or 'inaction'). This is likewise the way I treat the important cosmological idea of *wu-xing*, or the Five Phases.

I sometimes translate *shen* 神 in a variety of ways as 'spirit', 'numinal entity' or 'numinal being,' and sometimes I leave it untranslated. A *shen* is a phasal form of *qi* that normally lies outside of our sensory range, but it is not some different kind of metaphysical 'stuff'. It is *qi*, but its phasal configuration is not (or not always) detectable by our senses. *Shen* often project presence, even giving the sense of another self-consciousness in the way the presence of another person does. However, while *shen* is mostly used of numinal beings, it is sometimes used of something that is not self-conscious (e.g., some trees, caves, mountains, rivers are *shen*). I translate *gui* 鬼 as 'ghost' because, as far as I know, it is always used of entities that exhibit properties associated with ghosts in the West (e.g., transparent insubstantiality, telekinesis, association with those believed to have died, and the like). *Shen* and *gui* commonly betoken conscious entities along a continuum of being, extending from the nonsentient to the highest reaches of the empyrean, but they are certainly not always moral or entirely good or all evil in the ways in which a Western reader might take the terms 'demon' or 'God'. So I do not translate *gui* as 'demon' or *shen* as 'god' or 'God'. Some *gui* are charged with inflicting punishments, but this does not make them demons in the Western sense of some metaphysical sort of being that is different in kind from humans. They may be deranged and wild, but they are not always so. Using the term 'demon' to translate *guishen* can be seriously misleading. I translate *xian* 仙 as 'immortal'. *Xian* are self-conscious beings with greatly amplified powers over their phasal forms. One of these powers is the ability to live a long life in phases we can sense, or even to live indefinitely in and out of our sensory range. However, as we shall see, there is much more to a *xian* than merely power over death.

Jing 經, as in the title of the great Daoist text the *Daodejing*, is often rendered into English as 'scripture'. I use 'classic'. 'Text' is not strong enough to indicate the status and authority given to these works, but 'scripture' belongs to the religious language of the West and may be misleading. Admittedly, of course, *jing* is the Chinese character used by Buddhists to render the Sanskrit 'sutra'. Sutras in that tradition are 'words of the Buddha' and typically are what Westerners would know as 'scriptures'. Likewise, I am well aware that many Daoist *jing* are said to have come directly from *shen* or to have been written in marvelous ways (e.g., Bao Jing's [260–327 CE] observation of a text being written by a *shen* on the wall of his cave on Songshan Mountain). Usually, *jing* are composed when Daoist masters are in altered states of consciousness, but not always. In fact, Daoist masters continue even today to write in celestial scripts that vary according to the lineages in which they have received training, and some of these scripts have no natural language counterpart. Celestial script is used on talismans and charms, and even written in the air with incense sticks during rituals. But no standard *jing* of the tradition, and no text in the Daoist canon, is written entirely with any version of this celestial script. Some Daoist texts, especially the *Daodejing* and works in the Lingbao lineage vine, have been considered to possess talismanic or ritual powers when read or recited. Nevertheless, in spite of these extraordinary attributions to these texts, I want to avoid translating *jing* as 'scripture' so that I do not create a preconception in the mind of the reader. However, I am content to allow the reader to disagree and prefer to use 'scripture' if he or she chooses.

Throughout this text I speak of Daoist 'masters' when describing the teachers, founders and even ritual experts in the history of Daoism. In the classical texts of Daoism, such as the *Daodejing* and the *Zhuangzi*, teachers are simply 'masters' (*zi*). It is not until much later in Daoist history that the term *daoshi* (道士) becomes common. However, that appellation may be used of a Daoist master, and it probably could serve into the classical period (c. 300 BCE). I tried not to make fine distinctions between Daoist masters and those teachers and practitioners known as *fangshi* (方士), 'masters of techniques'. Often the *fangshi* were associated with expertise in arts and techniques that we might call occult or magical, but in my view this distinction has limited merit and, historically, it was in fact quite frequently merely a strategy for one master to discredit another. I feel that it may distract us from our overall goal to probe the historical uses of *fangshi* and *daoshi*, and I leave it to the reader to judge what Daoist masters taught and did from the discussion in Chapter IV: 'The Masters Who Nurtured the Trunk of Daoism'.

Chapter I
Telling the Story of Daoism

What Is Daoism?

Daoism is the oldest indigenous philosophic–spiritual tradition of China and one of the most ancient of the world's spiritual structures. The name 'Daoism' comes from the term *dao*, which is often used for a 'way' or a 'road' through the field or to one's village. It is also used as the 'way' to do something, such as the way a master craftsman carves a candlestick, makes a bell or even butchers an ox. *Dao* is used as the energizing process that permeates and animates all of reality to move in its ongoing process. However, as we shall see time and again in our study, *dao* itself cannot be described in words. *Dao* is not the supreme being of Daoism. Daoism has no supreme being, even if there is an extensive grammar about numinal self-conscious entities and powers for which the Chinese use the word *shen*. For example, the highest numinal powers of Daoism are called the Celestial Worthy of Primordial Beginning (*Yuanshi tianzun*) or the Jade Emperor (*Yuhuang Shangdi*), or the Perfected Warrior (*Zhenwu*). But these are expressions of *dao* in specific *shen*, they are not identical with *dao*.

Daoism is the spiritual tradition at the root of Chinese civilization. It defies characterization as either a philosophy or a religion. In fact, while these terms have been used by Western and Chinese scholars alike to understand Daoism, such categorization has regrettably only distorted the tradition, twisted it and perverted it by making it fit into conceptual modes to which it can conform only at the cost of its own destruction. Admittedly, until very recently it was common to speak of 'philosophical Daoism' (*daojia*) and 'religious Daoism' (*daojiao*), suggesting that the former was transformed into the latter or replaced by it. Western scholars did not begin this distinction, but the simple fact that Chinese commentators used it does not make it an accurate or productive way of approaching Daoism. Scholars today know things about Daoism and its origin that even the great Chinese thinkers of the past did not know. Some Chinese thinkers even had an interest in altering or reconstructing the Daoist tradition that they received. For example, Guo Xiang, the editor of the great Daoist text known as the *Zhuangzi*, systematically removed large blocks of material, reducing the text from the 52 chapters delivered to him to its present 33. He may have done this because he felt these materials contained 'superstitious' ideas and practices to which he and other educated intellectuals, such as his Confucian literati colleagues, objected (Knaul 1982: 54–5).

One way of thinking about whether to label Daoism as a philosophy or a religion is to follow the scholar Isabelle Robinet (1997) and consider 'religious Daoism' the practice of 'philosophical Daoism'. A growing repository of new discoveries about ancient Chinese texts, practices and artifacts have led scholars to appreciate more fully the dynamics of change and continuity in Daoist tradition and to conclude that this division between philosophical and religious Daoism is false and without merit. Indeed, to continue to make this distinction will systematically mislead us in our interpretations. Nowadays we pay attention only to what philosophy and religion have become, in their separate and often antagonistic domains. However, this book tells the story of what they were through the lives of the masters of Daoism in the time when practices and beliefs were ways to freedom and illumination, rather than schemes and structures for us to climb inside and analyze. If we are to understand it, we must look at Daoism as a living reality.

An Analogy for Understanding the Story of Daoism

Very early in Chinese history, some individuals invested their lives and energies in developing techniques for unifying and harmonizing their self-consciousnesses with *dao*, and thereby undergoing awe-inspiring biospiritual transformations. We can call these people 'masters of *dao*'. Sadly, very little is appreciated fully about who those people were and how their teachings are reflections of their practices. Their names are hardly known to anyone, but in the pages of the *Zhuangzi* and other Daoist texts both their names and traces of their activities are present. In Chapter IV, we will get a more detailed look at who these men and women were. The relationship between these masters and their students can be referred to as a lineage. We may think of the formation and interrelationship of the teacher-adept lineages on the analogy of a kudzu vine with each vine leading to a master, some grafting students onto shared masters, some continuing for decades or centuries and others dropping off and dying out, some contending with their teachers or other masters and others grafting into their lineage vine thought and practice from many others. On this analogy, Daoism is no single thing. It is the living tangled vines of teacher-practitioner lineages.

Climbing Kudzu Vine

There has been a great deal of scholarly debate both inside and outside of China, in the past and now, about this manner of sprouting, scrambling lineage lines that overlap, graft into each other and fall away. Scholars call this 'the problem of Daoist identity', and Livia Kohn and Harold Roth have compiled an extensive collection of points of view on this subject (2002). We will set this problem aside because it rests on the assumption that there is some single, identifiable set of teachings and practices that make up the essence of Daoism, and such an assumption cannot be supported by the history of Daoism. What that history reveals instead is that Daoism is much more like the living kudzu vine, ever changing and growing, with a composite and organic trunk and branches and stems reaching in many directions. Both inside and outside of China, and even within certain Daoist lineage vines, the purpose of the formulation of a catalog of traits designed to define the 'essence' of Daoism has been a polemical one designed to rule out as 'inauthentic' or 'unDaoist' certain beliefs and practices. But actually these 'inauthentic' vines often do belong to the stems, branches and, in some cases, even the trunk of Daoism.

I intend to trace the great vine of Daoism without essentializing it along the definition of any scholar, Chinese or Western, classical or modern, or even without relying on some specific formulation given by a particular vine or branch of the greater plant that is Daoism itself. The approach to Daoist identity that tries to delimit Daoism to a single set of doctrines or practices in order to say to some other lineage 'that's not real Daoism' will mislead us in our study of and appreciation for this great tradition. Daoism is the great changing and continuing, irrepressible, unstoppable, climbing and trailing pursuit of *dao* and its *de* that cannot be reduced to a few 'essential factors'. In the course of our study we shall see that not every stem presents all the characteristics of the vine from which it has grown, or at least it may minimize some teachings and practices so far as to make them inconsequential to its own historical manifestation. Likewise, the growth of some master–student lineage vines was short lived, while others stretched over long periods of time even into the present. Some lineages are connected to the fundamental trunk and roots of the tradition by strong master ties, and others cling tenuously onto the tips of the flimsiest of stems. Even the great Daoist texts, such as the *Daodejing* and the *Zhuangzi*, are in themselves visible graftings of the lineage vines and branches that preceded them and created them.

Daoism has grown over and around, and grafted into, Chinese popular religion, cultural custom and national identity. It has had a complex and overlapping relationship with vernacular religious culture, sometimes fully integrating ideas and practices, and sometimes various Daoist lineages distanced themselves from those popular practices even if they were still parts of many other vines and branches of Daoism.

It is impossible to disentangle Daoism from many aspects of Chinese culture itself. Daoism is wound around and over, and integrated with, China's calendar, traditional medicine, national artifacts and treasures, and even its holidays and festivities. For example, the Daoist calendar used for 'sacred time' in measuring the auspicious days for ritual events and festivals is identical to the traditional Chinese calendar. It is even the case that masters of *dao* celebrate a magnificent *jiao* ritual once every 60 years because this is the *jiazi* year on the calendar; the year that marks the beginning of a new cycle in the cosmos.

Chapter II
The Sprouting of the Trunk of Daoism

There are three phases in the development of the trunk of the great vine of Daoism in the classical period:

- The first phase (c. 450 BCE to 310 BCE) is represented by (1) some collection of textual blocks that now make up the *Daodejing*; (2) Chapters 1–7; and 8–10e, and 29 of the *Zhuangzi*; and (3) the *Inward Training* (*Neiye*) and *Techniques of the Heart* (*Xinshu*) essays in the *Guanzi*. All of these texts were probably being formed and modified, and in use at the Jixia Academy (see page 8).

- The second phase (c. 310–220 BCE) is represented by (1) the recently discovered texts from the Chu tomb at Guodian (see pages 10–11), including the versions of the *Daodejing* found there; (2) materials on the Five Phases associated with Zou Yan at Jixia and also found at Guodian; and (3) the materials from the Yellow Emperor-Laozi (*Huang-Lao Daoism*) and Zhuangzi Disciples lineages of the *Zhuangzi* (see pages 33ff. and 37ff.).

- The third and final phase (c. 220–139 BCE) is represented by (1) the surviving texts of the Huang-Lao manuscripts and the *Daodejing* silk manuscripts discovered at the burial site of Mawangdui (see page 10); (2) some composite version of the *Zhuangzi*, probably containing 52 chapters rather than our present 33; and (3) the work entitled *The Master of Huainan* (*Huainanzi*, 139 BCE).

These elements form the trunk of the Daoist kudzu. This trunk grew organically from a fibrous interweaving of lineages, pulling from the root system of practices and teachings of the masters of *dao*. We can actually see the trunk of Daoism taking shape in the texts of the *Daodejing* and *Zhuangzi*, both of which are already themselves composite.

The Jixia Academy

The Jixia Academy during the Warring States period (475–221 BCE) was a kind of ancient 'think tank'. Some of the teachers there were intellectuals who filled bureaucratic positions, others were literate descendants of knights whose smaller domains had been conquered by the rulers of the state of Qi. There were also present at Jixia practitioners of techniques and arts of the *dao* from the states of Yan and Qi. In fact, King Wei (358–320 BCE), who is credited with sending out the call for these teachers in the eighteenth year of his reign, is reported to have launched an expedition to locate the isles of the immortals at the instigation of these teachers, giving us insight into the kind of things these masters were practicing (Roth 2004: 22). According to the *Records of the Historian* by Sima Qian (145–90 BCE), during the reign of King Xuan (319–309 BCE) 76 teachers were given comfortable living quarters in the capital city of Linzi next to the Ji gate (thus the name *Jixia*).

The intellectual exchanges at the Jixia Academy lasted for about 100 years and the *Records of the Historian* tells us the names of 17 teachers who were there during that long period, including Zou Yan (305–240 BCE), the systematizer of Five Phase cosmology, and Zhuang Zhou (c. 365–290 BCE), the person associated with the earliest materials in the *Zhuangzi*. Many of the names given by Sima Qian are associated with the lineage known as Huang-Lao Daoism (see pages 33ff.). The great Confucian thinkers Mengzi (372–289 BCE) and Xunzi (310–220 BCE) were also associated with the Jixia Academy. If all this is taken as accurate, it is possible that Mengzi, Zhuang Zhou and Zou Yan could have overlapped at Jixia, and Xunzi might have been there at the same time as a young student before later returning as a master himself (*Records of the Historian* 46/10b; 74/4a, 2–6).

Early Shaping of the Trunk: The *Daodejing*

The long-standing tradition in China is that a philosophical master named Laozi was the author of the *Daodejing*, which means the 'Classic of *Dao* and *De*'. The identity of Laozi as a teacher and the originator of a work on the *dao* and its *de* can be traced into the other great classic of Daoism, the *Zhuangzi*. The *Zhuangzi* is the first text to use Laozi as a personal name. In that work, Laozi is often a character who is portrayed teaching and correcting Confucius, and Confucius is put in the role of giving Laozi great respect and honor. However, like many other names for persons in that text, Laozi was probably a fictional name used to give a voice to ideas within an influential lineage of teachers.[2] In Chinese, *lao* means 'ancient, old' and *zi* means 'teacher, master'. So 'Laozi' may stand-in for 'the ancient teachers' personified as one person.

Laozi

The tradition that Laozi was the author of a book on *dao* and *de* is embedded in the classical texts of China. Both the *Hanfeizi* (c. 230 BCE) and *Master of Huainen* (139 BCE) attribute the authorship of the *Daodejing* to Laozi, probably basing this ascription on the *Zhuangzi*. Then, Sima Qian provides a biography for Laozi in *Records of the Historian*, saying that when Laozi departed China to go to the West he gave a book of 5,000 characters, divided into two parts, to discuss the meaning of *dao* and *de*, to a person named Yin Xi, also known as the Guardian of the Pass (*guanling*). After delivering his teachings, Laozi went west and no one knew where he had gone; a later Daoist tradition said he went to teach the 'barbarians' in the West (i.e., the Buddha and the Buddhists).

In his biography, Sima Qian brings together a number of stories about Laozi. He says Laozi came from Quren village in Hu County in the state of Chu (modern Luyi district, Henan Province). He calls him Chong'er (lit., 'Double Ear') and Boyang ('Lord of Yang'). Actually the account conflates information on what seem to be four distinct people. First, there is the person called Li from the south of China; then, there is a historian by the name of Dan (Lao Dan) who served as librarian of the Zhou archives and was also called 'The scribe below the pillar'; third, Laozi is a master who met and taught Confucius how to perform religious rituals; and finally, there is a person who is called by the name of Laolaizi who Sima Qian says wrote a Daoist book in 15 sections.

In later Daoist history, Laozi was venerated as the personification of the eternal *dao*, the ultimate power that makes the universe processes exist. Like the universe at large, he changes and transforms in constant process. He is the original ancestor of *yin* and *yang*. He appears and disappears in every age.

The impact of the *Daodejing* has been monumental. According to one count, there are over 700 commentaries in Chinese on this work.[3] Our present *Daodejing* represents a collection of teachings used across lineages of Daoist teachers. It is divided into two parts and 81 chapters (*pian*) and until the recent archaeological finds at Mawangdui and Guodian, all translations of this work were based on the text edited by Wang Bi, a commentator who assembled the text between 226 and 249 CE. The two major divisions of Wang Bi's *Daodejing* are the 'Dao Classic' (*daojing*, Chs 1–37) and the 'De Classic' (*dejing*, Chs 38–81). However, this division probably rests on little else than the fact that the principal concept opening Chapter 1 is *dao* and that beginning Chapter 38 is *de*. In contrast, the much earlier Mawangdui versions of the text place the *dejing* first and the *daojing* second. In either case, D.C. Lau thinks that the division of the work was probably done to conform to the traditional story that upon leaving China a person named Laozi wrote a work in two books and presented it to Yin Xi, Guardian of the Pass to the West (Lau 1963: vii). As for the division of the text into 81 chapters, this, too, is not found in the earliest versions. Chapter divisions and even titles were added by the author of a commentary known as the *Heshanggong* (written in about the 200s CE).

Archaeological finds at Mawangdui and Guodian have shed new light on the early versions of the *Daodejing*. Mawangdui is the name for a site of tombs discovered near Changsha in modern Hunan province in 1973. The tombs contain many fascinating materials including the earliest manuscript of the Book of Changes (*Yijing*) and two *Daodejing* manuscripts. The *Daodejing* texts have been dated to before 195 BCE and consist of two incomplete editions on silk scrolls (*boshu*) now simply called 'A' and 'B'. These versions have two principal differences from that of Wang Bi (1) Some word choice divergences are present. (2) The order of the chapters is reversed, with Chapters 38–81 in the Wang Bi version coming before Chapters 1–37 in the Mawangdui versions. More precisely, the order of the Mawangdui texts takes the traditional 81 chapters and sets them out like this: 38, 39, 40, 42–66, 80, 81, 67–79, 1–21, 24, 22, 23, 25–37. Robert Henricks has published a translation of these texts with extensive notes and comparisons with the Wang Bi under the title *Lao-Tzu, Te-tao Ching* (1989). Contemporary scholarship associates the Mawangdui versions with a type of Daoism known as the Way of the Yellow Emperor and Laozi (*Huang-Lao Daoism*), which will be discussed on pages 33ff.

In 1993, more tombs were explored near the village of Guodian in the Jishan district of Hubei Province, not far from the city of Jingmen and only a few kilometers from the ancient capital of the state of Chu. Tomb No. 1 contained 730 inscribed bamboo slips. There are 71 slips in three bundle rolls containing material that is also

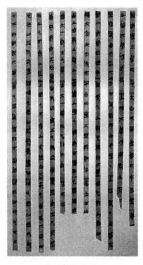

Bamboo Strips

found in 31 of the 81 chapters of the *Daodejing* and corresponding to Chapters 1–66. These bamboo strips are now the oldest versions of the *Daodejing* in our possession. They are called *Laozi A, B, C* or *The Bamboo Laozi* (*Zhujian Laozi*). These slips contain more significant variants from the Wang Bi versions than do those of Mawangdui. We believe the texts in this tomb formed the library of its occupant, the person we know by an inscription in the tomb as the 'Teacher of the Eastern Palace' (*donggong zhi shi*) (Allan and Williams 2000: 126). The tomb may date from as early as 300 BCE. If this is correct, we can be sure that versions of the *Daodejing* were already in existence and circulation in the period of the Jixia Academy and at, or before, the earliest parts of the *Zhuangzi*. In addition to the *Daodejing* bamboo slips, other often overlooked materials in this tomb are relevant to the early formation of Daoism. For example, Bundle Eight is concerned with the Five Phases of early Chinese cosmology and Bundle Thirteen is devoted to recipes for nourishing life, which is a common way of talking about the quest for health, longevity and even immortality in Daoism (see Chapter 3 of the *Zhuangzi*).

In all of its versions, the *Daodejing* is a collection of text blocks, and these are not arranged to develop any systematic argument. In this sense, the *Daodejing* is more like an anthology than a book with an overarching theme. The blocks were gathered and organized into chapters by one, or perhaps more than one, editor. In some ways, it is helpful to think of these blocks as beads on a string, and of the editor as a jeweler creating a necklace. Recently, some scholars have helped us detect the rough edges of the way many chapters have been edited from these smaller units. Consider these two fine translations of Chapter 8 as an illustration of what I mean:

Ivanhoe (2002)	LaFargue (1992)
8a. The highest good (*shan*) is like water. Water is good at benefiting the myriad creatures, while not contending with them. It resides in places that people find repellent, and so comes close to the Way. In a residence, the good lies in location. In hearts, the good lies in depth. In interactions with others, the good lies in benevolence. In words, the good lies in trustworthiness. In government, the good lies in orderliness. In carrying out one's business, the good lies in ability. In actions, the good lies in timeliness. Only by avoiding contention can one avoid blame.	8a. The highest excellence (*shan*) is like water. Water, Excellent at being of benefit to the thousands of things, does not contend It settles in places everyone else avoids. Yes, it is just about Tao. ★★★★★★ 8b. *Excellence in a house: the ground* 'Excellence in mind: depth Excellence in companions: Goodness Excellence in speaking: sincerity Excellence in setting things right: good management Excellence on the job: ability Excellence in making a move: good timing.' ★★★★★★ 8c. *Simply do not contend then there will be no fault.*

In the left column, we have an example of the text just as it is given in the P.J. Ivanhoe translation (2002). Using this version we might think of the chapter as a unity. But an alternative approach to the text is seen in the example on the right, taken from Michael LaFargue (1992). In the example on the right, the translator is calling attention to the component parts of the chapter that he believes were originally separate and only later gathered into the form we presently have in Chapter 8. LaFargue thinks the chapter contains three once separate sayings. One is about water and its usefulness as an analogy for understanding *dao*. It is followed by a teaching about excellence. Finally, there is a free-standing aphorism about the need to avoid contention.[4]

Sometimes even translators, agreeing that the chapters of the *Daodejing* are composite, differ on how a chapter should be divided.

Consider the following comparison between the ways D.C. Lau and LaFargue treat Chapter 15:

Lau (1963)	LaFargue (1992)
15a. Of old he who was well versed in the way Was minutely subtle, mysteriously comprehending, And too profound to be known. It is because he could not be known That he can only be given a makeshift description: Tentative, as if fording a river in winter; Hesitant, as if in fear of his neighbours; Formal like a guest; Falling apart like thawing ice; Think like the uncarved block; Vacant like a valley; Murky like muddy water. ★★★★★★	15a. The excellent *shi* 土 of ancient times penetrated into the most obscure, the marvelous, the mysterious. They had a depth beyond understanding. ★★★★★★ *15b. They were simply beyond understanding,* *the appearance of their forceful presence:* Cautious, like one crossing a stream in winter timid, like one who fears the surrounding neighbors reserved, like guests yielding, like ice about to melt *unspecified, like the Uncarved Block all* *vacant space, like the Valley everything* *mixed together, like muddy water.* ★★★★★★
15b. Who can be muddy and yet, settling, slowly become limpid? Who can be at rest and yet, stirring, slowly come to life? He who holds fast to this way Desires not to be full. It is because he is not full That he can be worn and yet newly made.	15c. Who is able, as muddy water, by stilling to slowly become clear? Who is able, at rest, by long drawn-out movement to slowly come to life? ★★★★★★ 15d. Whoever holds onto this Tao does not yearn for solidity. ★★★★★★ 15e. *He simply lacks solidity, and so what he is capable of: Remaining concealed, accomplishing nothing new.*

Lau believes Chapter 15 contains two originally separate passages. LaFargue thinks there are more text blocks in the chapter. He also tries to indicate certain editorial transitions designed to smooth the connections between the units that are traceable to the editor by placing lines he attributes to the editor in italics.[5]

One approach to studying the *Daodejing* is to isolate some of its most fundamental concepts and in what follows I use the translation by Philip J. Ivanhoe, including my own translations at certain points.

In the references, I offer the location in the text by giving its chapter with the number and its text block with a letter (e.g., 21a):

Dao 道 Chs 1; 4, 8b; 9; 14a, b; 16b; 18; 21a, b; 23b; 24; 25; 30; 31; 32; 34; 35b; 37; 38b, d; 40; 41a, b, c; 42a; 46a; 47; 48; 51a; 53a, b; 54b; 55; 56a; 59; 60; 62a; 65; 67; 77; 79; 81

The term *dao* is one of the most important concepts in the *Daodejing*. Sometimes it is used as a noun (i.e., 'the dao') and other times as a verb (i.e., 'daoing'). This is the way it changes meanings in the opening lines of Chapter 1:

> The *dao* that can be expressed in words (*daoed*) is not the
> eternal *dao*.
> The name that can be named is not the eternal name. (*DDJ*, 1a)

Many passages in the *Daodejing* make it apparent that *dao* cannot be put into words or named, and this is often known as the 'wordless teaching'. We will also notice this same point of emphasis in the *Zhuangzi* (14c, 156–8). Consider these passages:

> Music and good food will induce the people to stop by,
> But using words to talk about the *dao* is not satisfying.
>   (*DDJ*, 35b)

> There is a thing chaotic yet perfect, which arose before
>   Heaven and Earth.
> Silent and indistinct, it stands alone and unchanging,
> Going around it is tireless,
> We can take it as the mother of Heaven and Earth.
> I do not know its name.
> I have styled it *dao*. (*DDJ*, 25a)

> *Dao* is forever nameless. (*DDJ*, 32a)

In talking about the inability to explain *dao* and the inherent inaccuracy of putting a name to it such as 'reality' or 'God', the masters whose teachings are embodied in the *Daodejing* were pointing to its numinosity and ineffability. From *dao* all things have come:

> *Dao* produces the One;
> The One gives birth to two,

Two produces three.

Three produces the myriad creatures.

The myriad creatures shoulder *yin* and hold on to *yang*, and by
blending these *qi* they attain harmony. (*DDJ*, 42a)

In this brief statement of creation in the *Daodejing*, the text puts *dao*
prior to the first thing, what Daoist's call The Great One (Taiyi).
Dao gives rise to all things. It works in ways that we humans take to
exhibit design, but there is no statement that *dao* plans or has a will.

When one experiences *dao*, the sense of some presence is unmis-
takable. In Chapter 21a and b, the *Daodejing* speaks of this awareness
by using the characters *huang hu*.If we wonder whether this experience was regarded as a spiritual one, or as one we might have with
physical things, our best guide is to look elsewhere in Chinese texts
for the use of the expression *huang hu*. In the *Book of Rites* (*Liji*) that
records instructions for religious rituals in ancient China, these characters are used to refer to a state in which one encounters a spiritual or
numinal presence (*Book of Rites* 28.214). With this in mind, here is the
way Chapter 21 describes what happens in an encounter with *dao*:

The form of profound *de* (*kongde*) comes from the *dao* alone
As for *dao's* nature
it is *huang hu*
Hu! *Huang*!
There is an image within it.
Huang! *Hu*!
There is something within it.
Deep! Mysterious!
Within is numinal energy.
This numinal energy (*jing*) is undeniably real,
Within this [experience] lies its own proof.

According to the text, the whole world will come to follow the person who is able to hold on to this great image and its power (*DDJ*,
35a). And yet, the one who tries to describe this experience in language does not really know it; and the one who truly experiences it
does not try to explain it (*DDJ*, 56a).

The *Daodejing* teaches that when we try to make something hap-
pen in the world by our own reasoning, plans and contrivances, we
inevitably make a mess of it. But if we take our hands off of the

course of our lives and move with the *dao*, *dao* will untangle all life's knots, blunt its sharp edges and soften its harsh glare (*DDJ*, 56a). It is only when people abandoned oneness with the great *dao* (*da dao*) that they began to make distinctions in morality, politics, aesthetics and religion. Humans speak of beauty and ugliness; courage and coward-ice; good and evil. But these are discriminations of our own making, they do not belong to *dao*. The *Daodejing* makes this point in the passage below by specifically mentioning several of the distinctions made in Confucian moral and social philosophy: benevolence (*ren*), righteousness (*yi*), filial piety (*xiao*) and kindness (*ci*):

> When the great *dao* is abandoned, benevolence (*ren*) and
>   righteousness (*yi*) appear.
> When wisdom and erudition arise, great hypocrisy arises.
> When the six relationships [between persons] are out of
>   harmony, then you have filiality (*xiao*) and kindness (*ci*).
> When the state is in chaos, 'loyal ministers' appear on the
>   scene. (*DDJ*, 18)

We will see later that this disease of making distinctions is likewise condemned in the *Zhuangzi* (e.g., 2r, 45–6; 5a, 68–9; 5c, 72; 5d, 74). In Daoism, fighting and struggling over these human-made distinc-tions are the sources of all strife in the world (*DDJ*, 18, 38). The key is not to begin this process at all, or to empty oneself of it by forget-ting such distinctions and returning to the unity with *dao*, living out of a sense of its presence and its power, called *de*.

De 德 Chs 10b; 21a; 23b; 28; 38a, b; 41b; 49; 51a, b; 54b; 55; 59; 60; 63b; 65; 68; 79

There are some excellent recent essays on the meaning of *de* in Chinese thought.[6] In Chinese, it is used as 'excellence', 'virtue', 'power' or 'charismatic force'. So it is not a good idea to reduce the meaning of *de* to any one of these translations exclusively. In what follows, the term is left untranslated and this gives the interpreter a chance to place it in context and see the actual work it is doing in a passage. For example, the text says:

> To act with no expectation of reward;
> To lead without lording over others;
> Such is mysterious *de* (*xuande*). (*DDJ*, 10b; 51b)

If one moves in harmony with *dao*, he will have *de*. The *Daodejing* says:

> Cultivate *dao* in your person, and the *de* you develop will be genuine.
> Cultivate *dao* in your family, and the family's *de* will be more than enough.
> Cultivate *dao* in your village, and the village's *de* will long endure.
> Cultivate *dao* in your state, and the state's *de* will be abundant.
> Cultivate *dao* throughout the world, and the world's *de* will be pervasive. (*DDJ*, 54b)

Putting these passages together with the one mentioned earlier from Chapter 21, we can extend our reading. We can say that mysterious *de* [*xuande* (10b)] and profound *de* [*kongde* (21a)] expressed in one's power, wisdom, moral bearing and confident harmony with life's changes comes through the transformation that is a result of the experience with *dao* as *huang hu*. The reality of *dao* encountered in this experience, whether through individual meditation or in performance of ritual, is the source of the master's great *de*.

Wu-wei 無為 Chs 2c; 3c; 10a; 43; 47; 48; 57; 63a; 64b

De is not shown through striving, planning or training. It is exhibited with a sort of effortlessness for which Daoists use the concept *wu-wei*. 'The [people who possess the] highest *de* do not strive for *de* and so they have it' (38a). These characters 無為 (*wu-wei*) were rendered by the previous generation of translators as 'inaction'. Consequently, many interpreters understood *wu-wei* to mean that the *Daodejing* was recommending quiescence and inactivity as the way to practice the *dao*. But the *Daodejing* says clearly that persons should be active:

> Act, but as *wu-wei*.
> Be active, but don't let your conduct be intentional and deliberative (*wu shi*). (*DDJ*, 63a)

Wu-wei is a type of conduct, but it is not an intentional action or an omission to do something, rather it is a way of doing things that is unique to Daoism and Daoist master sages: 'Therefore, the sage *wu-wei*s things' (*DDJ*, 2c). *Wu-wei* is similar to a kind of natural or spontaneous conduct that occurs without deliberation and intention. It comes directly from the storehouse of *dao* and its limitless *de*. Below, we shall see several examples of how this conduct is felt by the agent doing it in the *Zhuangzi* in Chapters 3, 19 and 21.

This emphasis on acting naturally may seem somewhat problematic for a person steeped in the Western spiritual traditions. Often Westerners think that if someone does what is natural, this is undesirable. Westerners may take 'doing what comes naturally' as reverting to animality, or 'sinking to the lowest common denominator'. Non-Daoists do not value someone who acts spontaneously and naturally; they want persons to deliberate about what they are doing, act responsibly and weigh out the consequences. But in Daoism, moving naturally along with *dao* is not negative. It is the way out of the tangles we have created for ourselves by the institutions, rules and distinctions that clutter our minds and generate tension in our life together. The numinosity of *wu-wei* conduct lies in the fact that it accords in the situation with an efficacy that can only be attributed to the *dao* and could never have been a result of human wisdom, planning or contrivance. The person who is moved by the *dao* exhibits profound and mysterious *de*.

The *Daodejing* does not say that this efficacy ignores or has no connection with the virtues we use as distinctions in language. This is not the point of the text's thoroughgoing criticism of such discriminations. What it means is that following the demands and rules set up by convention *as though they were ends in themselves* will lead only to frustration and misery, whereas *wu-wei* conduct from an experience with *dao* will result in 'gaining the world', and things will be in harmony. In *wu-wei*, the individual is in harmony with the *dao* and this reveals itself in a person's *de*. Everything becomes well ordered (*DDJ*, 3c). Should barons and kings be able to express it (*de*), the myriad creatures would transform themselves (*DDJ*, 37b).

Emptiness, Stillness, Femininity Chs 5c; 6a; 11; 15c; 20; 28; 45; 48; 61

At first, the idea of emptiness sounds mysterious and vague, and it may not be clear how this idea applies to what we have said about *dao*, *de* and *wu-wei*. We may find it odd that emptiness is represented as full of power in many places in the *Daodejing*. In its analogies, the *Daodejing* says it is *what is not there* in a wheel that makes it useful, and *what is removed* that makes something such as a cup, pitcher or bowl effective. Only by *relying on emptiness* is a door or window what it is (*DDJ*, 11). The point is that since human discriminations and

distinctions fill the mind (lit. 'heart-mind' *xin*), we cannot act naturally, moving along with the *dao*. So, those who seek the *dao* and its
de do not desire the fullness of the world's knowledge, but they want
to make themselves empty. Being empty is a way of talking about
getting rid of the distinctions that tie us in knots and erupt in the
desires that are the source of our all human suffering, violence and
immorality. Thieves arise from stealing. Stealing arises from the idea
that this thing is mine, not yours. The greed that drives a thief comes
from our calling some people rich, powerful, or famous. If we emptied ourselves of these distinctions, there would be no more thieves
(see the *Zhuangzi's* discussion of Robber Zhi on pages 32, 33). We
use discriminations, such as success and failure, happiness and unhap-
piness, life and death, rich and poor, right and wrong, but all of these
distinctions are of our own making. The *dao* does not have any of
these. This is the context for the puzzling statement that perfected
rulers 'make sure that the people are without knowledge or desires;
and that those with knowledge do not act' (*DDJ*, 3b).

Emptiness means one reverts to a natural state, having forgotten human distinctions. The Daoist adept becomes like a valley
between mountains or uncarved wood that has not been tampered
with, bent or shaped (compare with *Zhuangzi*, Ch. 9). A valley
is a good analogy for emptiness because it is the void between
mountains. Uncarved wood is also an effective comparison to the
sage because the sage must act and live naturally, not be obsessed
with carving or refining himself according to the standards of the
world: 'If you are a valley for all the world, constant *de* will always
be sufficient, and you can return to being unhewn wood (*pu*)'
(*DDJ*, 28).

Being empty likewise indicates a disposition of receptivity. Just as
a bowl is ready to receive, so is the adept that seeks the presence of
dao. Such a one wants to receive *dao* and its *de*. This explains the
association of emptiness with the feminine. The *Daodejing* makes an
explicit analogical connection between emptiness, the valley and the
female:

> Know the male but preserve the female
> And be a ravine for all the world.
> If you are ravine for all the world, constant *de* will never leave
>   you. (*DDJ*, 28)

In sexual relations, the female receives. In the spirituality of the *Daodejing*, the person who becomes receptive to the presence of *dao* will have its constant *de*. To the would-be follower of the *dao*, the *Daodejing* asks:

> Opening and closing heaven's gate,
> Can you play the part of the female?

When the text speaks of opening and closing Heaven's gate it is describing entering into a state of spiritual awareness. Masters of the *dao* engaged in this experience on an individual level through quietude, stillness and meditation. They also entered this state through ritual action as well (see Chapter IV). If a person succeeds in playing the part of the female, then heaven will be opened, the state of *huang hu* awareness of *dao* will occur, and the person will be transformed by the boundless *de* experienced:

> Is not the space between Heaven and Earth like a bellows?
> Empty yet inexhaustible! (*DDJ*, 5c)

The transformation that results enables the person to *wu-wei* all his affairs with profound *de*. It is not surprising, then, that the *Daodejing* thinks of the extraordinary change occurring in the person who has become empty and receptive to the numinal power of the great image of *dao* experienced in *huang hu* as world changing:

> Hold on to the great image and the whole world will flock to
> you.
> Coming to you they will suffer no harm, be peaceful, secure
> and prosperous. (*DDJ*, 35a)

Correlativity Chs. 1; 2a, b, c; 22a, b; 29a, b; 30; 42a; 44; 48; 56a; 63b, c; 77, 81

The masters who were the sources of the *Daodejing* materials always moved their students away from the obsession to be fixated on opposites so common to thinking in terms of human discriminations. They did this by shifting the conception away from contradictions to correlations, using the Chinese cosmological ideas of *yin* and *yang*. The text says: 'The myriad creatures shoulder *yin* and embrace *yang*; and by blending these *qi* they attain harmony' (*DDJ*, 42a). This statement is the only explicit mention of *yin* and *yang* in the *Daodejing*. However, the theme of correlation is prominent in many places throughout the text as it warns against fixating on one distinction rather than another:

> Everyone in the world knows that when the beautiful is
>   obsessed with beauty, it is ugly.
> Everyone in the world knows that when the good is obsessed
>   with good, it is not good. (*DDJ*, 2)

Correlation was a part of the general cosmological theory of the Warring States. The image used most commonly from the Warring States period to the Song dynasty (about 1,500 years) for *yin* and *yang* was the tiger (*hu*) and dragon (*long*). Lacquer objects buried in tombs, roof tiles, mirrors and panels from sarcophagi from the Warring States through the Han use the tiger and dragon in this way (Little 2000: 128–32). Later in the Song dynasty the *Taiji* diagram began to replace the tiger and dragon. *Taiji* means 'Supreme Ultimate'. The first appearance of the 'Diagram of the Great Ultimate' (*Taiji tu*) by a Daoist was with Chen Tuan (c. 906–89 CE). In that figure, the white is *yang* and the black is *yin*. Within the black side, some white erupts, as also in the white side some black is present. This is a way of showing that *yin* and *yang* are not contradictions. With *yin* we should associate the female as passive, supple, warm and dark. With *yang* we should associate the male as aggressive, rigid, cold and light. In Chinese physics these forces proceed from *dao* and are forms of *qi* that give rise to the Five Phases and all objects in the process of reality. In correlational thinking, each contributes to the other and the way is

Dragon-Tiger Correlation   *Taiji Diagram*

found in the harmony and balance of both. One should never be only aggressive or competitive, sometimes one should be passive and compliant. No male should be without some female traits, and vice versa. Not even beauty should strive to be only beauty, because in this striving it will destroy itself. Correlativity in the *Daodejing* often functions as a criticism of human distinctions and judgments. To have and to lack generate each other. Difficult and easy give form to one another. The noble and the lowly give content to one another. Likewise, sometimes one leads, and sometimes one follows. Sometimes one is strong and sometimes weak (*DDJ*, 2b; 29b). Not everything that people call a gain is a gain, and not all losses are losses (*DDJ*, 44).

The *Daodejing* is not saying that an injury is not an injury, or that suffering is an illusion and unreal. It is saying that an injury is already moving toward health while it is still an injury. The correlative working of *dao* cannot be figured out by reason. Our plans and ways, human contrivances and 'how to' tactics, instead of bringing balance and harmony, will actually lead us into imbalance and greater disharmony. This is why Chapter 56 says the following:

> Those who know do not talk about it [*dao*]
> Those who talk about it [*dao*] do not know.
> [*Dao*] blocks the openings;
> Shuts the gates;
> Blunts the sharpness;
> Untangles the knots;
> Softens the glare;
> Merges with the dust;
> Brings wheels into the same track;
> This is known as profound unity (*xuan tong*). (*DDJ*, 56a)

If we think that life's occurrences seem unfair (a human discrimination), we should remember that heaven's net (*tian wang*) misses nothing, it leaves nothing undone (*DDJ*, 73). The *Daodejing* calls this correlative work of *dao* a deep mystery. 'Within this mystery is yet a deeper mystery (*xuan zhi you xuan* 玄之又玄). The gate of all mysteries!' (*DDJ*, 1):

> Those who are crooked will be perfected.
> Those who are bent will be straight.
> Those who are empty will be full.

Those who are worn will be renewed.

Those who have little will gain.

Those who have plenty will be confounded. (*DDJ*, 22)

Sage Chs 2c; 3a, b, c; 5b; 7; 10a; 12; 15a; 16b; 19b; 20 (1st person); 22b; 27; 28; 29b; 37; 46b; 47; 49; 51b; 55; 60; 63c; 64b; 66; 67 (1st person); 70 (1st person); 71; 72; 73; 76; 77; 79; 81

What is the image of the ideal person, the sage (*shengren*) in the *Daodejing*? Sages practice emptiness (*DDJ*, 11). They preserve the female (*DDJ*, 28). They shoulder *yin* and embrace *yang*, concentrate their internal energy *qi* and thereby attain harmony (*he*) (*DDJ*, 42a). They live naturally and free from desires, recognitions and standards given in the distinctions created by humans (*DDJ*, 37). They settle themselves down and know how to be content (*DDJ*, 46b). As we have seen, the *Daodejing* warns those who would try to do something with the world that they will fail. They will actually ruin it (*DDJ*, 29a). Instead of forcing their wills on life, sages are *yin*, pliable and supple, not rigid and resistive (*DDJ*, 76). Sages act with no expectation of reward (*DDJ*, 2c, 51b). They put themselves last and yet come first (*DDJ*, 7). They never make a display of themselves (*DDJ*, 22b, 24, 72). They do not brag or boast (*DDJ*, 22b, 24), and they do not linger to receive praise after their work is done (*DDJ*, 77). They manifest plainness and embrace simplicity, never thinking only of themselves (*DDJ*, 19b). They take the people's hearts as their own (*DDJ*, 49) and they are good at saving the people (*DDJ*, 27). They embody *dao* in practice, they have longevity of life (*DDJ*, 16b) and they create peace (*DDJ*, 32). Sages cause no injury (*DDJ*, 60). Heaven (*tian*) protects the sage and the sage becomes invincible (*DDJ*, 67):

Those who are steeped in *de* are like newborn infants;

Poisonous creature will not sting them;

Fierce beasts will not grab them;

Birds of prey will not carry them off:

Although their bones are soft and sinews pliable, their grip is firm.

They do not know the union of male and female and so their potency is high.

They can cry the whole day long, and yet not get hoarse.

This is because they are perfectly in harmony. (*DDJ*, 55)

The analogy between a newborn infant and the sage is illuminating. Sages, no matter their age, must move naturally and effortlessly, without deliberation, spontaneously, like an infant. But their movement is not infantile; it is the *wu-wei* of *de* from the *dao*.

Chapter III
The Composite Trunk of Daoism

Master Zhuang and the *Zhuangzi*

Most of what we know about Master Zhuang or Zhuangzi is taken from Sima Qian's *Records of the Historian*. According to his account of Zhuangzi, Master Zhuang's given name was Zhou. He lived during the reigns of King Hui of Liang (370–319 BCE) and King Xuan of Qi (319–309 BCE). He once served as an official in the 'lacquer garden' in the Town of Meng (Mengcheng), believed to be in the State of Song (now Henan Province). Zhuangzi was a contemporary of the great Confucian thinker Mengzi, and according to Sima Qian he was one of the masters who taught at the Jixia academy. Sima Qian tells us that Zhuangzi wrote a work of more than 100,000 characters and it was mostly filled with fables. This seems fairly accurate because the *Zhuangzi* is, indeed, filled with interesting stories and characters, even with talking animals, trees and skulls. The text is a rich treasure house of style and Chinese philosophical and religious thought.

The present text of the *Zhuangzi* was edited by a scholar official named Guo Xiang (d. 312 CE), and it contains 33 chapters. Most of these, like the *Daodejing*, contain many component text blocks put together by an editor as one might place beads on a string. However, unlike the case of the *Daodejing*, we know that there was a much larger and older *Zhuangzi*. This 'lost *Zhuangzi*' consisted of 52 chapters and it is mentioned on a list in Imperial bibliographies dating from about 110 CE. The 'lost *Zhuangzi*' was undoubtedly older than the compilation of this list, but we do not know by how much (Watson 1968: 13).

The current text is traditionally divided into three major sections: the Inner Chapters (*neipian*) (Chs 1–7), Outer Chapters (*waipian*) (Chs 8–22, c. 180 BCE) and Mixed Chapters (*zaipian*) (Chs 23–33, c. 250 BCE). We are not sure whether it was Guo Xiang or some earlier editor who divided the *Zhuangzi* into these sections (Watson 1968: 13; and Roth 1991: 80). Actually, these neat divisions of the text are not very helpful in identifying where a specific text block within the chapter originated in the flow of Daoist history. The text reflects a variety of literary styles, uses of poetry, short prose essays and references to movements and figures of much later historical context than that of Zhuang Zhou. It also contains a number of text blocks written about Zhuang Zhou in the third person, and there are clear internal differences in teaching between many text blocks, reflecting that there must have been several source lineages for the materials.

Contemporary scholars, such as Angus Graham (1986), Liu Xiaogan (1994) and Harold Roth (1991), have all suggested revised models for understanding the structure of the text of the *Zhuangzi*, but each of these has its detractors. Accordingly, when I am identifying material in the *Zhuangzi*, I will make use of the literary critical convention of marking the component text block of a chapter by small alphabetical letters. Throughout our study of the *Zhuangzi*, I most often rely on the translation by Burton Watson (1968), including my own translations at certain points. In the references, I offer the location in the text (e.g., 7a) and follow with the pagination in Burton Watson (e.g., 7a, 92).[7]

The Inner Chapters

Chapters 1–7, containing a number of text blocks that may be attributed to Zhuang Zhou, represent the oldest material in the book. These materials are probably connected with Master Zhuang's teachings during his time at the Jixia Academy (c. 330–301 BCE). But these chapters in their present form contain blocks easily seen as not traceable to Zhuangzi himself because Zhuangzi is described in the third person (e.g., 1h, 34–5; 1i, 35; 5g, 75–6).

Cosmology of the Inner Chapters

In Chapters 1–7, several text blocks reveal a cosmological worldview that is not unique to the masters of *dao* lineages of the Warring States period, but certainly belongs to them. Many text blocks reflect the cosmology that lay in the background of the Five Phase worldview that was taking shape at the Jixia academy (2a, 36–7; 2c, 37–8; 2d, 38; 2x, 49; 6c, 83–5; 6d, 86–7; 6h, 91; 7e, 94–7).

What was the Five Phase (*wu-xing*) Worldview?

Although he built upon ideas that predated him, Zou Yan (c. 305–240 BCE) was the earliest architect of the specifics of the cosmology that underwrites the *Zhuangzi*, the components of which are the power of *qi*, its correlative forces of *yin* and *yang*, and the Five Phases of phenomena which explain the movement of objects into and out of our sensory range (solids, liquids, gases and the like). He explained existing things by an appeal to the ways in which the Five Phases (water, fire, wood, earth and metal). All things are going through innumerable and infinite permutations of *qi* energy and the phases of objects are not fixed. In this worldview, everything is in process; and what is great in size or longevity in comparison to one thing is not so in relation to another. The process of reality is like 'the Great Clod breathing in and out *qi*'.

The Inner Chapters present the source of all things as itself empty, wriggling, turning. It is energy and not a thing. It is neither a *what* nor a *who* (7e, 97). Each of the objects and entities of reality makes its own sound, but Zhuangzi asks without answering: 'Who does the playing?' (2a, 36–7). The Inner Chapters are not content to allow this question to remain dangling. Zhuangzi says: 'This comes close to the matter. Although I do not know what makes them [the things of reality] the way they are. It would seem as though they have some True Master, and yet I find no trace of him. He can act – that is certain. Yet I cannot see his form. He has identity but no form' (2c, 37–8).

In the cosmology of the Inner Chapters, since every one of the existing things we experience is in process we may wonder whether the 'I' has any 'I' to it (6e, 88–9). Of course, when applying this to the human self, there is no question that we have awareness, that there is consciousness. The only question is whether there is some *thing* that has this consciousness, whether there is a self that underlies it, has some identity that is other than the consciousness itself. In the Daoist worldview, the whirl and process of change sometimes combines the Five Phases of *qi* into consciousness, even self-consciousness. But on the question of whether there is a self/mind/soul that underlies consciousness, Daoists have no single answer, just as they have divergent views on a host of other questions as well.

One thing the Inner Chapters makes clear is that masters of *dao* are able to control the phasal changes they undergo and take on different forms, providing themselves and others with experiences out of the ordinary. This is one of the messages of the story of the encounter between Huzi (Master Hu), his disciple Liezi and a village shaman (7e, 94–7). This cosmology lies behind the *Zhuangzi*'s teaching that persons and objects are being constantly made and remade like metal in a Great Forge (6c, 84–5).

The Daoist Ideal in the Inner Chapters

The text blocks of Chapters 1–7 may represent memories of Zhuangzi about his teachers or those masters about whom his disciples heard (e.g., Xu You 1e, 32–3; Lianshu 1f, 33–4; Ziqi 2a, 36–7; Wang Ni 2r, 45–6; Changwuzi 2s, 46–7; Qu Boyu 4c, 62–3; Carpenter Shi 4d, 63–5; Bohun Wuren 5b, 70–1; Nu Yu 6b, 82–3; Sizi, Yuzi, Lizi, Laizi 6c, 83–5; 6d Zi Sanghu, Meng Zifan, Zi Qinzang 6c, 86; Yuzi and Sangzi 6h, 91; Wang Ni and Putizi 7a, 92; Jie Yu 7b, 92–3; Lao Dan 7d, 94; Huzi 7e, 94–7). While it is almost certainly not Zhuang Zhou's writing, the small essay in 6a, 77–82 is a description of the Daoist ideal known as the Perfected Person (*zhenren*) and is probably based on traditions about these persons. *Zhenren* cannot be harmed because life and death, profit and loss and the like are distinctions which they have set aside (2r, 45–6), just as the *Daodejing* also recommends. They are like still water and do not allow the turbulence of life to agitate them into violence, pride or other destructive action. Their internal 'spiritual storehouse (*lingfu*)' is unaffected by whatever happens (5d, 74). For them, all things are equal; that is to say that there are no differences in reality between success and failure, beauty and ugliness and such. These are our distinctions; they do not belong to *dao* (5a, 68–9; 5c, 72). In all of this, we are walking on ground we have already surveyed in the teachings of the *Daodejing*.

The *zhenren* does not love life and hate death, he forgets these distinctions entirely, and delights in the transformations of life (6a, 81). This is the meaning of the famous story called 'Three in the morning':

> When the monkey trainer was handing out acorns, he said, 'you get three in the morning and four at night.' This made all the monkeys furious. 'Well, then,' he said, 'you get four in the morning and three at night.' The monkeys were all delighted. There was no change in the reality behind the words, and yet the monkeys responded with joy and anger. (2k, 41)

This same point is brought home again in the Inner Chapters by showing that whether something is good or bad depends greatly on a relative perspective. Men who sleep in cold and damp places awaken with their back aching, but a loach does not find it miserable. A person who must climb a tree shakes with fright, but monkeys do not. So, can the question 'What is the proper place to live?' be answered with a universal truth? The answer is 'no'. It depends on one's perspective (2r, 45).

The masters of *dao* taught their disciples that joy, anger, grief, delight, modesty and such distinctions are like mushrooms springing up and being replaced by another the next day (2c, 37–8). One master asks: 'How do we know that loving life is not a delusion and that holding on to what we think is happiness or moral right is not merely grasping at something that has no existence beyond our own distinctions?' (2t, 47). The story of Lady Li demonstrates this point well:

> Lady Li was the daughter of the border guard of Ai. When she was first taken captive and brought to the state of Qin, she wept until her tears drenched the collar of her robe. But later, when she went to live in the palace of the ruler, shared his couch with him, and ate the delicious meats of his table, she wondered why she had ever wept. How do I know that the dead do not wonder why they ever longed for life? (2u, 47)

In contrast to others, *zhenren* have the wordless teachings that can open up oneness with *dao*. It seems that this is a reference to the sort of spiritual experience or altered consciousness that we have noticed in the concept of *huang hu* in *Daodejing* 21 (see page 15). It seems we should draw this close connection because of the seriousness with which the Inner Chapters treats 'getting the *dao*'. Whenever *zhenren* 'get the *dao*', they become like the numinal powers of the universe: the Big Dipper (*beidou*), the Yellow Emperor (*Huangdi*) and the Queen Mother of the West (*Xiwangmu*) (6a, 82). They can enter Kunlun (i.e., the Daoist paradise that houses the Jade Palace of the Yellow Emperor and the gardens of the Queen Mother of the West where the peaches of immortality grow). *Zhenren*, whose flow of *qi* and Five Phases have been brought within their control, can wander reality in different forms (6d, 87).

Zhuangzi as a Master of Dao in the Inner Chapters
From these chapters we get a look at how Zhuangzi himself functioned as a teacher (2b) and at the role of debate and dispute at Jixia.

There are several text blocks in which Master Zhuang is pitted against the great Jixia logician Master Huizi in accounts provided about Zhuangzi in the third person (1h, 34–5; li, 35; 5g, 75–6).

Huizi

Nine *Zhuangzi* chapters mention Master Hui (Huizi or Hui Shi). Most of the passages, except those in Chapter 33, portray Huizi as a friendly rival of Zhuangzi, who often criticizes the Daoist perspective and has a different point of view.

One text block says that Zhuangzi was accompanying a funeral when he passed by the grave of Huizi. Turning to his attendants, he said, 'There was once a plasterer who, if he got a speck of mud on the tip of his nose no thicker than a fly's wing, would get his friend Carpenter Shi to slice it off for him. Carpenter Shi, whirling his hatchet with a noise like the wind, would accept the assignment and proceed to slice, removing every bit of mud without injury to the nose, while the plasterer just stood there completely unperturbed.' Lord Yuan of Song, hearing of this feat, summoned Carpenter Shi and said, 'Could you try performing it for me?' But Carpenter Shi replied, 'It's true that I was once able to slice like that but the material I worked on has been dead these many years.' [Thus, Zhuangzi said] 'Since you died, Master Hui, I have had no material to work on. There's no one I can talk to any more'. (24g, 269)

Even if the Inner Chapters record a good deal of rational debate between Zhuangzi and other Jixia scholars, there is no mistaking the fact that Zhuangzi did not believe that victory in a rational argument was equivalent to having the truth:

> Suppose you and I have had an argument. If you have beaten me instead of my beating you, then are you necessarily right and am I necessarily wrong? If I have beaten you instead of your beating me, then am I necessarily right and are you necessarily wrong? Is one of us right and the other wrong? Are both of us right or are both of us wrong? If you and I don't know the answer, then other people are bound to be even more in the dark. Whom shall we get to decide what is right? Shall we get someone who agrees with you to decide? But if he already agrees with you, how can he decide fairly? Shall we get someone who agrees with me? But if he already agrees with me, how can he decide? Shall we get someone who disagrees with both of us? But if he already disagrees with both of us, how can he decide?

> Shall we get someone who agrees with both of us? But if he already
> agrees with both of us, how can he decide? Obviously, then, neither
> you nor I nor anyone else can decide for each other. Shall we wait for
> still another person? (2v, 48)

The power to master life and the ability to control one's transformations is not an achievement of reason. It comes from oneness with
dao, so that one flows in life spontaneously and effortlessly, without
thought, just like the famous butcher of the Inner Chapters, Cook
Ding, who cuts up an oxen without ever hitting a bone or dulling
his knife (3b, 50–1). Like Cook Ding, the *zhenren* moves effortlessly
with the *dao* (3b; 5f, 75) and is content to follow along rather than
tamper, strategize and plan out his life (3c, 52; 3d, 52; 6h, 91). The
master does not try to follow the world's views of success, power,
influence and achievement. In this sense the *zhenren* makes himself
'useless' by the standards of the world and its institutions (4d, 63–4;
4e, 65–6; 4g, 66–7).

The Inner Chapters on Rulership
The text blocks in Chapters 1–7 show a decided view that their
source masters had no use for positions as officials or rulers. Instead,
they recommended that the world be left to the process of the *dao*
that orders things itself, without man's help (1e, 32–3). Indeed, trying
to force the world into a pattern is something the *zhenren* must avoid.
Political machinations run counter to what is natural. Moving with
the *dao* is the proper way of life. Of politicians who rely on principles,
laws and structures, Jie Yu said:

> This is a bogus virtue! To try to govern the world like this is like try-
> ing to walk the ocean, to drill through a river, or to make a mosquito
> shoulder a mountain! When the sage governs, does he govern what is
> on the outside? He makes sure of himself first, and then he acts. He
> makes absolutely certain that things can do what they are supposed to
> do, that is all. (7b, 93)

Even the great sage ruler Yao, when he visited the four masters of
Gushe Mountain, realized that there was no need for government
and that the affairs of human politics could be forgotten by the one
who followed the *dao* (1g, 34). This same point is made by The
Nameless Man of Yin Mountain in 7c, 93–4.

Daode Chapters.

Chapters 8–10e and 29 should be taken as a unit, consisting of materials formerly designated as the Outer and Miscellaneous Chapters. Chapters 8–10e represent a clear break in the text and form a coherent essay, often using the first person and employing illustrations of its points internal to the essay. The essay is not interrupted by any disconnected text blocks. As such, it is likely that the essay was written by a single individual who made use of texts and themes also found in the *Daodejing*.

One of the most important literary evidences of the distinctiveness of this material is that the writer often uses the compound *daode*. Yet the *daode* sections make no mention of the Daoist conduct concept of *wu-wei* prominent in the *Daodejing*, the stress is instead on returning to naturalness and embracing one's 'inborn nature' (*xingming*). The use of the concept of 'inborn nature' in the *daode* section is another of the reasons we should set the material off from that of Chapters 1–7. In Chapters 1–7, this compound of terms is never used (Liu 9). However, the writer of the *daode* essay says: 'My definition of expertness has nothing to do with benevolence and righteousness; it means being expert in regard to your *de*, that is all. My definition of expertness has nothing to do with benevolence or righteousness; it means following the true form of your inborn nature, that is all' (8a, 103).

There is an argument throughout the *daode* materials that human society has been on a steady decline from the distant past when persons followed *dao* and possessed its *de*. Stories – such as that of Robber Zhi, first introduced in 10c and then told in great detail in Chapter 29 – are specifically designed to show that holding elite Confucian values – such as benevolence and righteousness, and making distinctions such as private property – are the source of confusion, unlawfulness and disorder. We see here a consistent rejection of the cardinal Confucian values of benevolence and righteousness, just as we noticed in the *Daodejing*. These values represent a falling away from oneness with *dao*.

The writer of the essay in Chapters 8–10e often says that it was not until the *dao* and its *de* were cast aside that the Confucian emphasis on benevolence and righteousness entered, and the distinctions made by men created disorder and disharmony (e.g., 8a, 101; 9a, 105, 106). Prior to that time, in the age of Perfect Virtue (*zhende*), there was harmony and everything moved according to its inborn nature. The author makes the interesting argument that the distinctions made by Confucians are actually the sources of greed, theft, murder, rape and violence of all sorts. He says when people learn the ways of the Confucian sages (*shengren*) in making distinctions of wealth and success, thieves like Robber Zhi will exist. If there are no such discriminations, then there will be no need for stealing and theft, and no robbers (10b, 109).

The *daode* materials are critical of Confucian ideals because devotion to them cuts away one's inborn nature and confuses the world:

> If we must use cords and knots, glue and lacquer to make something firm, this means violating its natural virtue. So the crouchings and bendings of rites and music, the smiles and beaming looks of benevolence and righteousness, which are intended to comfort the hearts of the world, in fact destroy their naturalness. (Ch. 8a, 100)

In Chapter 9, the author makes the point that the domestication of horses destroys their nature, and 'as far as inborn nature is concerned, the clay and the wood surely have no wish to be subjected to compass, curve and plumb line' (9a, 104–5). The author says Confucians huff and puff after benevolence and stand on their tiptoes to reach righteousness, but if the *dao* and its *de* had not been cast aside, no one would have ever even called for benevolence and righteousness, everyone would have lived by 'inborn nature' (105). The master–disciple lineage in which this material originated also likens Confucian self-cultivation with its stress on social rules, etiquette and morality to having a piece of useless flesh between our toes (Ch. 8, 98).

What shall we make of this part of the book? While it is not traceable to Zhuang Zhou himself, the sentiments and even the actual refrains of the *Daodejing* that the author uses may very well have been contemporaneous with Zhuang Zhou and the students he had at Jixia. There was gathered at Jixia a great assembly of masters and students, and we do not know whether some early materials of the *Daodejing* were formed or compiled before, during or after the heyday of the academy or the time Zhuang Zhou was there.

Huang-Lao Chapters (Chs 11; 12a, 126–8; b, 128–9; 13a, 142–8; 14a, 154–5; c, 156–8; e, 161–2; f, 163–4; g, 163–5; h, 165–6; Chs 15; 16; 18a; 19a, 22a)

Angus Graham calls the creators of this material 'Syncretists', and it has been traditionally associated with the Outer Chapters division. We should notice that each of these chapters begins with a short essay that is, in some cases, followed by a series of text blocks containing parables and stories of the sort we see elsewhere in the book. Just whether and how these blocks are connected by the writer/editor(s) to the essay preceding them is a matter of much debate.

The materials in these sections of the *Zhuangzi* give us the first signs of ideas associated with what Sima Qian later called Yellow Emperor-Laozi Daoism (Huang-Lao). This lineage vine developed during and after the heyday of the Jixia Academy. The earliest look that we get at the characteristics of this important vine in Daoist history is in the *Zhuangzi* itself. In the next chapter, we will see that the *Master of Huainan* (139 BCE) may represent a later statement of this vine in a distinct form.

One of the indicators of the presence of a Huang-Lao lineage vine in the *Zhuangzi* is the prominent role given to the Yellow Emperor in a set of text blocks that can also be isolated by style and theme. Indeed, in the *Zhuangzi*, all the blocks in which the Yellow Emperor is a main character are in the materials we have identified with these chapters. Aside from the presence of the Yellow Emperor, another marker of the distinctiveness of these materials is the prominence given to *wu-wei* in its text blocks. These materials may also be distinguished from the Inner Chapters, the Daode Chapters and the Zhuangzi disciples (see pages 37ff.), because the Huang-Lao textual materials do not reject rulership. On the contrary, they embrace the role of ruler and teach that the true ruler should govern by *wu-wei*, following the model of the Yellow Emperor.

The Daoist Ideal in the Huang-Lao Vine Materials.
In the textual materials transmitted by the Huang-Lao teachers, the term 'sage' (*shengren* and not *zhenren*) is used when speaking of their Daoist ideal. 'Sage' is not used for the Daoist ideal in the Inner Chapters and Daode Chapters. The characteristic mode of conduct that identifies the sage in the Huang-Lao materials is *wu-wei*. Like the *zhenren* of Chapters 1–7, the sage does not make distinctions, value riches, or worry about early death. The sage's ability to move through life by *wu-wei* is directly traceable to the fact that he takes his stand 'in the original source and his understanding extends to the spirits' (12a, 128). In the face of the ebb and flow of life's experi-

---

The Yellow Emperor

Who was the Yellow Emperor referred to in the *Zhuangzi* and in Sima Qian's name for the vine of Daoism we first see in *Zhuangzi*? According to tradition, the Yellow Emperor was the third of ancient China's mythological emperors. As the legend goes, he was born in 2704 BCE and became emperor in 2697 BCE. Tradition holds that his reign saw the introduction of wooden houses, carts, boats, the bow and arrow, writing and governmental institutions. His wife was reputed to have taught women how to breed silkworms and weave silk.

---

ences, the sage is 'like a quail at rest', and totally unmoved in emotion or thought.

We noted Zhuangzi's criticism of reason and logic in Chapters 1–7, and the Huang-Lao text blocks likewise teach that one should set aside knowledge. The Yellow Emperor figures prominently in this section's text blocks that reject rational knowledge:

> The Yellow Emperor went wandering north of the Red Water, ascended the slopes of Kunlun, and gazed south. When he got home, he discovered he had lost his Dark Pearl. He sent Knowledge to look for it, but Knowledge couldn't find it. He sent the keen-eyed Li Chu to look for it, but Li Chu couldn't find it. He sent Wrangling Debate to look for it, but Wrangling Debate couldn't find it. At last he tried employing Shapeless, and Shapeless found it. The Yellow Emperor said, 'How odd! – in the end it was Shapeless who was able to find it!' (12b, 129)

Whereas in Chapters 1–7, the friendship and disputation between Zhuangzi and Huizi form the background for a rejection of the use of argument and debate, in the Huang-Lao materials this teaching is brought home through a series of text blocks that are very critical of Confucius and usually portray Laozi as his teacher and master.

Laozi and Confucius Text Blocks

12g, 132–3	Dialogue with Confucius (called by his personal name, Qiu), in which Laozi attacks rhetoricians (such as Confucius) and those who try to make plans and strategies for trying to do something. Their fate will be disastrous like that of the nimble monkey and rat catching dog. They must forget all this.

13c, 149–50	Dialogue with Confucius about the twelve classics he wants to put into the royal library, but when Laozi finds that the central thrusts of those works is the distinctions of benevolence and righteousness, the flags that only bring confusion to men, he refuses to accept them.
14e, 161–2	Dialogue with Confucius who complains that he has not found the *dao* in benevolence and righteousness, and Laozi tells him that this is not surprising, that he should instead rest in *wu-wei*.
14f, 162–3	Dialogue with Confucius in which Laozi again condemns running around trying to practice benevolence and righteousness and recommends instead being natural, like the white of the goose and the black of the crow.
14h, 165–6	Dialogue with Confucius as Qiu over the fact that no ruler listens to him as he takes his six classics to them. Laozi says that it is a good thing they do not listen, and he criticizes the six classics as worn-out paths, with the dialogue concluding by Confucius realizing that he must act naturally.

The Huang-Lao Text Blocks on Rulership

In making its point about rulership, this section takes its hero the Yellow Emperor and says that in his early period of rule he used benevolence and righteousness to meddle with the minds of men. What followed was a history of consternation and confusion, all the way down to the Confucians and Mohists who are mentioned by name (11c, 117). But in the teaching block 11d, we find the story about the Yellow Emperor visiting Master Guang Cheng on top of the Mountain of Emptiness and Identity (Kongtong). When the Yellow Emperor learned the essence of the Perfect Dao, he 'withdrew, gave up his throne, built a solitary hut, spread a mat of white rushes, and lived for three months in retirement' (11d, 119). When the Yellow Emperor returned to rule thereafter, he followed *wu-wei* and became an immortal. The Yellow Emperor creates disaster when he rules as a Confucian would, meddling with people's minds, but when he rules in *wu-wei* he is glorified.

The Huang-Lao lineage masters tried to synthesize their ideas with the *daode* lineage and with the teachings of the Inner Chapters, but they also worked hard to show how following *dao* did not require a rejection of rulership. Consider this attempt at harmonizing lineage vines in a passage from the opening essay of Chapter 13 (13a, 142–8):

> Emptiness, stillness, limpidity, silence, *wu-wei* are the root of the ten thousand things. To understand them and face south is to become a ruler such as Yao was; to understand them and face north is to become a minister such as Shun was. To hold them in high station is the *de* of emperors and kings, of the Son of Heaven; to hold them in lowly station is the way of the dark sage, the uncrowned king. Retire with them to a life of idle wandering and you will command first place among the recluses of the rivers and seas, the hills and forests. Come forward with them to succor the age and your success will be great, your name renowned, and the world will be united. In stillness you will be a sage, in action a king. Resting in *wu-wei*, you will be honored; of unwrought simplicity, your beauty will be such that no one in the world may vie with you.

In this passage, the much honored Confucian sage kings Yao and Shun are not blamed for the confusion and disorder of the world, but their success and greatness is attributed to the fact that they practiced the ways of Daoism: *wu-wei*, emptiness and stillness. Any true ruler should follow their example.

Zhuangzi Disciples Chapters

Chapters 17–28 and 32 represent a still different set of material. Text blocks from this section have been classified traditionally as coming from both the Outer and Miscellaneous Chapters. They are associated with the earliest disciple transmitters of Zhuang Zhou's teachings. Here are some of the evidences why this is true: (1) With the exception of Chapters 19 and 23, each of the chapters in this section contain passages that directly record Zhuang Zhou's activities and teachings in the third person, just as we might expect from his disciples. In fact, in the *Zhuangzi* there are 25 records of Zhuang Zhou's activities outside of Chapters 1–7. This cluster of text blocks contains 23 of these. (2) Liu Xiaogan (1994) has done an intensive conceptual and linguistic study of these chapters, and he has traced 90 passages in which these chapters are identical with or correspond closely to Chapters 1–7 of the book that are closely associated with Zhuang Zhou himself. (3) Since the 90 instances of connection with Chapters 1–7 are spread across Chapters 17–27, it is reasonable to conclude that these materials were probably gathered by a lineage vine of masters who traced themselves back directly to Zhuang Zhou as their master. (4) Like Chapters 1–7, but in distinction from the Daode Chapters and the Huang–Lao materials, these blocks use the term *zhenren* to speak of the Daoist ideal.

The Zhuangzi Disciples on Rulership

The Zhuangzi disciples return to the rejection of rulership that we saw in Chapters 1–7 and away from the Huang-Lao lineage effort to embrace rulership if practiced in *wu-wei*. To explain why Zhuangzi was never a ruler, the disciples provide us with an account of the master fishing on the Pu River when two ministers from the King of Chu come to ask him to rule over all the territories of Chu (17e, 187–8). Zhuangzi refused, saying he would rather be like a turtle content to have his tail in the mud than be the long dead sacred tortoise in the palace of the king. This distaste for official position and government rulership is very clear throughout this material. For example, Zhuangzi tells his old logician friend Huizi, who reappears in this material but is absent from the *daode* and Huang-Lao materials, that he has no desire to rule (17f, 188).

Chapter 28 contains a long series of text blocks all dealing with rulership. Some of these are designed to show that when they were approached with the offer of rulership, famous Daoist masters refused it. Consider this one:

> Shun tried to cede the empire to Shan Juan, but Shan Juan said, 'I stand in the midst of space and time. Winter days I dress in skins and furs, summer days, in vine-cloth and hemp. In spring I plow and plant – this gives my body the labor and exercise it needs; in fall I harvest and store away – this gives my form the leisure and sustenance it needs. When the sun comes up, I work; when the sun goes down, I rest. I wander free and easy between heaven and earth, and my mind has found all that it could wish for. What use would I have for the empire? What a pity that you don't understand me!' In the end he

would not accept, but went away, entering deep into the mountains, and no one ever knew where he had gone. (28c, 309–10)

Other passages teach that it is only the person who does not want to be a ruler who is really fit to be one:

> The men of Yue three times in succession assassinated their ruler. Prince Sou, fearful for his life, fled to the Cinnabar Caves of Danxue, and the state of Yue was left without a ruler. The men of Yue, searching for Prince Sou and failing to find him, trailed him to the Cinnabar Cave, but he refused to come forth. They smoked him out with mugwort and placed him in the royal carriage. As Prince Sou took hold of the strap and pulled himself up into the carriage, he turned his face to heaven and cried, 'To be a ruler! A ruler! Could I alone not have been spared this?' It was not that he hated to become their ruler; he hated the perils that go with being a ruler. Prince Sou, we may say, was the kind who would not allow the state to bring injury to his life. This, in fact, was precisely why the people of Yue wanted to obtain him for their ruler. (28f, 311)

There are several text blocks according to which Daoist masters would rather run away into hiding or even commit suicide rather than rule (28d, 310; 28h, 312; 28i, 313–14; 28s, 321–2).

Zhuangzi as a Master of the Dao in the Disciples' Material

It is probable that many of the text blocks concerning Zhuangzi in this section were formed after his death, or at least after the time he departed from the Jixia circle of masters and scholars. Perhaps the disciples were pressed to defend Zhuangzi's teachings by persons from the other schools of Chinese tradition. An important example of how the disciples do this is the dialogue between the great logician Gongsun Long and Duke Mou of Wei:

> Gongsun Long said to Duke Mou of Wei, 'When I was young I studied the teachings of the ancient kings, and when I grew older I came to understand the conduct of benevolence and righteousness. I reconciled difference and sameness, distinguished hardness and whiteness, and proved that not so was so, that the unacceptable was acceptable. I confounded the wisdom of the hundred schools and demolished the arguments of a host of speakers. I believed that I had attained the highest degree of accomplishment. But now I have heard the words

of Zhuangzi and I am bewildered by their strangeness. I don't know whether my arguments are not as good as his, or whether I am no match for him in understanding. I find now that I cannot even open my mouth. May I ask what you advise? ... [Duke Mou answered], 'still you try to use your knowledge to see through the words of Zhuangzi. This is like trying to make a mosquito carry a mountain on its back or a pill bug race across the Yellow River. You will never be up to the task!' (17d, 185–7)

What we see here is not only the valorization of Zhuangzi as a teacher but also an estimate of the profundity of his teaching. In the background is the friendly competition between Huizi the logician and Zhuangzi himself, so apparent in Chapters 1–7, and his rejection of argument and rational analysis.

The Daoist Ideal in the Disciples' Text Blocks

Just as we have seen in Chapters 1–7, the materials preserved and created by Zhuangzi's disciples condemn the making of distinctions. We find numerous text blocks embracing the sort of perspectivism we see in the stories of Lady Li (2u, 47) and 'Three in the Morning' (2k, 41). Chapter 17 opens with a dialogue between The Lord of the River and Ruo of the North Sea in which Ruo reminds the Lord that '... no line can be drawn between right and wrong, no border can be fixed between great and small ... From the point of view of *dao*, things have no nobility or meanness ... Looking at it this way, we see that struggling or giving way, behaving like a Yao or like a Jie, may be at one time noble and at another time mean. It is impossible to establish any constant rule' (17a, 179). In one of the most famous passages in this section of the work, Zhuangzi has a conversation with an old skull, meant to reinforce the teaching that we cannot be sure whether we should rely on a single perspective as the truth:

When Zhuangzi went to Chu, he saw an old skull, all dry and parched. He poked it with his carriage whip and then asked, 'Sir, were you greedy for life and forgetful of reason, and so came to this? Was your state overthrown and did you bow beneath the ax, and so came to this? Did you do some evil deed and were you ashamed to bring disgrace upon your parents and family, and so came to this? Was it through the pangs of cold and hunger that you came to this? Or did your springs and autumns pile up until they brought you to this?'

When he had finished speaking, he dragged the skull over and, using it for a pillow, lay down to sleep. In the middle of the night, the skull came to him in a dream and said, 'You chatter like a rhetorician and all your words betray the entanglements of a living man. The dead know nothing of these! Would you like to hear a lecture on the dead?' 'Indeed,' said Zhuangzi. The skull said, 'Among the dead there are no rulers above, no subjects below, and no chores of the four seasons. With nothing to do, our springs and autumns are as endless as Heaven and Earth. A king facing south on his throne could have no more happiness than this!' Zhuangzi couldn't believe this and said, 'If I got the Arbiter of Fate to give you a body again, make you some bones and flesh, return you to your parents and family and your old home and friends, you would want that, wouldn't you?' The skull frowned severely, wrinkling up its brow. 'Why would I throw away more happiness than that of a king on a throne and take on the troubles of a human being again?' (18d, 193–4)

These materials are consistent with Chapters 1–7 in teaching us not to resent the transformations we undergo in the Great Forge of the *dao* or be too quick to use human distinctions to categorize them (6c, 84–5). The disciples report that Zhuangzi does not resent the transformations of life even when his wife died (18b, 191–2).

Chapters 1–7 make it clear that the *zhenren* have remarkable capabilities. The Zhuangzi disciples also reinforce this teaching, but they even attempt to explain how this is possible. In doing so, they introduce us to the figure of Barrier Keeper Yin in order to teach that the remarkable feats of the *zhenren* are a result of the control of *qi*; they have nothing to do with cultivated skills (19b, 198). In this context the disciples gather a series of text blocks, all of which are designed to show that the *zhenren's de* is not an outcome of rational knowledge or even repeated practice (19c, 199–200; 19d, 200; 19e, 201; 19i, 204; 19j, 204–5; 19k, 205–6; and 19m, 206–7). The *zhenren's de* comes from oneness with *dao*, so that one flows in life spontaneously and effortlessly, without thought, in *wu-wei,* just like the famous butcher of the Inner Chapters, Cook Ding, who cuts up an oxen without ever hitting a bone or dulling his knife (3b, 50–1). The Zhuangzi disciples gather stories about conduct analogous to *wu-wei* such as extraordinary swimmers and divers (19d, 200; 19j, 204–5); the ferryman in the gulf of Shangshen who handled his boat with commensurate skill

(19d, 200); the amazing hunchback cicada–catching man (19c, 199); Ji Shengzi, the game cock trainer for King Xuan (19i, 204); Bohun Wuren's test of Lie Yukou's skill in archery (21i, 230–1); Qing who makes bellstands that seem to be the work of the spirits (19k, 205–6); and Chui, the artist who can draw freehand as true as a compass or T-square (19m, 206).

The disciples preserved this series of text blocks in order to refute the idea that being a *zhenren* was the result of self-cultivation, practice or developed skill.

Barrier Keeper Yin

We are unsure from where and when this character originated. In Chapter 33 of the *Zhuangzi*, Barrier Keeper Yin is presented, along with Laozi, as a *zhenren* of the ancient period (33, 371–3). Later traditions after the *Zhuangzi* taught that it was Barrier Keeper Yin who asked Laozi to give him a set of teachings as Laozi was leaving China, and so Laozi transmitted to him the *Daodejing*.

Unassigned Chapters

Chapters 30 and 31 are unassigned. Liu Xiaogan does not believe Chapter 30 has any distinctively Daoist themes and should simply be ignored. Graham thinks that Chapters 30 and 31 represent a collection of material from what he calls the 'individualist' school of Yang Chu in c. 200 BCE (Roth 1991: 80–2). It seems best to conclude that since Chapter 30 lacked any commentary by Guo Xiang and has little or nothing to do with the teachings of Zhuangzi, it should simply be set aside. Chapter 31, while trading on the appeal of thinking of Zhuang Zhou as 'The Old Fisherman' in the chapter name, is actually little more than a systematization of what is wrong with the Confucian way and the conditions under which Confucius could be taught. The author has the Old Fisherman tell Confucius to avoid 'the eight faults' and 'four evils'. This kind of grouping of ideas into serial categories probably shows a late developing practice and does not contribute any insight not already presented in other parts of the work.

The World Chapter

Chapter 33, with which the book ends, is a survey of the world of Chinese philosophy around the time of the transition from the Qin to Han dynasty. It contains descriptions of most of the major thinkers of classical Chinese philosophy, including Zhuangzi himself and the 'techniques of the Dao'. It was likely added by one of the later editors of the material. Since Chapter 33 may be the last material added to the *Zhuangzi*, the brilliant analysis of Liu Xiaogan can help us give a date for the compilation of the work by reference to it. Liu has demonstrated that at least 30 passages from 14 different chapters of the received *Zhuangzi* had been quoted by *Mister Lu's Spring and Autumn Annals* (*Lushi chunqiu*) and the *Hanfeizi*, before 241 BCE. The length of the passages account for about 42 per cent of our present 33-chapter *Zhuangzi*. This would have been impossible if the *Zhuangzi* had not already been in a substantial form and widely circulated before 241 BCE when *Mister Lu's Spring and Autumn Annals* was completed.

Chapter IV

The Masters Who Nurtured the Trunk of Daoism

Masters of the *Dao* in the *Daodejing* and *Zhuangzi*[8]

What can we learn about the life and work of the masters of the *dao* in the period prior to and including the fourth century BCE, based on the information embedded in the text blocks of the *Daodejing* and *Zhuangzi*? Who were the masters who created the teachings that became the great trunk of Daoism?

Being in a lineage following a master of the *dao* was like being in a new family. Lineage lines were long, as the great female master of the *Zhuangzi*, Nu Yu, makes clear to us. Nanbo Ziqi, seeing that she was old but had the look of a young woman, asked Nu Yu from whom she had learned such power of transformation. She replied, using Daoist names for her teachers: 'I heard it from the son of Aided-by-Ink, and Aided-by-Ink heard it from the grandson of Repeated-Recitation, and the grandson of Repeated-Recitation heard it from Seeing-Brightly, and Seeing-Brightly heard it from Waiting-for-Use, and Waiting-for-Use heard it from Exclaimed-Wonder, and Exclaimed-Wonder heard it from Dark-Obscurity, and Dark-Obscurity heard it from Participation-in-Mystery, and Participation-in Mystery heard it from Copy-the-Source!' (6b, 83) Lineage lines were also overlapping. Gengsang Chu did not hesitate to send his student Nanrong Chu to Laozi for guidance (23a, 248–54). We also know that masters consulted with each other and compared practices and teachings, often becoming friends, such as masters Si, Yu, Li and Lai, or masters Zi Sanghu, Meng Zifan and Zi Qinzang (6c, 83; 6d, 86).

The Worldview of Pre-Qin Masters of the *Dao*

The masters from whom the materials that found their way into the *Daodejing* and *Zhuangzi* came made no difference between what we call religion and what we know as philosophy. Neither of these conceptual frames would have made much sense to them. Their world was a unified whole. It was not made up of two realms, such as nature and supernature or the material and spiritual. These masters realized the limitations of their own sensory awareness and tried to overcome them. Masters of this period believed that one's current configuration of the Five Phases might take the form of a body, but such a form could be altered and manipulated, transformed into a different expression entirely.

The specifics of the worldview that lay behind these beliefs were associated with the work of Zou Yan at the Jixia Academy. He was the earliest architect of the worldview, the components of which are the power of *qi*, its correlative forces of *yin* and *yang*, and the Five Phases of phenomena that explain the movement of objects into and out of our sensory range. He believed that all things are going through innumerable and infinite permutations of *qi* energy and the phases of objects are not fixed but in process. Whether we can speak of this system as distinctively Daoist is doubtful because it was the undergirding supposition of virtually all classical Chinese understanding of the cosmos, and many archaeological findings have confirmed this claim as true.

Findings in the material culture of this period have supported the interpretation that this worldview was firmly established at the time of the formation of the *Daodejing* and *Zhuangzi*. In 1998, archaeologists excavated a funerary shell sculpture with the images of a tiger and dragon beside a corpse in a Neolithic era burial at Puyang (Henan Province). The dragon-tiger symbolism is a trope for *yin* and *yang*, and in much later Daoist history for lead (*qian*) and mercury (*shui yin* 水銀). These were the most common chemicals in the alchemy that masters of the *dao* used to control their transformations and increase their longevity and powers (Sun and Kistermaker 1997: 116). Likewise, the Warring States period (474–221 BCE) tomb of Yi of Zeng at Suixian (Hubei Province), discovered in 1978, contained a lacquer box with painted designs depicting the Big Dipper constellation (also called Northern Dipper or North Star) surrounded by 28 'mansions' (lesser stars) and flanked by a tiger and dragon, suggesting the belief that numinal entities mentioned in the *Zhuangzi* (e.g., the Big Dipper 6a, 82) exert influence over the cosmic process of our lives (Little 2004: 710–11). This piece may now be seen in the Provincial Museum in the city of Wuhan, Hubei Province.

The physics of *yin-yang* and the Five Phases represent the theoretical substrate lying underneath many text blocks in the *Zhuangzi*. One passage in which this view of reality is quite evident is from the Inner Chapters (6c, 84):

> Master Si, Master Yu, Master Li, and Master Lai were all four talking together ... . There was no disagreement in their hearts and so the four of them became friends ... Suddenly Master Lai grew ill. Gasping and wheezing, he lay at the point of death. His wife and children gathered round in a circle and began to cry.
>
> Master Li, who had come to ask how he was, said, 'Shoo! Get back! Don't disturb the process of change!' Then he leaned against the doorway and talked to Master Lai. 'How marvelous the Creator is! What is he going to make of you next? Where is he going to send you? Will he make you into a rat's liver? Will he make you into a bug's arm?'
>
> Master Lai said, 'A child, obeying his father and mother, goes wherever he is told, east or west, south or north. And the yin and yang – how much more are they to a man than father or mother! Now that they have brought me to the verge of death, if I should refuse to obey them, how perverse I would be! What fault is it of theirs? The Great Clod burdens me with form, labors me with life, eases me in old age, and rests me in death. So if I think well of my life, for the same reason I must think well of my death. When a skilled smith is casting metal, if the metal should leap up and say, "I insist upon being made into a Mo-ye [i.e., the greatest of all swords]!" he would surely regard it as very inauspicious metal indeed. Now, having had the audacity to take on human form once, if I should say, "I don't want to be anything but a man! Nothing but a man!" the Creator (*zaohua*) would surely regard me as a most inauspicious sort of person. So now I think of heaven and earth as a great forge, and the Creator as a skilled smith. Where could he send me that would not be all right? I will go off to sleep peacefully, and then with a start I will wake up.' (6c, 85)

Just whether all masters believed there was a Creator who controls the process of the transformation of things as does a great smith tending a giant forge is not altogether certain. However, it was not a question they tried to avoid. In the Huang-Lao materials of the *Zhuangzi*, Chapter 14 begins with a series of questions worthy of a twenty-first-century philosopher:

Does Heaven turn? Does the Earth sit still? Do sun and moon compete for a place to shine? Who masterminds all this? Who pulls the strings? Who, resting inactive himself, gives the push that makes it go this way? I wonder if there is some mechanism that works it and won't let it stop? I wonder if it just rolls and turns and can't bring itself to a halt? Do the clouds make the rain, or does the rain make the clouds? Who puffs them up, who showers them down like this? Who, resting inactive himself, stirs up all this lascivious joy? The winds rise in the north, blowing now west, now east, whirling up to wander on high. Whose breaths and exhalations are they? Who, resting inactive himself, huffs and puffs them about like this?

These sentiments should be read with the theory of the Five Phases as the background. In the Five Phase physics, all present forms transform and they are always becoming other things. People become ghosts and *shen* and all the entities of reality interact in the giant forge. An adept may be transmuted into a *zhenren* or *shen*. Adapting and controlling this process is the key to longevity and *de*.

Nourishing Life in the Practices of Pre-Qin Masters of the *Dao*

Masters of the pre-Qin period practiced healing and life-prolonging techniques called 'nourishing life' (*yangsheng*). In fact, this term is used as the title of the third chapter of the *Zhuangzi*. Persons who mastered these arts, such as Nu Yu (*Zhuangzi* 6b, 83), were believed to live long and not age or sometimes not die (i.e., they were *xian*, immortals). The first literary description of a person who has become an immortal is in the opening chapter of the *Zhuangzi*:

> In the mountain of far off Gushe there lives a spirit man (*shenren*) whose skin and flesh are like ice and snow, who is gentle as a virgin. He does not eat the five grains but sucks in the wind and drinks the dew; he rides the vapour of the clouds, yokes flying dragons to his chariot, and roams beyond the four seas. When the spirit (*shen*) in him concentrates itself it keeps creatures free from plagues and makes the grain ripen every year. (1f, 33)

There is a further account of a *zhenren* immortal in the second chapter of *Zhuangzi*:

Wang Ni replied, 'The Perfect Person (*zhenren*) is godlike (*shen yi*). Though the great swamps blaze, they cannot burn him; though the great rivers freeze, they cannot chill him; though swift lightning splits the hills and howling gales shake the sea, they cannot frighten him. A man like this rides the clouds and mist, straddles the sun and moon, and wanders beyond the four seas. Even life and death have no effect on him, much less the rules of profit and loss!' (2r, 46)

Terms for longevity (*shou*) and long life (*changsheng*) are first found in Zhou bronze inscriptions long before either the *Daodejing* or the *Zhuangzi*. Writings providing information about the activities necessary to bring about longevity date into the 400s BCE (Yu 1964: 87). The techniques included the use of herbs and management of diet by avoiding the five grains (i.e., rice, two types of millet, sorghum and wheat). These methods that cause good health and longevity are also those that are the fundamental basis for immortality. During the Eastern Zhou dynasty, immortality was thought of as not dying (i.e., 'no death', *wusi* or *busi*). Just as there were herbs and potions for curing and preventing illness in the period of the Eastern Zhou (770–476 BCE), master teachers also located and developed 'medicines of immortality' (*xianyao*) (Engelhardt 2004). These medicines could be found in remote mountain areas. They were cooked or sometimes carried in bags or gourds by masters of the *dao* who were believed to have the proper knowledge of alchemy. Masters of various lineages identified elements that could be processed into potions to drink, powders to be sprinkled on food or dropped in teas or soups, and mash to be pressed into a pill. The earliest mention of alchemical elixirs for longevity and immortality is in connection with lineage masters who were employed by rulers and comes from the 300s BCE (DeWoskin 1981: 166).

The techniques lineage masters used for health and longevity also included methods to guide *qi* through physical exercises (*tugu naxin*) and gymnastic movements known as 'guiding and pulling' (*daoyin*). These exercises seem to have been associated with what the *Zhuangzi* refers to as 'bear hangings' (*xiongjing*) and 'bird stretching' (*niaoshen*) (15a, 167). Today they are known as *qigong*. The exercises mentioned in the *Zhuangzi* were designed to help *qi* circulate for health and power. They seem to have been originally modeled after animal behaviors and movements. Animals are excellent examples of *wu-wei*.

Daoyin Exercises

They move naturally and spontaneously with *dao*, and so they express the *de* appropriate to their 'inner nature'.

Assuming control over one's transformations, and becoming an immortal (*chengxian*) was the goal of a master and of his adepts. Being an immortal was more than having physical longevity. It was also a transformation in the powers of a *zhenren* and in the range of experiences about which they could be aware (Engelhardt 2004: 75). In the *Zhuangzi*, two examples of such techniques stand out: Laozi sitting in solitude stillness like a tree when Confucius approached him (21d, 225–6) and Cheng of North Gate's experience when the Yellow Emperor played ritual music (14c, 156–8). In both of these instances, Laozi and Cheng concentrated their *qi* and the result was great *de*. They were able to do, see and hear things the ordinary person could not.

In this way, the ideal of Daoism, its goal for humanity, is very different from what one might find in Confucianism, Buddhism, Christianity and other traditions. *Zhenren* are not trying to extinguish desire and avoid suffering as in Buddhism, and they are not seeking forgiveness from a supreme deity whom they have wronged and offended as in Christianity. They are seeking nothing less than oneness with the power to transform their being, to control their Five Phase form and its power. In the *Zhuangzi* Master Hu transformed himself several times in order to overwhelm Ji Xian (7e, 96–7).

How shall we take teachings about *zhenren* and immortals (*xian*)? When we read that *zhenren* had remarkable powers to withstand cold and other adversities and to change their form, it seems that these persons were possessed of truly extraordinary abilities. But verification and confirmation of such abilities was always a subject of great concern. As the great vine of Daoism grew, many followers of the *dao* took these descriptions literally. By the time of the Han dynasty, as we shall see, collections of biographies of such persons were made and the stories tell of incredible accomplishments. However, another reading of these passages is possible, one that takes these passages more metaphorically. It is possible that these descriptions may mean that *zhenren*, because they treat all things as equal, forget distinctions and embrace the changes of *dao*, are *unaffected* by fire, flood, cold, hunger and the like. In this case, what is extraordinary about the *zhenren* is the way they have emptied their minds and controlled their *qi*, and not that they display transnormal abilities.

The Residence of Masters of the *Dao* in Mountain and Cave

Daoist Mountains

All major Daoist lineages are linked in some way with a sacred mountain. Early masters went into the mountains to communicate with the *dao* and develop their skills. Mountains were where the *qi* energy of the universe was particularly rarefied. In the *Zhuangzi* we can see the masters were associated with mountains. Four masters lived in the Gushe Mountains (1g, 34): Jianwu 'got the *dao*' on Mt Tai (6a, 81), the master called Nameless Man lived on Mt Yin (7c, 93–4), the Yellow Emperor is portrayed as seeking the *dao* from Guangchengzi in the Kongtong Mountains (11d, 118–19) and visiting Taiwei at Juzi Mountain (24c, 265), and Zhuangzi retreats to the mountains (20a, 209). Master Gengsang Chu lives in the mountains of Weilei (23a, 348), Xu Wugui lives in the mountains (24a, 261), Nanbo Ziqi lives in a cave in a mountain (24k, 271), and Shan Juan went to the mountains rather than rule the empire (28c, 309–10). In later Daoist history, the founders of new lineage vines were often associated with mountains. Zhang Daoling, the founder of the Way of the Celestial Masters, reported having a direct encounter with a spirit being that was the personification of *dao* on Crane-Call Mountain (*Hemingshan*). Master Kou Qianzhi had his spiritual experience on Mt Song (*Songshan*) in Henan Province. Ge Hong wrote his greatest works while living at Luofu Mountain (*Luofushan*). A group of masters established themselves in a community called *Louguan Tai* on Zhongnan Mountain (*Zhongnan shan*), southwest of the city of Chang'an (Xi'an). At that place, Wang Chongyang, founder of the Complete Perfection lineage (Quanzhen), said he met the numinous immortal Lu Dongbin. The lineage of Highest Clarity (*Shangqing*) was centered on Maoshan Mountain (Maoshan), southeast of modern Nanjing in Jiangsu Province.

The Five Sacred Mountains of Daoism

From the Warring States onward, the Five Marchmounts (*wuyue*) sacred to Daoism are often depicted on richly decorated and inlaid incense burners (*boshan lu*). The five sacred mountains of Daoism were codified by the time of the Warring States as Taishan (Shandong, east); Hengshan (Shanxi, north); Huashan (Shaanxi, west); Hengshan (Hunan, north); and Songshan (Henan, centre) (Little 2000: 148). What many regard as the most beautiful of these burners was excavated in 1968 during the Cultural Revolution from the tomb of imperial prince Liu Sheng (d. 113 BCE), in Mancheng, Hebei Province. On that burner, the mountain is surrounded by whirling lines made of inlaid gold, symbolizing *qi* energy. The piece may be seen in the Hebei Provincial Museum, Shijiazhuang city (Little 2004: 713).

Daoist masters built altars (*tan*) on the mountain sites where the sacred had erupted into their conscious experience. They 'read' the earth's landscape texture (*diwen*) and used arts first called 'planning residences' (*tuzhai shu*) that later became known as the science of 'wind and water' (*fengshui*) to locate the appropriate spot for a hut, cave or burner to make elixir. Later in Daoist history, 'true' charts and diagrams of holy mountains were cherished by lineages and their masters. Likewise, later Daoist writings codify the practices of early masters and provide specific instructions about how to determine sites for altars and instructions called 'opening a mountain' (*kaishan*) or 'mountain methods' (*shanfa*). Almost always the site was linked with its proper star constellation, thereby enabling the focus of sacral energy. The masters built altars, activated them with rituals, and in so doing they turned these places into 'the gates of Heaven' where numinal realities entered into the master's awareness. Afterward, when the master closed the gate, the place and altar would appear entirely normal to passers-by. There is evidence of these types of altars in inscriptions on bronze vessels as early as the Shang dynasty (Hahn 2004: 685).

Daoist Cave Refuges

Caves on mountains provided those seeking to know the *dao* with shelter for living, cooking and practicing inward stillness away from villages and towns. They were called 'earth lungs' (*difei*), and later masters speak of them as filled with 'refined breath' (*jingqi*) because they are places thought to concentrate the *qi* from which all things receive their power to live and take form. Masters and their students often made their way up mountains and into caves that could be accessed only by ropes and stone ladders. As someone approached these caves, they would notice markings placed by the master to protect the space and warn those who drew near to the focused *qi* in that site.

In Daoist belief, a cave is *yin*, its mountain is *yang*. The cave is a physical place, but it is also a metaphor for overcoming the distinction between the exterior and interior. Like *yin* and *yang*, exterior and interior are not opposites; they are in a relationship of correlation to each other. On another level, entering the cave is like entering the womb. It is windowless and enclosed, a self-contained shelter. This is why caves came to be called 'grotto heavens' (*dongtian*). When the *Daodejing* asks rhetorically whether a disciple can 'become as an infant' (*DDJ*, 10), it may be playing off the analogy between the cave and the womb. In a cave, the seeker of *dao* may enter into *huang hu* and emerge newly born, and with a mind emptied of human distinctions and paradigms. In the cave, seekers of the *dao* meditate, dream, visualize *shen* beings and conduct alchemical experiments and rituals. They become like little children and they walk out supple, spontaneous and able to move with *de* in effortless action (*wu-wei*) as one with *dao*. In the *Zhuangzi* Prince Sou of Yue fled for safety to the cinnabar caves where masters of the *dao* lived (28f, 311). Nanbo Ziqi resided in a cave because living there aided spiritual incubation, stillness and the emptying of his mind (24k, 271).

Common people and prospective students would go to the caves where the master lived, seeking healing, power and longevity. In a much later fifth-century CE Daoist writing, caves are ranked into the

ten great and 36 lesser grotto heavens (Verellen 1995: 278). In the
Tang dynasty (618–907 CE), many new Daoist temples were constructed at cave sites. Moreover, of 100 local gazetteers surviving into
the modern period providing information about the geography and
customs of southeast China, 90 list caves with Daoist names, indicating they are holy sites (Hahn 2004: 695).

Healing Techniques of Masters of the *Dao*

Zhenren, who learned the techniques of transformation, included
healing as one of their powers. They healed not only themselves but
also others. Such practices in this period, as in later Daoist history,
were reflections of the compassion of the masters of the *dao*. As we
have seen on page 48, it was believed that one of the *zhenren* of the
Gushe Mountains could, by concentrating his *qi*, protect creatures
from disease and pestilence and provide a plentiful harvest every year
(1f, 33). The method of healing used by a master of the *dao* was not
centered in anatomy in a Western sense, but in the body's energy
system (*qi*) and how the body was itself a microcosm of the processes
of reality in ever-changing combinations of the Five Phases. Masters
used herbs and elixirs for healing, and there are many examples of
common people and rulers who sought the masters whenever they
were ill. The earliest currently known mention of herbal healing, *qi*
therapy and alchemical elixirs refers to their use to assist rulers in the
300s BCE. These practices surface again around 133 BCE when Li
Shaojun suggested that Han Emperor Wudi's attempts to overcome
ill health and attain immortality would have benefitted from ingestion of cinnabar transmuted into an elixir (Pregadio 2004: 166). Early
masters made no hard and fast line between herbal pharmacology
and alchemy, nor between physical health and the prerequisites for
immortality.

However, some illnesses were believed to have their sources in
causes that would sometimes not respond to herbs and medicine, but
required the enhanced powers of masters of the *dao*. Consider the
Zhuangzi's story of the Duke Huan of Qi's encounter with a ghost
while hunting near a marsh in the mountains. After seeing the ghost,
the duke became ill and incoherent. Master Huang Gao'ao was called
in to help him. When the duke asked if ghosts really exist, Master
Huang answered:

'Indeed they do. By the mountain pools, there is Lu. There is the Ji in the stove. The heap of clutter and trash just inside the gate is where the Leiting lives. In the northeast corner the Bei-a leap about, and the northwest corner is where the Yiyang lives. In the water is the Wangxiang; on the hills, the Shen; in the mountains, the Kui, in the meadows, the Pang-huang; and in the marshes, the Weiyi.'

The duke said, 'May I ask what a Weiyi looks like?'

Master Huang said, 'The Weiyi is as big as a wheel hub, as tall as a carriage shaft, has a purple robe and a vermilion hat and, as creatures go, is very ugly. When it hears the sound of thunder or a carriage, it grabs its head and stands up. Any one who sees it will soon become the prince of princes.'

Duke Huan's face lit up and he said with a laugh, 'That must have been what I saw!' Then he straightened his robe and hat and sat up on the mat with Master Huang, and before the day was over, though he didn't notice it, his illness went away. (19h, 203–4)

It may very well be that this text is included in the *Zhuangzi* to poke fun at the belief that ghosts can cause illness. But it nevertheless testifies to common beliefs about the powers of masters of the *dao*. We get a good look at the beliefs underwriting this narrative in a work called the *Classic of the Mountains and Seas*. This is a writing that was in use before the formation of the *Zhuangzi*. The book is a sort of encyclopedia of flora, fauna, mountain trees and rock formations, but it also contains a number of stories about the mysterious powers and entities in the eerie world of the mountain forests and remote streams. However, in a period in which it was believed that the forms of all things were governed by the energy of the Five Phases, it was widely thought that anomalous appearances of beings and phenomena were everywhere and that such entities often hid in the mountain regions. These creature-spirits were usually said to be bizarre combinations of natural, human and animal forms because their Five Phases were associated with disruptions of *qi* and its *yin* and *yang*. For example, mountain spirits were reported to be nine-tailed foxes, snakes with human heads, and figures possessing human bodies with branches growing out of them. These spirits were often attached to certain locations, and masters of the *dao* were used by rulers, landowners and common people alike to assist in identifying these spirits, making spells to bind them, and providing protective talismans for venturing into these areas (von Glahn 2004: 82–9). In the account from *Zhuangzi* Duke Huan does not want Master Huang to simply identify the spirit he saw by the marsh; he wants Huang to bind the spirit and, thereby, return him to health.

Spellbinding

Although Master Huang Gao'ao was not required to spellbind the spirit of the mountain marsh Duke Huan saw, an example of the sort of thing the Duke wants him to do is in the remarkable work entitled *Spellbinding (jie)* that provides techniques and methods for dealing with a host of problems. This work is an account of ghosts and *shen* entities written on 45 bamboo slips. It is closely dependent on the doctrine of the Five Phases. The text was discovered during the excavation of Tomb 11 at Shuihudi, Hubei Province in 1975–6. The burial of the tomb occupant is dated as 217 BCE, but the work placed in the tomb is surely much older.

Spellbinding contains 70 separate entries for the techniques of managing a great number of difficulties. We can look at a few of them following the convention of the separate entries made on the slips:

2. When without cause, a ghost spirit (*guishen*) attacks a person and does not desist – this is the Stabbing Ghost. Make a bow from peach-wood; make arrows from non-fruiting jujube wood, and feather them with chicken feathers. When it appears, shoot it. Then it will desist.

19. When a person's wife or concubine or his friend dies and their ghost returns, wait for it with an ignited torch made of nutgrass on a nonfruiting jujube-wood shaft. Then it will not come again.

49. When a ghost baby continually calls to people [in the house] saying, 'Give me food' – this is the Ghost Who Was Mourned as a Suckling. Some of its bones are on the outside of the house. Cover them with yellow soil. Then it will desist.

Masters of the *Dao*: Arts of Talisman and Petition Writing

One example of the power of a master to write talismanic petitions is the exchange between Zhuangzi and the skull he passes beside the road on his way to the state of Chu. When querying the skull about its satisfaction in its present state, Zhuangzi asks the skull, 'If I got the Arbiter of Fate to give you a body again, make you some bones and flesh, return you to your parents and family and your old home and friends, you would want that, wouldn't you?' However, the skull frowned severely, wrinkling up its brow: 'Why would I throw away more happiness than that of a king on a throne and take on the troubles of a human being again?' (18d, 193–4). Zhuangzi is portrayed in this passage as proposing to write a petition to the Arbiter of Fate, a celestial official believed to be in charge of the health and lifespan of all persons. Of course, the point of this story is not to teach about petitions or even to suggest that Zhuangzi wrote them. The point is that we cannot be sure whether a change in life is good or ill or even whether death is better than life. However, the reference to this practice of petition writing indirectly gives us a window into the kinds of things masters of the *dao* were believed to be able to do at the time of the development of the *Zhuangzi* text.

A report found in a late Warring States era tomb dated prior to 269 BCE provides a great deal of illumination about the world view that formed the context for Zhuangzi's proposal and for the art of petitions known to the masters of the period. The report recounts the story of a man named Dan who committed suicide around 300 BCE after stabbing another man. His patron, General Xi Wu (d. 293 BCE), felt that Dan had not lived out his full lifespan. So he arranged for a plea written on a talismanic petition to be sent to The Scribe of the Director of Lifespan (*siming shi*), whose name is given in this text as Gongsun Qiang. In his lifetime, Gongsun Qiang was an official who figured prominently in the fall of the state of Cao in 487 BCE, but at the time of the writing of the petition he was believed to be ruling among the spirits. According to the account, following Xi Wu's request, and fully three years after his suicide, Dan was indeed sent back and arose from the grave. The narrative says that after about one week Dan could hear and eat again, but his body still showed the signs of his death for quite some time (Cedzich 1993: 26).

This story of revived Dan confirms that a belief in a celestial bureaucracy existed in the fourth and third centuries BCE, of which Zhuangzi's Arbiter of Fate is a part, as is The Scribe of the Director of Lifespan. Masters were believed to know how to address petitions to them in order to secure their support and numinal power. Donald Harper has provided a study of four examples of petitions whose purpose was to inform officials in numinal phases of the coming arrival of a deceased person (Harper 1994).

Talismans (*fu*)

Talismans are fundamental elements of Daoist communication with the forces and beings that exist in phases of reality that are not visible to us. Originally, talismans were messages written on oblong pieces of wood. Later, they were inscribed on bronzes, and today they are written on colored paper (usually yellow). The writing is mixed with figurative symbols and sometimes in unknown or secret characters or language. Talismans were thought to possess cosmic energy and power to protect an area or a person, express an edict from the *shen*, or make requests of *shen* to check the records of newly deceased (e.g., to show a deceased person mercy or to aid in the healing of the sick, or the arrangement of events to create auspicious happenings). The most ancient talismans we have excavated to date are those in tomb No. 3 at Mawangdui that date before 168 BCE.

Spiritual Experiences of the Masters of the *Dao*

Early masters were not strictly speaking what we know in the West as mystics, although they were known for gaining knowledge and power received in an altered state of awareness that could sometimes be called mystical. Awareness of something that was ineffable was a part of their experience. As the *Zhuangzi* says, 'What a pity! That the men of the world should suppose that form and color, name and sound are sufficient to convey the truth of a thing. It is because in the end they are not sufficient to convey truth that those who know do not speak, those who speak do not know' (13f, 152). Chapter 2 of the *Zhuangzi* says that in these states an individual's consciousness goes visiting into other phases (2b, 37). Later accounts report masters visualizing numinal beings or sensing a presence. In the *Zhuangzi*, when Tian Gan was searching for a master of the *dao* along the south of Yin Mountain on the banks of the Liao River, he met Nameless Man who told him the following:

> I'm just about to set off with the creator. And if I get bored with that, then I'll ride off on the Light and Lissome Bird out beyond the six directions, wandering in the village of Not-Even-Anything and living in the Board-and-Borderless field … Let your mind wander in simplicity, blend your spirit with the vastness, follow along with things the way they are … (7c, 91–2)

The testimony of masters to these experiences is not merely a poetic or literary device. These are reports of experiences with numinal presence and an immediate awareness of reality that infuses the master with *de*.

One way this awareness came to a master was through a state of stillness and quietude empty of the machinations of language, reason, ideas and inferences. Consider this beautiful example from the *Zhuangzi*:

> Confucius went to call on Lao Dan [Laozi]. Lao Dan had just finished washing his hair and had spread it over his shoulders to dry. Utterly motionless, he did not even seem to be human. Confucius, hidden from sight, stood waiting, and then after some time presented himself and exclaimed, 'Did my eyes play tricks on me, or was that really true? A moment ago, Sir, your form and body seemed stiff as an old dead tree, as though you had forgotten things, taken leave of men, and were standing in solitude itself!' Lao Dan said, 'I was letting my mind wander in the Beginning of things.' … Confucius said, 'I would like to hear by what means this may be accomplished.' [Lao Dan replied] '… In this world, the ten thousand things come together in One, and if you can find that One and become identical with it, then your four limbs and hundred joints will become dust and sweepings; life and death, beginning and end will be mere day and night, and nothing whatever can confound you …' (21d, 225–6)

Ritual Practices of Masters of the *Dao*

The Laozi legends put him in the line of masters we have already introduced. One of the earliest stories about Laozi is that Confucius sought him out for instruction in funeral rituals.

Confucius Visits Laozi

There are many fine paintings and other works of art that depict Confucius' visit to Laozi. One of these is an Eastern Han dynasty ink rubbing of a stone panel from the Wu Liang Shrine, Jiaxiang county, Shandong province, which is now in the Field Museum, Chicago (USA).

We should make clear just what such funeral rituals included. They were not about putting flowers on the grave or eulogizing a person. These rituals consisted of such important tasks as sending talismanic petitions to the numinal powers and offering incantations to keep the dead from intruding into this phased reality in order to protect family and villagers from a ghostly return. If we think that surely Confucius would not be interested in things such as this, we do well to remember that our evidence for Confucius' participation in religious sacrifices and rituals is both adequate and clear. One of the most interesting is *Analects* 10.14: 'When the villagers were performing the end of the year exorcism (*nuo*), he would stand on the Eastern steps dressed in full court regalia.' The ritual referred to in this analect is probably the New Year's exorcism in which the entire populace participated and which is described in the *Rites of Zhou* (*Zhouli*), Chapters 48 and 54. Its purpose was to drive away evil spirits and bad influences from the previous year.

The Laozi text blocks in the *Zhuangzi* represent that he had disciples other than Confucius and it seems he transmitted skills in ritual to them. In *Zhuangzi* Chapter 23a, Gengsang Chu is one of these. Gengsang Chu has taken what he has learned from Laozi and begun a training program with his own students on another mountain (23a, 248–54). Indeed, his task, like that of Laozi, is to transform (*hua*, 23a, 251) his disciples. By virtue of his great impact during the three years he was among them, the villagers on the mountains of Weilei wanted to turn over to him the rituals of soil and grain and make him their 'impersonator of the dead' (*shi*). Clearly, performing rituals and speaking for the ghost spirits of the departed is presented as something readers would have believed possible of the kind of disciples Laozi was producing. Of course, in the *Zhuangzi*, Gengsang Chu is displeased with their desire to install him in this role. However, this displeasure is not because he was asked to do rituals, but rather because the people wanted to make him a sort of 'local worthy' and give him a position of fame and acclaim, and he was taught by Laozi that the true sage should remain hidden and never give in to the desire for fame.

Masters of the *dao* were believed to be able to bring the *dao* and numinal beings into their own awareness and that of other persons by the use of ritual. The Huang-Lao materials of the *Zhuangzi* relate a fascinating story about a time when the Yellow Emperor played ritual music. When he played this music, *yin* and *yang* were in harmony, the ghosts and spirits kept to their proper places, and the spirits in the constellations did what was appropriate (14c, 156–7). Although the Yellow Emperor should not be regarded as a master who actually lived, he is portrayed doing the kinds of things that living masters were believed to do. In fact, the activities of living masters were probably the model for attributions of such techniques to the Yellow Emperor. The ritual music of the Yellow Emperor could produce spiritual states in the master who played the music and in those who heard it. Cheng of North Gate reports having such a numinal experience:

> Cheng of North Gate said to the Yellow Emperor, 'When Your Majesty performed the Xianchi music in the wilds around Lake Dongting, I listened, and at first I was afraid. I listened some more and felt weak, and then I listened to the end and felt disoriented. Overwhelmed, speechless, I couldn't get hold of myself.'
>
> 'It's not surprising you felt that way,' said the Emperor. 'I performed it through man, tuned it to Heaven, went forward with ritual principle, and established it in Great Purity … now with clear notes, now with dull ones, the *yin* and the *yang* will blend all in harmony, the sounds flowing forth like light, like hibernating insects that start to wriggle again, like the crash of thunder with which I awe the world. At the end, no tail; at the beginning, no head; now dead, now alive, now flat on the ground, now up on its feet, its constancy is unending, yet there is nothing that can be counted on. That's why you felt afraid.
>
> …You stand dazed before the four-directioned emptiness of *dao*, … It flowed and scattered, and bowed before no constant tone … Wordless, it delights the heart-mind. Therefore Shennong sang its praises thus: "Listen – you do not hear its sound; look – you do not see its form. It fills all Heaven and earth, enwraps all the six directions".' (14c, 156–8)

The setting for this ritual observance is the lakeside. There the Yellow Emperor played ritual music and it produced in Cheng of North Gate a spiritual state of awareness, similar to that reported in *Daodejing* 21: 'Listen – you do not hear its sound; look – you do not see its form.'

Pacing the Dipper and the Step of Yu (*Yubu*)

Pacing the Dipper is a Daoist ritual dance that is pre-Qin in origin and it is done in the style of the Step of Yu mentioned in the *Day Book* (*Ri Shu*), a bamboo slip text dated 217 BCE and excavated in 1975 at Shuihudi, Hubei Province. The Step of Yu is also referred to in the largest medical text discovered at Mawangdui: *Fifty-two Healing Methods* dating to 164 BCE. In the dance, the master walks his way into the presence of the numinal powers closest to the Supreme Unity (Taiyi) whose presence is in the Big Dipper (cf. *DDJ*, 42a). So the Step of Yu is closely associated with what is known as 'Pacing the Dipper' or 'Pacing the Guideline'. The Chinese character for 'guideline' (*gang*) originally referred to the star at the end of the handle of the Big Dipper and the character for 'star' (*dou*) referred to the Dipper itself. The basic function of the dance is to symbolize the transformation and empowerment of the master caused by a spiritual journey to the source of the power of the universe, the Supreme Unity.

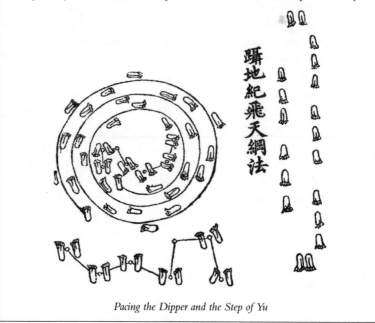

Pacing the Dipper and the Step of Yu

Divination Practices among Masters of the *Dao*

Divination, often associated with fortune-telling, is the gaining of information, insight or the hidden significance of events or phenomena usually by means of the interpretation of omens, dreams, physiognomy or other powers. In ancient China, divination was not specifically or exclusively associated with masters of the *dao* (Sakade 2004: 541).

However, in the *Zhuangzi* there are passages that mention divination probably of the milfoil type (*shizhan*) (e.g., 21, 229) and also of the Turtle Shell Oracle Bone (*jia gu*) technique (26, 298–9). There are also several examples of gaining knowledge through dream experience scattered in all strata of the *Zhuangzi* (2u, 47; 4d, 64; 14d, 158–9; 18d, 193; 21h, 230; 26f, 298). There are two accounts of physiognomy (*xiangshu*) reported without disapproval (7e, 94–7; 24o, 273–4). There are references suggesting the use of the stars to obtain insight into events because they are in ranks, such as the way in which the *shen* of the Big Dipper control things as in Dipper astrology (*qizheng*) (6a, 82; 13c, 149–50). The *Zhuangzi* makes reference to the technique of choosing auspicious days (5a, 69) that may show the tolerance or even the use of the method of calendrics (*dunjia*) on the part of masters of the *dao*. We can have little doubt that sites were chosen on mountains, especially for digging caves by means of the practice of geomancy (*kanyu jia*) that would later be known as *fengshui*.

Divination by use of milfold stalks was used as early as the Zhou

Replica of the Turtle Shell Oracle Bone

dynasty, gradually replacing the more ancient practice of Oracle-bone divination that died out in the Han (Smith 1991: 19–22). In milfold divination, 50 stalks were cast on the ground, divided into piles, and counted off in sets of four to yield either a *yin* (even) or *yang* (odd) number. Each cast thus created a *yin* or *yang* line, until six lines were determined. The result corresponded to one of the 64 hexagrams of the *Book of Changes* (*Yijing*). A hexagram is a combination of two trigrams that were talismanic arrangements of marked lines believed to reveal the *yin* and *yang* energy patterns of the universe, and thought to have been disclosed to one of the mythic three founders of China, Fu Xi. The *Book of Changes* text multiplied this pattern beyond the original eight trigrams that were arranged in an octagonal shape with one trigram on each side and known as the *bagua*. Once a hexagram was determined, the *Book of Changes* could be interrogated for guidance in decision-making. These techniques of calendrics, physiognomy, geomancy, hexagram calculation and Dipper astrology continued to be part of the arts of masters of the *dao* throughout most of Daoist history. Marc Kalinowski (1990) has shown that 40 texts in the Daoist canon are concerned with divination methods.

A composite picture of the masters who created the *Daodejing* and *Zhuangzi* has emerged from our survey. They not only lived in the mountains but also were thought to change in appearance and exhibit spirit-like behavior. They altered their diets and practiced breathing methods and gymnastic exercises that concentrated their *qi*. They were healers and were believed to know the rituals and practices necessary to communicate with numinal beings and protect persons from disease and starvation. When we put this together with their abilities to enter altered states of consciousness and receive *dao's de* as *Daodejing* 14 and 29 represent, we have a fairly complete picture of the sorts of masters who created the great classical texts of Daoism. With this picture in mind, we can have no doubt that they were not merely discursive philosophers or lower-level officials of government. If we looked for Western analogs to these figures in roughly the same time period, we would be seeking not Socrates, Plato and Aristotle, but Parmenides and Empedocles.[9]

Chapter V
Growth of the Daoist Vine During the Qin and Han Dynasties

The Huang-Lao Lineage Vine

During the period from the Jixia Academy (c. 300s BCE) to the creation of the Huainan Academy (c. 160s BCE, see page 67), the Yellow Emperor, whom we have already met through the Huang-Lao materials in the *Zhuangzi*, became associated with a number of texts, including the following:

- The now-lost *Yellow Emperor's Old Willow Divination by Dreams.*

- An attempt to synthesize medical techniques with the doctrine of the Five Phases known as the *Yellow Emperor's Inner Classic.*

- The *Dietary Proscriptions of the Divine Agriculturist (Shennong) the Yellow Emperor* concerned with identifying foods that are helpful or else must be eliminated from the diet of one who would seek longevity and immortality.

- The *Yellow Emperor's and Three Kings' Techniques for Nourishing Yang*, which was devoted to methods for controlling *qi* and harmonizing the balance of *yin* and *yang* through sexual methods.

- The *Wondrous Mushrooms of the Yellow Emperor and His Various Disciples*, which was a work on mountain herbs and other medicinal plants and their uses.

- The *Yellow Emperor's Classic of the Golden Bookcase and Jade Scales*, which is devoted to techniques for addressing numinal officials who rule over longevity and death, acquiring their help in gaining prosperity and auspicious benefits in life, and providing methods for expelling and identifying harmful spirits.

Significance of the Yellow Emperor Medical Texts
at Mawangdui

In the 1973 finds at Mawangdui tombs in Changsha, Hunan province, mentioned earlier in our discussion of the *Daodejing*, 15 medical manuscripts written on silk and bamboo strips were found in tomb No. 3. Although the burial is dated to 168 BCE, the manuscripts themselves derive from the period between the Jixia Academy and the formation of the Huainan Academy group of scholars. The texts are built on medical theories and practices that make use of the theory of *qi*, *yin* and *yang* interaction and the Five Phases, the fundamentals of which we have already discussed with respect to the *Zhuangzi*. These should not be understood simply as medical texts. They are, from the point of view of the Huang-Lao lineage vine, profoundly spiritual and transformative techniques. All of them are rooted in *qi* theory and its implications for regenerating and energizing the phasal consciousness of one's being.

Recipes for the 'nourishing of life' (*yangsheng*) are a central concern of these texts. These works offer a more developed written explanation of practices mentioned in the *Zhuangzi*, both in its chapter by that name and in other places in the text. According to these manuscripts, the functions of the body need to be regulated and ordered (*zhi*) to ensure longevity and the balance of *yin* and *yang* that makes for good health. Moreover, as we shall see, good health and harmony internally were believed to lead to the ease and naturalness of a moral life.

The Mawangdui manuscript entitled *The Rejection of Grains and Absorption of Qi* describes how to eliminate grains (*bigu*) and balance other ordinary harmful foodstuffs (*quegu*) by replacing them with medicinal herbs, and building robust *qi* through special breathing and gymnastic exercises. We have already seen that *zhenren* were associated with the removal of grains from their diets and with *qi* building exercises in the *Zhuangzi* (1f, 33; 15a, 167). So what we notice in this text is an extension of, not a radical departure from, the *Zhuangzi*.

Eliminating grains, practicing breathing and performing gymnastic exercises are referred to as 'guiding *qi*' (*xingqi*) in these texts. These healthful practices move *qi* in an optimal circulation of power within the body (*xiao zhoutian*). In these manuscripts, clearly the body is thought of as a network of flowing *qi* energy. In fact, five texts in this collection of 15 outline a system of *qi* conduits or meridians (*jingmo*) in the body.

The *qi* meridian network of the Mawangdui medical books is elaborated in the *Yellow Emperor's Inner Classic*, mentioned on page 65. That text taught that the *yin* conduits run on the inside of the body just under the skin, and the *yang* meridians are external, meandering along the surface of the skin. Each conduit has a number of clearly defined energy directional centres accessible through the skin called 'caverns'.

These centres are now called acupuncture points (*kongxue*; *qixue*). We believe the masters of this period used needles, massage or simply hand and finger pressure to influence the flow of *qi* through these points.

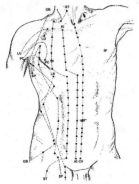

Acupuncture Network

A text found at Mawangdui simply called the *Gymnastic Chart* (*Daoyin tu*) has color illustrations of human figures performing the *qi* work noted on page 50, which was later known as *qigong* exercises. We can connect this work and its illustrations to the *Zhuangzi* because the author uses some of the same names for these exercises as those employed in the *Zhuangzi*: 'bear hanging' and 'bird stretch' (15a, 167).

The *Mawangdui* medical texts also teach a method for healing as a part of their repertoire of techniques for long life: the ingestion of talisman water (*fushui*). This practice is described in *Techniques for Fifty-Two Ailments*.

Note: The medical texts from Mawangdui did not have titles and I use those given in the *Han Dynasty Tombs at Mawangdui Silk Texts Naming Catalog* in Donald Harper (1999).

Texts ascribed to the Yellow Emperor were valued not only for their association with him but also because of the talismanic power they possessed. Ying Shao tells tales of how the chanting of some texts staved off trouble and illness. He describes how Han dynasty Emperor Wu hired a shaman (*wu*) to curse a man named Dong Zhongshu (179–104 BCE), but by chanting the same Huang-Lao texts Dong escaped and caused the shaman to die instead.

The Huainan Academy and the *Master of Huainan*

According to the *Book of the Early (Former) Han* (44.2145) Liu An, the prince of Huainan (in modern Anhui province), and uncle of

Han Emperor Wudi, gathered several thousand masters of the *dao* and other experts to Huainan in the 160s–120s BCE because he wanted to learn their arts and techniques and support them in the creation of written works related to these abilities. The *Book of the Early (Former) Han* refers to one of these works, which is now apparently lost, as a text concerned with becoming a spirit immortal (*shenxian*) by the use of 'the yellow and white' or alchemy (*huangbai*) (Csikszentmihalyi 2004: 56). But the *Master of Huainan*, which we will henceforth refer to as the *Huainanzi*, also known as *The Great Brilliance of Huainan* (*Huainan honglie*), was arguably the most important text composed by the masters gathered at Huainan. Some traditions say the work was composed by the 'Eight Gentlemen' (*bagong*) of Huainan.

The Eight Gentlemen of Huainan
Jin Chang
Lei Bei
Li Shang
Mao Bei
Su Fei
Tian You
Wu Bei
Zuo Wu

The *Huainanzi* was presented by Liu An to his nephew, Emperor Wu, on the occasion of Liu An's visit to court in 139 BCE. Liu An wanted to influence the political direction of the state and the trajectory of the emperor's rulership to be more like what we saw in the Huang–Lao materials of the *Zhuangzi*. He sought to do this in a time when the political momentum was moving quickly toward the establishment of Confucianism as the imperial ideology (Vankeerberghen 2001: 12).

The *Huainanzi* is largely a political treatise on rulership, but its political objectives are pursued through a series of 21 essays (*xun*) ranging from cosmology and astronomy to inner *qi* cultivation and spiritual transformation. Although it was not written for a general readership, but for the imperial court of the Han, nevertheless it has a great deal in common with many text blocks in the *Daodejing* and the *Zhuangzi* (especially its Huang–Lao lineage materials). The work extends the Huang–Lao lineage vine into new areas by bringing into visibility much that belongs to Daoism and that is undisclosed or lying in the background in the *Daodejing* and *Zhuangzi*.

Healing and Nourishing Life in the Huainanzi

One way the *Huainanzi* brings into visibility practices seen in the *Zhuangzi* is its description of the healing and healthful practices of abstaining from the five grains and eating *qi* in order to nourish life and obtain longevity and immortality. The *Zhuangzi* makes it clear in the Inner Chapters that the *zhenren* has *de* because he does not eat the five grains and he knows how to control his *qi* (1f, 33). The *Huainanzi* text expands on the way these techniques can be used to create a transformation of the person. The text says: 'Those who eat *qi* achieve spirit illumination and are long lived; those who eat grain have frenetic minds and are short-lived' (Ch. 4). One of the most important contributions of the *Huainanzi* is the way it connects moral action and physical well-being into a holistic theory of health that teaches that behavior influences *qi* energy, thereby integrally connecting the physical, spiritual and the moral:

> Happiness and anger are aberrations of *dao.*
> Worry and sadness are deficiencies of *de.*
> Likes and dislikes are excesses of the mind ...
> In a human being:
> Great anger damages the *yin.*
> Great joy collapses the *yang.*
> Weak *qi* causes dumbness.
> Shock and fright bring about madness.
> When worry, sadness and angry rage abound, illness develops.
> When likes and dislikes abound, misfortunes follow one another.
>   (1/12b6–13a2)
> ...
> The reason
> That people are able to see clearly and hear acutely,
> That the body is able to be strong, and the hundred joints can bend
>   and stretch flexibly,
> That one's discrimination can determine white from black, ugliness
>   from beauty, and similarities and differences
> Is because *qi* infuses these activities
> And the *shen* directs them (1/17a1–6).

In these passages, the *Huainanzi* clearly is teaching the correlational relationship between robust *qi* and human emotions and even moral dispositions (e.g., anger). The emotional states of worry and sadness are caused by deficiencies of *de*. If we draw out the implications of these teachings, we might conclude that the masters of Huang-Lao believed one way of living an emotionally and morally healthy life was to strengthen *qi* energy.

Zhenren in the Huainanzi

The *Huainanzi* follows closely the picture of pre-Qin masters provided at the end of Chapter IV. Of the *zhenren*, it says:

> Those we call 'zhenren' are people whose natures are united with
> *dao*.
> They possess it, but appear to have nothing,
> They are filled by it, but appear to be empty.
> They rest in this unity
> And know not duality.
> They concentrate on what is inside
> And pay no attention to what is outside ...
> They ramble outside this dusty world
> And wander by *wu-wei*
> Unfettered and unhindered,
> They harbor no contrived cleverness in their minds.
> Hence death and life are great indeed, but they do not alter them ...
> they forget emotions ...
> Vast and empty, they are tranquil and without worry.
> > Great swamps may catch fire, but they cannot burn them.
> > Great rivers may freeze over, but they cannot chill them.
> > Great thunder may shake the mountains, but it cannot panic them.
> > Great storms may darken the sun, but they cannot harm them ...
> They take life and death to be a single transformation, and the myriad
> things to be of equal in value.
> They merge their *qi* with the foundation of great purity and roam
> freely beyond the boundless ...
> Emerging from and entering the process of reality, they command
> ghosts and *shen* entities.
> This is how their *shen* is able to ascend to *dao*. This is the roaming
> around in life of the *zhen[ren]*. (7/5a2–6a9)

This extended passage shows us that according to the *Huainanzi* the *zhenren* possess the *dao* and make their way through life in *wu-wei*. By holding on to *dao*, nothing can harm them. These are themes we have seen before in both the *Daodejing* (e.g., Ch 35s, 67) and *Zhuangzi* (1f, 33; 2r, 46; 5f, 75; 12d, 130). Likewise, *zhenren* regard life and death as a single continuous transformation and all things are equal, which is the most prominent emphasis in *Zhuangzi* Ch. 2.

The Huainanzi on Rulership

The Huang-Lao method of governance revealed in the *Zhuangzi* stressed the principles of *wu-wei* and noninterference, while not teaching that the *zhenren* should avoid rulership entirely. This same ideology found expression in the *Huainanzi*. Indeed, the culture-creating acts establishing order and institutions performed by sages – such as Yao, Shun, Yu and even Confucius – are associated in both of these texts with *wu-wei* conduct, moving with the *dao*. In fact, not even acquiring wealth or gaining an official position is condemned, if it is done in, or a result of, *wu-wei* (Vankeerberghen 2001: 97). Accordingly, the *Huainanzi* directly addresses the nature of *wu-wei* because it is so important to the ruler:

> What do we call *wu-wei*? When a wise person does not use his position to conduct his own affairs; when a brave person does not use his position to engage in reckless exploits; when a benevolent person does not use his position to impress with acts of bounty, this is what we can call *wu-wei*. (9/75/20–1)

As we can see, the *Huainanzi* does not reject the Confucian virtue of benevolence as was done in the *Daodejing*, the Inner Chapters, the Daode Chapters and Zhuangzi disciple materials of the *Zhuangzi*. It approves of benevolence, but says that one's aim in benevolence cannot be to show the world how benevolent one is. The *Huainanzi* seeks to correct the followers of Confucius for teaching benevolence in the wrong manner. This is perhaps exactly what we might expect from a work compiled during the ascendancy of Confucian influence, but which also strives to convey its sense of the truth in terms of following the *dao*.

The Huainanzi on Human Nature and De

The *Huainanzi* also develops the idea of inborn nature that played a prominent role in the *Daode* Chapters of *Zhuangzi*. In the *Huainanzi*, as in those materials in *Zhuangzi*, the reader is taught that all things have their own nature (*xing*). For humans, our inborn nature is compared to our guiding star. On an individual basis, this means the star under which we are born. Every person has a birth star. But, more importantly, there is the 'Big Dipper' or 'North Star' (*bei-dou*) that is a symbol for the celestial forces that guide the universe amid the confusing multitude of forces that would draw persons and things away from *dao* (11/96/1–2). There is a difference between humans and other things. While all other things in reality move *only* according to their nature, humans can make a decision against their inborn nature, disrupting their being with turbulent emotions and confusions, and committing immoral actions that will divert the harmony of *qi* necessary for health and longevity. This is why the *Huainanzi*, like the *daode* materials' emphasis on 'inborn nature' in the *Zhuangzi* (8a, 103), calls on its readers to 'return to their nature' (*fan xing*). In both of these sets of materials, becoming a *zhenren* means not straying from one's inborn nature. When humans fail to guard their inborn nature, the physical acts of seeing, hearing, moving, appearance and the ability to exercise moral discernment all go awry. The greater the distance a person's will is from his inborn nature, the less likely that he will possess *de*, be able to communicate with the *shen* and have health and longevity. In contrast, the *zhenren* circulates 'straight *qi*' (*zheng qi*, 14/137/20), not *qi* diverted from the flow of inborn nature.

It is within this context that one of the important emphases of the *Huainanzi* should be understood. The text teaches that there is a kind of 'action and response' (*ganying*) present in the movement of *dao*, revealing that all things in the universe are interrelated and influence each other. Morality, health, longevity, power and success are all interrelated. Failure to follow one's inborn nature and allow *qi* to flow undiverted will bring disappointment and disaster, as well as illness and early death. So, the text says:

> For this reason, whenever one is about to take up an affair, one must first stabilize one's intentions and purify one's spirit.
> When the spirit is pure and intentions are stable
> Only then can things be straight [*zheng*]. (11/96/7–12)

A person whose *qi* is straight, flowing from his inborn nature into *wu-wei* conduct, will have remarkable *de*. When this individual is a ruler, great bliss will follow in the kingdom:

> When pure sincerity is stimulated inwardly, bodily *qi* will move Heaven; then auspicious stars appear, the yellow dragon descends, the well-boding phoenix arrives, sweet springs flow, good grains sprout, the river does not flood, and the sea is not stirred by waves. (20/210/20–1)

Masters of the *dao* mentioned in the *Huainanzi*, such as Master Kuang and the female master known simply as Commoner's Daughter (*Shunu*), are described as having tremendous *de* because 'concentrating their *qi* and disciplining their intentions ... they were able to merge above with the Nine Heavens and activate [control over that which was outside of them]' (6/49/27–8).

The *de* of the *zhenren* comes not only from healthful living and inner concentration but also from the activity of ritual in ways similar to those we have already seen in the *Daodejing* (Chs 5, 10, 14, 21) and *Zhuangzi* (14c, 156–7). Borrowing language that sounds similar to that of *Daodejing* 14, the *Huainanzi* says:

> Now with regard to ghost spirits (*guishen*)
> we look for them but they are without form;
> we listen for them but they are without voice;
> we perform the *jiao* sacrifice to Heaven and the *wang* sacrifice to the mountain and river *shen*.
> By prayer and sacrifice we seek prosperity;
> By the *yu* sacrifice and the *dui* [trigram of the *Yijing*] we seek rain;
> With tortoise shell and milfoil we decide matters.
> The *Book of Odes* says, 'Just when the spirits might descend cannot be calculated. So, how can you treat them with disdain?' (20/211/5–7)

Rituals are thought to be effective in the *Huainanzi* because *zhenren* 'employ ghost spirits as their servants' (*yishi guishen*, 7/57/10). As an example of the *de* of the great legendary Kings Fu Xi and Nu Wa, the text tells us that they led a group of numinal beings when they climbed to 'the Ninefold Heaven' (6/52/24).

People such as these *zhenren*, and even the Confucian sage kings, are given as examples in the *Huainanzi* because they have transformed themselves from humans into *shen*. Chapter 9 says that their 'essence as a human being has been developed to the utmost (*zui*) and they have become spirits (*zhi jing wei shen*)' (9/68/1–12). In the *Huainanzi* this meant that the ruler who underwent a 'transformation in spirit' (*shen-hua*) would bring peace and harmony to the land and its people.

Clearly, then, there is a definite connection between what is said of the *zhenren*, the inner nature and *de*, and the *Huainanzi's* political objectives for rulers, such as Emperor Wu to whom the book was presented. As an exemplar of the ideal Daoist ruler, the text offers Shennong:

> He [Shennong] nurtured the people; the people in response were simple and steady, straight and sincere.
>
> They did not engage in anger and strife but [regarded their] goods as sufficient.
>
> They did not labor until exhaustion but they completed their accomplishments.
>
> They availed themselves of the gifts of Heaven and Earth and lived in harmony and unity.
>
> Thus his [Shennong's] transformation of the people was truly spiritual. (9/67/17–23)

Who Was Shennong?

Shennong was a cultural hero of Chinese legend said to have lived in about 2700 BCE. Traditionally, he is regarded as the Father of Chinese agriculture and medicine. The name 'Shennong' may also be taken as a title: 'The *Shen* Agriculturist'. He is associated closely with the Yellow Emperor and the development of the pharmacology of *qi* energy. In fact, he is sometimes taken as a master with vast knowledge of medicine who advised the Yellow Emperor, and sometimes as the Yellow Emperor himself, as the ambiguity of the title of one work shows: *Dietary Proscriptions of the Divine Agriculturist the Yellow Emperor.* He is said to have assembled the earliest Chinese pharmacopoeia, including over 365 medicines derived from minerals, plants and animals. He is also credited with originating the technique of acupuncture.

The *Huainanzi* says that Shennong was one with *dao*, and his personal 'spiritual transformation was numinous' (*bianhua ruo shen*, 9/67/23). Shennong is used as the ideal pattern for a ruler in the *Huainanzi's* political theory because he did not rely on punishment or execution to control the people, but governed as a master of *dao* and transformed their spirits. (9/68/11)

If a ruler fails in his own spiritual transformation, the consequences are frightening because another kind of action and response (*ganying*) will follow:

> Then sun and moon will be feeble and eclipsed, the five planets will deviate from their courses, the four seasons will encroach upon one another, the day will be dark and night will be light, mountains will collapse and rivers will dry up, and there will be thunder in winter and frost in summer. (20/210/20–1)

Response to Daoism in the Qin and Early Han Dynasties

Some of the methods and texts that emerged from Huainan were seen as dangers to the state and to the rulers' increasing interest in centralizing control. There were numerous critics of the teachings of these new synergistic teachings. Several intellectuals of the last years of the Han dynasty found the emphasis on the spirits in Huang-Lao and the *Huainanzi* to be disturbing and misleading. In *Records of the Historian*, Sima Qian was skeptical of the Huainan masters of the *dao* and thought that they preyed on the desires of the rulers (12.482). He considers these masters to have been charlatans who misled the rulers and manipulated them by telling them fantastic tales and making unsubstantiated claims. Sima Qian tells us that both the first emperor of the Qin dynasty, Qinshihuang (r. 221–210 BCE), and Han Emperor Wu (r. 141–87 BCE) were obsessed with the pursuit of immortality and the techniques necessary to it. Both of these emperors made expeditions into the ancient states of Qi and Yan (modern day Shandong and costal Hebei and Liaoning, respectively) to locate the immortals and learn their secrets. They wanted to find the paradise islands on which immortals were said to live. Qinshihuang also turned west in search of Kunlun Mountain, where it was believed that the immortal Queen Mother of the West (*Xiwangmu*) lived. He readily indulged masters who would instruct him in the pursuit of immortality.

Qinshihuang's Necropolis

From the late fifth century BCE onward, vertical-shaft tombs for the elite were replaced by ones having spacious chambers, because it was believed that the dead would go on living in their tombs. These tombs replicated the world of the living, and the scale and amenities included in them matched the deceased status in the world of the living. Wealthy rulers built majestic mausolea, and Qinshihuang's is undoubtedly the greatest of all. When Qinshihuang built his fabulous necropolis (city of the dead) near Chang'an (Xi'an), he created a massive army of life-size terracotta soldiers as guardians. This extraordinary accomplishment, however, may not be as significant as the creation of his own mausoleum, which has not yet been excavated. The reason this is so may be learned from Sima Qian's description of the construction of the tomb in his *Records of the Historian*.

'They dug through three subterranean streams and poured molten copper for models of palaces, pavilions and officials, as well as fine vessels, precious stones and rarities. Artisans were ordered to design crossbows so that any thief breaking in would be shot. The ceiling was inlaid with pearls to simulate the sun, stars [constellations] and the moon, the floors and walls were lined with bronze to keep out water. All the country's streams, the Yellow River [Huang He] and Yangzi [lit., "Long River", *Chang Jiang*] were reproduced in mercury and by some mechanical means made to flow. The heavenly constellations were shown above and the regions of the earth below. The candles were made of whale oil to ensure an eternal flame.'

Qinshihuang included rivers of mercury in his tomb because mercury was the most highly valued elixir substance for those seeking immortality during this period. The properties of mercury appeared to be mysterious when it was produced from burning cinnabar. It seems to be solid, liquid and to give off gas, exhibiting behaviors of many states of being and revealing its transformational qualities. It was believed to possess a pure energy that when ingested could aid in the transformation of the Five Phases of a human being. Qinshihuang's mausoleum has never been opened, but in an article in the February 2006 *China Daily*, Duan Qingbo, an archaeologist and researcher from the Shaanxi Provincial Archaeology Institute, reported that studies have shown the mercury density in the soil around the site to be more than ten times that of the nearby area. So perhaps Sima Qian's account is reliable.

Emperor Wu, whom we should remember was Liu An's nephew, was told by masters guiding him that the performance of special rituals, use of various medicines and elixirs, and inner cultivation of his *qi*, would transform him from a human being into an immortal in the same way that Shennong and the other *zhenren* mentioned in the *Huainanzi* had done in the past. Li Shaojun was one master who received patronage from Emperor Wu, enabling him to develop alchemical medicines for immortality. It was Li who told the emperor that he should ingest mercury in an elixir (*Records of the Historian*, Ch. 28, also Pregadio 2004: 171). Another master was Dongfang Shuo. Tradition ascribes to him a work describing how to find materials for elixirs of immortality and methods for travel in the mountains where such precious items existed. The text became extremely famous and widely used in later Daoist history as well. It is entitled *The Chart of the True Shape of the Five Sacred Mountains*. Both Li Shaojun and Dangfang Shuo are mentioned in the earliest collection of the lives of immortals made in about 77 BCE by Liu Xiang, entitled *Biographies of the Immortals* (*Liexian zhuan*), and later in Ge Hong's *Biographies of Shen Immortals* (c. 316 CE).

Powers of Immortals

According to text and tradition, immortals possessed extraordinary powers, many of which were attributed to early masters in the *Zhuangzi*, the advisors to Qinshihuang and Emperor Wu and the early biography collections. They were believed to be skilled in transformations (*bianhua*). The writings report that these people were shape shifters who could change their own bodies into many appearances, merge into the surroundings, and appear simultaneously in different places. A great number of other powers were associated with immortals: changing the form of objects (e.g., turning white rocks into goats); making food and wine from inedible objects; lacking the signs of aging (e.g., having black hair, all their teeth (regrown sometimes), and youthful complexions; covering great distances of space and time in a flash; possessing phenomenal strength; being impervious to temperature; passing through or entering solid objects such as walls, or diving into the earth; and flying and levitating. Some immortals were believed to possess wondrous physiognomies, such as large foreheads. Other stories claimed that they could talk to and control animals (such as tigers, snakes or monkeys), move objects without touching them, read another person's thoughts, control spirits, restore broken bones, prevent the cutting of skin by sword or knife, cure poisonous bites and relieve drought. Many accounts say that immortals knew the language of spirits and could write what is secret to normal people, thereby directing spirits to do their bidding with talismans. The writing of their talismans is sometimes said to be invisible or to disappear if read by a skeptic, and at other times it is indelible and cannot be removed. Immortals were thought to be able to see inside people and visualize their organs in order to heal them. They were believed to perform acupuncture without need of needles, know the secrets of herbs and the recipes for elixirs of immortality, and even bring the dead back to life. Stories tell that they could exorcize evil spirits and command them, protect the innocent and predict the future.

The cult of immortality coming out of the Han period diffused from the aristocracy into lower levels of the society. Among the elite, the mortuary art often portrayed the occupant of the tomb ascending to the paradise of Kunlun Mountain and being met by immortals, including the Queen Mother of the West who would greet them with kindness and compassion. The discoveries of inscriptions and implements in Han era tombs of those who were not in the elite class also reveal that the belief in immortality and the entities associated with it was widespread. These tombs contain lacquer paintings of the movement of *qi* and winged figures (*yuren*) of immortals sailing through their transmutation into other phases. An excellent example of such a figure comes from a tomb dating to the late Han period (25–220 CE) in the outskirts of Luoyang and is now in the Luoyang Museum in Henan province.

One of the most significant of examples of the seriousness with which the quest of immortality was undertaken in the Han was the appearance of the above-mentioned work, *Biographies of the Immortals*. This work provided tales of immortals in brief form, rarely exceeding 200 characters.

Biography or Hagiography?

A hagiography is a writing about someone who is considered to be a hero or sacred person. There are many hagiographies of Christian, Buddhist and Islamic saints. When scholars feel a life story has shown a disregard for the facts, lacks critical merit or allows reverence for the subject to supersede the accuracy of the account, they use the term hagiography rather than biography. It is probably more appropriate to speak of the tales of the immortals as hagiographies, rather than biographies.

These early accounts of the immortals are actually not proper life stories, but were more like hagiographies. The author provides the name, home town (or 'no one knows where this person came from') and the period in which the subject person lived. However, little additional information is given. The biographies are arranged in chronological order. The 72 individuals included in this work are now among the most famous in Chinese history, numbering among them such heroes of Daoism as Master Redpine (Chisongzi), The Yellow Emperor (Huangdi), Pengzu, Laozi and Yin Xi.

Masters of the *dao* also played a significant role with respect to departed members of ordinary families. In place of bronzes and precious regalia, masters made for the common people miniature replicas of items made out of nonprecious materials (e.g., ceramics, straw, fabric) called *mingqi*. It was likewise a belief among the Han that the dead were subject to judgment and punishment for their wrong deeds (von Glahn 2004: 45). In fact, a pantheon of hierarchially ranked spirit beings became a part of Daoist belief and practice. The *shen* in the underworld meted out punishments and penalties according to their records of the deeds of the deceased, and some of these punishments might even bring harm to a person's descendants. The Lord of Mt Tai (*Taishang fujun*), Daoism's sacred peak in the east, located in Shandong province, was the presiding *shen* over the disposition of the dead, and the nearby Haoli Mountain was believed to be the entrance into the residence of the dead (von Glahn 2004: 52). The Lord of Mt Tai was charged with oversight of lower ranking *shen* officials who performed tasks such as recording good and evil acts of individuals, keeping track of their appointed hour of death, controlling their punishments and maintaining the records of their descendants. To these officials petitions could be addressed by a master of the *dao*. We may see such activity in the Han as an extension of the sort of petition Zhuangzi suggests he can write to the Arbiter of Fate (18d, 193–4), and to the one General Xi Wu was alleged to have written to The Scribe of the Director of Lifespans around 300 BCE on behalf of a man named Dan (see *Masters of the Dao: Arts of Talisman and Petition Writing* in Chapter IV).

Chapter VI
The Earliest Branches of Daoism

Establishing Communities of Daoist Practitioners

The Daoist movements of the late Han dynasty were not merely lineages. For the first time in history, lineage masters sought to establish well-organized and administrated communities. This is an interesting development because there is a great deal in the teachings of the *Daodejing* and *Zhuangzi* that empowers individualism, rather than community. Indeed, some teachings, including the criticisms we see of Confucianism's cardinal ideals of benevolence and righteousness and the strong statements against making discriminations in law and morality, seem actually to contradict the kinds of actions necessary to build community. It seems clear that trying to live as a Daoist within a city or town was very difficult, and many masters may have felt it was impossible to do. This may partially explain why masters sought the life of isolation as mountain recluses, and often refused any summons to court and political involvement.

The failure of efforts to influence the Han officials to embrace a Daoist rulership model that we see in the aftermath of the *Huainanzi*'s presentation to Emperor Wu may explain the desire to form more substantial communities. It became increasingly clear that Han imperial rulers were not going to follow the rulership program of the *Huainanzi*. Liu An was even forced to commit suicide. As the Han evolved, Confucianism was becoming the intellectual currency of China for political and social order.

However, the empire was weakening and regional power centers were developing. The opportunity for asserting new models of communities was present and some lineage masters seized it. The earliest efforts to form Daoist governments were driven not only by the fact that the Han was declining and civil unrest and discontent were widely present, but also that there was hope for a new era of peace and harmony. The two Daoist movements we study below were both committed to this belief that a new era was dawnings and that it would be ushered in by people committed to following the *dao* and who knew the practices and arts of its *de*.

The Daoist Vine Flowers into a Community: The Yellow Turbans and the *Great Peace Classic*

The Yellow Turban (*Huangjin*) lineage of Daoism is also known as the movement of Great Peace (*Taiping*) after its principal text, the *Great Peace Classic*. Hence, the movement was also called the Way of Great Peace (*Taiping dao*). The book entitled *The Later Han*, which covers the period from about 25 CE to 200 CE, is our most reliable source of information about what is known as the Yellow Turban rebellion. The revolution began in Shandong province in 184 CE under the guidance of Zhang Jiao. In the fourteenth century, quasi-historical novel *Romance of the Three Kingdoms*, written by Luo Guanzhong, the author describes events in the turbulent years from the end of the Han Dynasty to the Three Kingdoms period (220 BCE–80 CE). In the first chapter of the book, the novel says that Zhang Jiao was wandering in the mountains gathering medicinal herbs when he came across an old man who had a strikingly youthful countenance, and was carrying a walking stick (signs of a *zhenren* master or immortal). The old man invited Zhang Jiao into his cave and presented him with a book in three volumes that the man said had been written by celestial beings. The name of the book was *Great Peace Classic*. Upon receiving the text, Zhang Jiao practiced its arts and techniques until he learned how to make talisman water to heal the sick, use spells to control ghosts and chant rituals for transformation. He built an army of over 150,000 followers who were devoted to him and the kingdom he promised to establish. He attracted many of his followers because of his reputation for healing. Tradition says that his healing arts saved huge numbers of lives during a regional plague.

His followers took their name from the yellow turbans they wore. In the Five Phase system, yellow is the color of the Earth Agent that rises in the cosmic order of things after the red of the Fire Agent. The Han rulers claimed the Fire Agent ruled their destiny (Robinet 1997: 54). The idyllic era of the Yellow Turbans was to arise after the disappearance of the Red Agent, and it would be one of Great Yellow Peace.

One teaching of the *Great Peace Classic* makes it particularly clear why the Yellow Turbans undertook mass organization, attacked the government and even resorted to armed uprising and rebellion, all of which are behaviors that seem contradictory to Daoism as we have seen it develop. The text, at least in its present form, introduces a concept of 'inherited evil' (*chengfu*) to describe the way in which generations of individual and state malpractices had accumulated evil and led to natural disasters and widespread epidemics of horrific illness. The theory behind this idea is the 'action and response' notion that we saw in the *Huainanzi*. To stave off the continuation of such dangers, a new community had to be constructed, and the present leaders and ways of doing things had to be overturned.

Zhang Jiao divided his followers into 36 administrative regions and took the title 'Great Sage and Good Master' (*Daxian Liangshi*). Yellow Turban communities required a set of rules by which to organize themselves, but the origination of the formation of moral precepts for a Daoist community was not sociological or political. It was medical and cosmological! Echoing the 'action and response' sentiment, the Yellow Turbans taught that all things in the universe are interrelated and influence each other. Morality, health, longevity, power and success are all interrelated. Failure to follow one's inborn nature and allow *qi* to flow undiverted will bring disappointment, illness, disaster and early death. The rebellion was finally quelled only when regional lords appealed for imperial troops.

The Daoist Vine Flowers into a Community: The Celestial Masters and the *Xiang'er Commentary on the Daodejing*

What is known as the Way of the Celestial Masters (*Tianshi Dao*) was founded by Zhang Ling, most commonly known as Zhang Daoling in the province of Shu (current Sichuan) at roughly the same time as the Yellow Turbans. In fact, historians often associate the Celestial Masters with the Yellow Turbans, and there is a tradition that Zhang Daoling was the grandfather of Zhang Jiao, founder of that movement.

However, the precise nature of the connection between these two movements is still unclear. Like the Yellow Turbans, the Celestial Masters were seeking to create a utopian state of Great Peace that would replace the Chinese imperial institution that they believed would be swept away in a series of disasters and travails of apocalyptic proportions. However, unlike the Yellow Turbans, the Celestial Masters was not a revolutionary movement. They waited on the coming cosmic transformation of *dao* by building communities of their own, while not coming into conflict with imperial power.

'Celestial Master'

The term 'Celestial Master' occurs first in *Zhuangzi* 24c, 266, where the Yellow Emperor uses the term to praise a young boy herding horses whom he meets while on a journey in search of the 'Great Clod'. There is also a Celestial Master in the *Great Peace Classic*, but there he is a numinal being who instructs the *zhe*nren and responds to their questions (Kleeman 2007: 982).

The Celestial Master lineage was led by Zhang Daoling, his son Zhang Heng, and most prominently by his grandson, Zhang Lu. Even today, there is still a Celestial Master who claims to be a direct descendant from Zhang Daoling, and the overwhelming majority of non-monastic Daoist masters within China still identify themselves as part of this tradition. In Ge Hong's 'Biography of Zhang Daoling', in the *Biographies of Shen Immortals* (c. 316 CE), we learn something about the background and motivations of the first Celestial Master:

> Zhang Daoling was a man of Pei. He was originally a student in the Imperial Academy and was broadly conversant in the Five Classics [of Confucianism]. As he grew older, he sighed, 'This is of no benefit to my lifespan [i.e., immortality].' Consequently he studied the *dao* of longevity. He obtained the *Nine Cauldron Elixir Formula of the Yellow Emperor* (not an extant text) and wanted to compound it, but exhausted his wealth on the drugs needed for it. Ling's family had heretofore been poor. He wanted to make a living by farming the fields and raising livestock, but he was not good at either and consequently gave up this approach. He heard that most of the people of Shu were pure and sincere and open to moral instruction, and that, moreover, there were many famous mountains there. So, accompanied by his disciples, he entered Shu and lived on Crane Call Mountain (*Hemingshan*), where he composed twenty-four scrolls of Daoist documents. (*Taiping Guangji* 8, entry 3; quoted in Kleeman 1998: 67)

While he was living on Crane Call Mountain, 50 kilometers west of Chengdu, in modern Sichuan province, the reports say that Zhang Daoling had an extraordinary experience. Ge Hong provides a description of Zhang's encounter with Laozi in this way:

> Suddenly there was a heavenly being (*tianren*) descending with a thousand chariots and ten thousand riders in golden carriages with feathery canopies drawn by countless dragons on the outside, and tigers on the inside. Sometimes this being called himself the Scribe below the Pillar; at other times he called himself the Lad of the Eastern Sea. He gave Ling the newly emerged 'Way of Orthodox Unity and the Awesome Covenant' (*Xinchu zhengyi mengwei zhi dao*). After this, Ling was able to heal illnesses. (*Taiping Guangji* 8, entry 3; Kleeman 1998: 66)

There's no mistaking who this heavenly being was. Laozi was known in other texts as 'the Scribe below the Pillar'. Moreover, notice the images in the description of Laozi's entourage. His chariot has a feathered canopy because birds are associated with immortals. They fly, and so do immortals. And, of course, the animals drawing the chariots are not horses. They are dragons 'on the outside' and tigers 'on the inside'. As we saw previously, the tiger/dragon image was used as a *yin/yang* reference. So, even though Laozi is not mentioned by name, no one familiar with the traditions about Laozi would make a mistake in identification. Later Celestial Masters' adherents also understood this *shen* being to be Laozi, identifying him as Supreme Lord Lao (*Taishang Laojun*). Following this source, then, it seems that in 142 CE, Laozi appeared to Zhang Daoling while he was living on Crane Call Mountain and installed him as the first Celestial Master, giving him the power of the 'Covenant of Orthodox Unity'.

The Deified Laozi

Laozi was worshipped as a numinous being as early as the 150s CE. The earliest material evidence we have that associates Laozi as equivalent to the *dao* is the 'Stele of the Sage Mother', which says: 'Laozi, the *dao*: born prior to the Shapeless, grown before the Great Beginning, He lives in the prime of the Great Immaculate, and floats freely through the Six Voids' (Little 2000: 165). In about 185 CE the work entitled *Classic of Laozi's Transformations* taught that Laozi as the *dao* had manifested himself in human form on nine occasions in order to save humankind.

Zhang Daoling gathered tens of thousands of households as his disciples. His lineage vine became more than a community; it was a kind of Daoist theocracy. The cohesion of the community was achieved by means of regular assemblies featuring ritual activities, communal meals and meetings for the administration of practical concerns. The assemblies informed the spirits of the needs in the community, provided forums for the propagation of precepts governing private and communal life and honored what the Celestial Masters called the Three Offices (*sanyuan*, i.e., Heaven, Earth and Water), the most powerful numinal forces in the universe. Like the Yellow Turbans, the Celestial Masters taught that doing what was morally right would bring health and prolong life, as well as make it more prosperous and successful, whereas doing evil would shorten it and lead to illness, tragedy and failure. The Three Offices were believed to be the ultimate overseers of this process.

The Celestial Masters' administrative centers operated under a code of order (*tiaozhi*) that required communal sharing of rice, silk, vessels, paper, brushes, firewood and a number of other goods. Indeed, perhaps the best-known practice of the Celestial Masters was their annual tithe of five 'pecks' (about nine liters) of rice that was distributed among members of the community. This practice explains why the movement was also known as 'Way of the Five Pecks of Rice' (*Wudoumi Dao*). A common misconception is that the Celestial Masters were primarily peasants. While there were great numbers of commoners in the communities of the Celestial Masters, both textual and archaeological evidence confirms that the followers of this movement were not restricted to lower social strata (Wu 2000: 78). The Celestial Masters were motivated by their belief that they were the chosen 'seed people' (*zhongmin*) of the coming new age of Great Peace. They believed the 'seed people' would repopulate a new world after the conflagration toward which *dao* was moving because of the disorder and wrong deeds that had built up over time and were most apparent in the late Han Dynasty. They made converts with appeals like this one from probably the earliest extant text of the Celestial Masters, the *Code of Nuqing for Controlling Ghosts*:

> Enter into my living energy and you will become a *zhenren*. On the day of Great Peace [*taiping*] you will fly away into heaven. Even if you cannot fly, you will live to an old age and not die. Then you will

become a terrestrial immortal and will get to see Great Peace. (quoted in Kleeman 1998: 74)

Charts and Diagrams (*tu*)

Numinal charts and diagrams are much less numerous in the archeological record and also less frequently used in Daoist practice than are talismans. However, they are of three basic types: plats of numinal places, such as the Five Sacred Mountains, or the underworld of Fengdu; patterns that reveal the functioning of the universe and its upcoming movements, such as those associated with the *Yijing* or the Diagram of the Great Ultimate (*Taiji tu*); and representations of the body, such as acupuncture charts, or the Diagram of Interior Lights (*Neijing* tu), which shows the organs of the body and how they are affected by alchemical processes (Despeux 2004a: 498–9).

The administrative framework of the Celestial Masters consisted of 24 centers of organization called *zhi*. The organization of the centers followed the model of a sacred chart called the *Chart of United Energy* written in the tradition of Dongfang Shuo's *Chart of the True Shape of the Five Sacred Mountains* (see page 77). The chart required that the 24 communal divisions be centered around the 25th that was the abode of Lord Lao on Mount Kunlun. These centers also constituted a hierarchically structured network of holy places, many that were associated with deeds and events in the career of the community's founder Zhang Daoling. Receiving the *Chart of United Energy* was part of the ritual of promotion to leadership in the community.

Zhang Daoling

The most extensive hagiography of Zhang Daoling's life is in the thirteenth-century *Comprehensive Mirror of the Immortals Who Embodied the Dao Through the Ages*.

To bring order to the new Celestial Masters' communities, Zhang Daoling and others ordained the community members and ranked them hierarchically. Those at the highest leadership rank were called libationers (*jijiu*). The libationers led spiritual rituals and employed techniques and powers for the benefit of the community. They practiced healing, wrote talismans and were believed to be able to control ghost spirits and direct the celestial powers to bring peace, health and prosperity. They were also the 'merit inspectors' of the community and served as the ruling political officials of the centers. At their

initiation to the rank of libationer, these people received a set of secret
texts (*weijing*) that enabled them to possess powers not belonging to
others in the community. This uniqueness in their role is all the more
significant when we remember that every member of the Celestial
Master community was a master of sorts. All adult members of the
Celestial Masters' community could perform rituals and teach, even if
the more complex rituals involving tremendous numinal power were
reserved for libationers. The sorts of practices one could perform
depended entirely on one's Register (*lu*). Registers contained lists of
shen over which a master had power and control. Libationers could
control *shen* as their Registers allowed. All the rampaging ghosts of
popular religion were reconceived in Celestial Masters' communities
as 'ghost soldiers' (*guibing*) subject to the authority of Celestial Officers
on the Registers of Celestial Masters' libationers. The background of
this practice was the procedure in ancient China in which the nobles
received from the king, along with the deed certifying their land titles,
a list of subordinates who were in their service (Schipper 1994: 61).

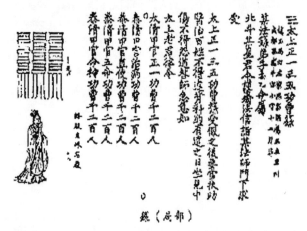

Sample of Celestial Masters' Register

Celestial Masters believed that a master who possessed a Register
could invoke the spirit officers, warriors and generals listed on it to
protect his body or to assist his techniques, making the master more
powerful and effective. The greater the number and the more powerful the *shen* under one's control, the higher rank in the community
one possessed. One could gain new powers over the years. At one's
ordination and investiture (promotion), the list of spirits over which
one had authority was worn as a part of the clothing. Children were

first initiated at the age of six years old and every child had a Register, albeit a small one. It is not surprising, then, that the first title given to a person wanting to enter the community from the outside world was 'Register student' (*lusheng*) (Little 2000: 306). Marriage between community members brought with it the union of two sets of Registers, and created greater strength than either spouse could have separately. The *Formal Registers of the Awesome Covenant of Orthodox Unity* lists 14 kinds of Registers – including those for infants, generals and others – as well as Registers classified by type, such as to protect the body, provide longevity and control evil powers. Registers were in continuous use by various Celestial Masters lineages until the Qing dynasty (late 1800s CE) and it is still common for the lineage of Celestial Masters called Zhengyi in Southern China to speak of distinctions between Registers among their masters and themselves.

Within each of the 24 administrative centres (*zhitou dajijiu*) were 'lodges of righteousness' (*yishe*) and 'hostels' (*ting*) that helped meet the physical and material needs of the members. The hostels functioned as inns for travelers journeying from one center to another to study, work and find new residence. They served meals and offered lodging. Rice and meat were hung in the lodges and were available free for the taking, although those who took more than they needed would be punished by the spirits (*Romance of the Three Kingdoms* 8/263). Leading libationers in the administrative centers also distributed food to the needy in the Celestial Masters' communities.

Marriage in the Celestial Masters' Communities

The marriage rite that joined Registers was called 'merging *qi*'. In this rite, the act of sexual penetration in intercourse came only after a lengthy series of visualizations of *shen* beings and *qi* massages of one partner by the other. Intercourse was accompanied by an incantation designed to unite the *qi* force of the partners and join the Registers of *shen* powers each could summon.

The *Xiang'er Commentary on the Daodejing* expands our understanding of marriage and sexuality in Celestial Masters' communities in this way. 'The *dao* of *yin* and *yang* [i.e. sexual intercourse] is congealing the *qi* to produce life. At the age of fifty, having filled one's [reproductive] role, one should stop. Even when one is young, though one possesses [the capabilities for reproduction], one should cease [from intercourse] and conserve [*qi*] ... If one from youth follows the path of lessening *qi* [as in avoiding ejaculation], one will live a long time' (lines 55–8, translation by Bokenkamp 1997b).

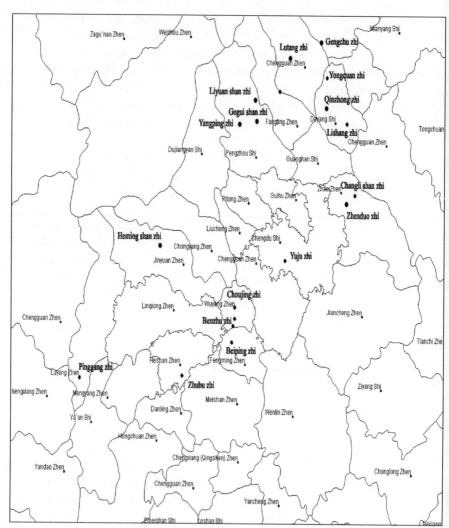

Celestial Masters Centres in the Chengdu Plain with reference to Modern
Counties shown in **bold**

Celestial Masters' adherents practiced methods they received from earlier lineages including abstaining from grains, ingesting *qi* through breathing, strengthening *qi* by gymnastic exercises and drinking talismanic water. In fact, drinking talisman water became a major technique of healing in this community because talismans were a central part of the ritual activities used by the libationers.

Two modifications in healing and longevity techniques were new with the Celestial Masters. First, healing was no longer administered by a master merely on an individual basis; instead, rituals and talismans with activated power were believed to have efficacy for the entire community. Communal rituals were done through the recital of a document known as the 'Text in Five Thousand Words'. The recitation of this text was led by a master known by the title 'Libationer in Charge of Controlling Evil' (*Jianling Jiju*). Second, according to the later Daoist writer Lu Xiujing (406–77 CE), the Celestial Masters' communities did not use acupuncture or drugs, but healed exclusively with talismanic water, formal petitions to spirits and reliance on the confessions of sins by their members (Engelhardt 2004: 76).

Both the Celestial Masters and the Yellow Turbans integrated confession of wrongdoing into their understanding of healing, because both movements saw a connection between morality, health, longevity and the transformation of the person into a *zhenren*. In this way, both of these new extensions of the vine of Daoism showed some continuity with teachings we have already seen in the *Huainanzi*.

However, there was a difference between the Huang-Lao lineage and that of the Celestial Masters on the theory behind the workings of 'action and response'. In Huang-Lao, as is shown in the quote on page 69, actions that represented 'aberrations' or 'deficiencies' of *dao* and *de*, or that had 'damaged' *yin* or 'collapsed' *yang*, caused illness in a natural and cosmic 'act and response' (*ganying*) manner (see our previous discussion of *Huainanzi* 11/96/7–12 on page 72). Whereas, for the Celestial Masters, numinal beings were the causes of illness, either as mischief on the part of a deranged spirit or as punishment for one's immoral actions. Celestial beings who resided in the stars, or in the underworld of Fengdu, could shorten people's lives, inflict illness on them or cause them to fail in life pursuits as just punishments for wrongdoing. They could punish not only individuals but also families and even entire villages.

The Celestial Masters believed that human conduct was under the constant surveillance of the numinal beings of the Three Primes. Accordingly, they created 'chambers of quietude' (*jingshi*) in which individual members of the community could meditate and confess their wrongdoing. Upon the emergence from the chamber a penitent would report to a practitioner known as a 'ghost official' (*guili*), who would write down the offenses the penitent wanted to confess and apologize for and then send them as a petition (*zhang*) to the Three Offices. The message to the Heavenly Office was placed on a mountain; that to the Earthly Office was buried in the ground; and that to the Water Office was thrown into water. Sometimes the penitent would perform a ritual demonstrating remorse by smearing his body with mud and charcoal and reciting his immoral actions with hands bound behind his back (Von Glahn 2004: 66).

Confession was a result of the self-examination (*ziyin*) done in 'the chamber of quietude'. It was also self-regulating. Confession was not made *to* the community 'ghost official' or to a priest of any sort. Moreover, if one wanted to lie to oneself or pretend that one had done nothing wrong, the principal person harmed would be oneself. If one left the chamber of solitude having resolved to alter his life, and actually did so, then it was likely that the community would notice this change and the person's fortunes would increase. The penitent would gain respect and people would seek such a one for business, friendship and even leadership. Perhaps in keeping with the rigorous moral tone of their 24 centers, the Celestial Masters prohibited divination, consulting almanacs for taboo days and performing blood sacrifices (*xueshi*).

Rituals of Blood Wine (*xuejiu*)

The fact that the Celestial Masters are believed to have explicitly rejected blood sacrifices is important. They thought of the covenant between their libationers and the *shen* beings as embodied in text and talisman, so they did not use rituals of blood. This was one way they chose to separate themselves from the ritual practices of other lineages and from popular expressions of religion as well. It was commonly believed in China during this period that engaging in rituals designed to control ghost spirits was very dangerous work. People thought that ghost spirits entering a space might cause a lot of trouble. Accordingly, blood sacrifices were made to create a unity with more powerful numinal powers and protect the master performing the rituals of the community. We cannot be sure just which blood sacrifices the Celestial Masters rejected, but the term they use for bloody sacrifices, *xueshi*, is a category name for a number of rituals of which blood wine is one.

However, we do not even know for sure whether the blood wine ritual was done during the period of Celestial Masters, and, if it was, how the perform-ance was enacted. The main source of information about it is a collection of instructions about ritual methods entitled *Daoist Methods, United in Principle*. This text does not now exist apart from the Ming Daoist canon (1445 CE). While the text was probably made for the canon, it likely represents a collection of much older methods. In any event, the blood wine ritual it describes can serve as an example of the kind of thing done in other lineage vines to which the Celestial Masters may have objected.

One form of ritual protection involved the use of blood wine. According to descriptions of the performance of this ritual, the master would first pace the Step of Yu (*Yubu*; see the earlier discussion in 'The Masters Who Nurtured the Trunk of Daoism'), chant invitations to the *shen*, and burn talismanic protection charms. After this, taking a chicken in the left hand, the master would chop off its head with a ritually purified sword and allow the blood to drip into a cup of wine, using the sword to mix the two substances together. The master would then make an oath to serve Heaven and protect the people. The master would command the numinal beings to send ghost soldiers (*guibing*) to help him in his work. After completing the oath, the master would drink the blood wine that was also offered to the spirits. Arriving at unity with the numinal powers signi-fied by the sharing of the blood wine, a master could control ghost spirits, ban-ish them from the community, listen to the complaints of ghosts against people in the community and decide their merits, and send them back to their place. Depending on the lineage and its tradition of ritual practice, other animals could be used, and some traditions even report the masters cutting their fingers and using their own blood.

The work of libationers with respect to the dead was immensely important. They would address a petition to the numinal beings on their Registers, requesting kind treatment for a deceased and ask-ing that the dead person be permitted into celestial bliss. Then, this document would be burned at the funeral (Miller 2003: 25). We may take the following petition as an illustration of the sort of thing the Celestial Master libationers did:

> The Celestial Master sealed up the tomb of the deceased Xu Wentai of Dingyi district and dispatched orders to the Tumulus Adjutant, the Lord of the Tomb, the Infernal 'Two-Thousand-Bushel' Officers, the

Spirits Above and Below the Tomb, the Guardian of the Centre, the
Spirits to the Left and Right of the Tomb, the Libationer of the *Hun-*
Spirit Gate, and the Elders of Haoli Mountain stating: 'The family of
Xu Wentai, including his sons, grandsons, and all later generations,
no longer has any connection with the deceased. The dead return to
the world of *yin*, while the living belong to the world of *yang*. The
living have their villages, while the dead have their own place. The
living owe fealty to Xian in the West, while the dead become subjects
of Mount Tai in the East. If in the underworld Xu is found guilty of
crimes, let this wax figure substitute for him in performing convict
labor. Never again, in a thousand autumns, in ten thousand years,
shall Xu again make any imposition on the living, but only give aid to
the living sons and grandsons of the Xu family. May their fortune and
fame increase, their property and wealth multiply many thousandfold,
and let their progeny be fruitful'. (quoted in Von Glahn 2004: 56–7)

This petition is a multi-purpose one designed to exempt the living
from any moral debts still owed by the deceased, to release the
deceased from punishment in the numinal underworld and to protect
the living from their deceased relative.

The Celestial Masters' libationers issued 'writs of grievance from
the grave' (*zhongsong*, Von Glahn 2004: 66). This kind of spiritual
document was a testimony written by someone in touch with the
spirit of a deceased person who had a complaint against a living relative or an entire family. It was typically addressed by the deceased to
his or her unfilial children. If the libationer determined the complaint
was legitimate, a penance could be prescribed. Daoist masters could
defend the living against an invalid complaint from a deceased relative
by performing rituals and sending petitions to Celestial Officials of
the Three Offices.

Arguably the single most important text of practical guidance
for Celestial Masters' communities was the *Xiang'er Commentary on
the Daodejing*. It is the earliest known Daoist interpretation of the
Daodejing. Although mentioned in a number of Daoist works, there
was no known copy of it until a fragmentary manuscript was found
at Dunhuang. The Dunhuang version dates to about 500 CE, but the
original materials upon which it is based probably date to about 200
CE. The commentary goes so far as to say that in Laozi the *dao* 'took
humanity as its name'. It encourages all followers to allow the *dao* to
flow freely in them just as Laozi did.

Xiang'er taken literally as 想爾 means 'thinks of you', as though *dao* thinks of an adept devoted to it. Kristopher Schipper thinks *Xiang'er* is the name of the author of the commentary (Schipper and Verellen 2004: 75). However, tradition attributes the commentary either to Zhang Daoling or Zhang Lu. The simple act of reciting the text itself was believed to bring extraordinary powers, heal disease, open one's vision so that one could see the *shen* numinal beings and even grant longevity (Bokenkamp 1997b: 29).

The *Xiang'er Commentary* is concerned with remaking society into a kingdom of Great Peace by the *dao* and its *de*. Followers of the Celestial Masters believed that the *Daodejing* contained the rules by which to live in harmony with the *dao*. So, the purpose of this commentary was to standardize the interpretation of the *Daodejing* for their communities and give structure to the 24 centers. The commentary explains that in order for each person to reach oneness with the *dao* and its *de*, every member of the community must have this desire (Bokenkamp 1997b: 39). The text calls upon people to eradicate deviant tendencies and actions and to embrace 'clarity and stillness' (lines 197–200). It tells one to make one's body the sacred place where Heaven's gate is opened and the location where things of the earth and heaven may intersect: 'Entering into the space between heaven and earth, [the *dao*] comes and goes within the human body, that's all. It is there everywhere within your skin, not just in a single spot' (lines 107–8).

In this commentary, the common belief of the Celestial Masters that there is a close connection between physical disease and moral action is made explicit: 'The heart is a regulator. It may hold fortune or misfortune, good or evil ... When the heart produces ill-omened and evil conduct, the *dao* departs, leaving one empty. Once one is empty, deviance enters, killing the person' (lines 4–6). So, spiritual encounter in 'clarity and stillness' or in 'opening the space between Heaven and Earth' is not sufficient. The accumulation of moral merit is also needed for spiritual transformation. Later Daoist sources refer to the 'Nine Principles' of the *Xianger Commentary* and to its 'Twenty-seven Precepts'. Unfortunately, neither of these is given as a specific list in our surviving fragment. However, other texts list them as follows:

The Nine Practices are:

> Practice lacking falseness.
> Practice subtleness and receptivity.
> Practice maintaining the feminine. Do not initiate actions
>   [i.e., practice *wu-wei*].
> Practice lacking fame.
> Practice clarity and stillness.
> Practice good deeds.
> Practice being without desires.
> Practice knowing how to cease striving.
> Practice yielding to others.

The 'Twenty-seven Precepts' of the *Xiang'er Commentary* are:

> Not to delight in excess, since joy is as harmful as anger.
> Not to waste essence or *qi* energy.
> Not to harm the dominant *qi* energy.
> Not to eat beings that contain blood delighting in their
>   fancy taste.
> Not to hanker after merit and fame.
> Not to explain the teaching or describe the *Dao* to outsiders.
> Not to forget the divine law of the *Dao*.
> Not to try to set things in motion.
> Not to kill or speak about killing.

> *These are the highest nine precepts.*

> Not to study false texts.
> Not to covet high glory or vigorously strive for it.
> Not to pursue fame and praise.
> Not to do things pleasurable to ears, eyes or mouth.
> Always remain modest and humble.
> Not to engage in frivolous undertakings.
> Always be devout in religious services, of respectful mind,
>   and without confusion.
> Not to indulge in fancy garb or tasty food.
> Not to overextend oneself.

> *These are the medium nine precepts.*

> Not to strongly pursue riches and honor if poor and humble.
> Not to do evil.

Not to set many taboos and avoidances.

Not to pray or sacrifice to demons or spirits of the dead.

Not to strongly oppose anyone.

Not to consider oneself always right.

Not to quarrel with others over what is right and wrong.
   If in a debate, concede first.

Not to praise oneself as a sage of great fame.

Not to take delight in soldiering.

These are the lowest nine precepts.

Those who follow the 'Twenty-seven Precepts' including the highest nine, will become spirit immortals. Those who follow the lower 18 will double their life expectancy. Those who follow the lowest nine will extend their years and never meet with adversities.

The Celestial Masters opened the office of libationer to women. 'Lady' Wei Huacun (251–344 CE) is the best known of these. She was a libationer who performed rituals, including submitting petitions and creating talismans (Despeux 2004b: 387). She received revelations about the numinal realm of Highest Clarity (*shangqing*) and was instrumental in the development of that lineage vine of Daoism, as we shall see later.

While the Yellow Turbans died out as a community, their practices and teachings grafted onto various aspects of the Celestial Masters' vine and showed up time and again in later Daoist history. The Celestial Masters' movement, on the other hand, was able to remain largely independent of imperial domination for over 25 years. Gradually, libationers of the centers replaced government officials or exercised a dual authority. Around 200 CE, this situation began to disintegrate as libationers competed for power. Finally, in 215 CE the general Cao Cao (155–220 CE) moved royal forces into Hanzhong, and Zhang Lu surrendered. And yet, unlike the Yellow Turbans who were treated harshly and virtually extinguished, Zhang Lu's family was very well connected to the regional governor. His mother had had free access to the governor's home and family because of her knowledge of healing techniques and her abilities as an impersonator of the dead and spirit medium. Sources say she knew 'the ways of ghosts' (*guidao*) and how to bind them. So Zhang Lu was treated well and his children even intermarried with the Caos. In fact, after Zhang Lu submitted to Cao Cao in 215 CE, he was granted a title and lands. Several of his sons and generals also received positions and land. Nevertheless, Celestial Master centers were broken up and families were dispersed northward. One wave of about 200–300,000 individuals was resettled from Hanzhong to Chang'an (Xi'an) and its surrounding areas. In the five-year period that followed (215–20 CE), another 80,000 Celestial Masters from the Hanzhong region moved of their own volition into the Luoyang and Ye areas. In this way, the Celestial Master belief system was dispersed widely beyond the southern area of Sichuan. Nevertheless, the movement continued in Southern China among groups of families and villages. These dispersions created the lineage vines of Northern and Southern Celestial Masters.

Chapter VII
The Spread of Celestial Masters' Daoism

The Northern Celestial Masters

An early look at the tasks facing the Northern Celestial Masters as they tried to establish themselves in a new area after 215 CE can be gained through a 'letter' meant to be circulated to the various community cells in the northern part of China. This text has been recently translated as *Commands and Admonitions for the Families of the Great Dao* (Bokenkamp 1997a). It is included in the canonical collection entitled *Commandments of the Celestial Master from the One and Orthodox Canon*. The *Commands and Admonitions* was written in the first person and is meant to encourage Celestial Masters' families to obey the moral rules and follow the beliefs of the early movement in Sichuan. Some scholars believe Zhang Lu was the letter's author. However, there are three specific dates given in the text and the one that corresponds to the release date of the work is February 255 CE, well after Zhang Lu's death in 216 CE.

The *Commands and Admonitions* uses the expression *jueqi* of community members who wrote or spoke in the voice of a spirit. As noted earlier, some among the Celestial Masters practiced spirit mediumship. In fact, an official position in the community was charged with the task of determining the veracity of mediumistic utterances (i.e., the *lingjue*, Bokenkamp 1997a: 151). The *Commands and Admonitions* was presented to the Northern Celestial Masters' communities as the first-person voice of Zhang Lu's spirit speaking through the author in a mediumistic way. Such a view is supported by the speaker's report: 'I have circulated day and night, traveling around within the four seas and journeying beyond the eight extremities, all from the desire to cause the ruler to be humane and his ministers loyal, fathers magnanimous and sons filial' (Bokenkamp 1997a: 152). This sort of cosmic journeying is mentioned in Daoist texts of beings who have transformed into numinal spirits, and the readers of the text would likely have made this interpretation.

While the authorship and nature of the *Commands and Admonitions* as a mediumistic text are subjects of debate, there is no mistaking its call for a return to the earliest Celestial Masters' early structures. The text traces the revelations of *dao* in a manner similar to the *Classic of Laozi's Transformations* (see page 85) and says that the last manifestation of Laozi was to Zhang Daoling. It says that Laozi bestowed on Zhang Daoling the true covenant guidelines between humans and the numinal powers. Moreover, the underlying basis for the commands in this work is the oversight of the numinal beings of the Three Offices, who know all of the people's good and evil deeds and may deduct years for infractions. However, if the people follow the covenant given to the Celestial Masters, they will enter the ranks of the 'seed people' (see page 86). The author says:

> Morning and evenings you should practice 'clarity and stillness.' Root out all covetousness, abandon the pursuit of personal profit, and rid yourself of desire. Be liberal in supplying others and in giving way to them. Drive from your heart excesses of jealousy, joy, and anger so that your emotions are constantly equal and your eyes and belly are in accord. Aid the kingdom [the Northern Wei] in strengthening its mandate. Abandon all your past evil pursuits. Those who, from today on, practice good actions will find that disaster and disease melt away from them, and they will become seed people of the later age. (18b, in Bokenkamp 1997a: 181)

The people are warned to return to the traditional practices for training and ordaining libationers. Apparently these procedures had been displaced by hereditary appointment or political machination. The people are, likewise, admonished to give places of libationer leadership only to the men and women who follow *dao* and display its *de*. In all these ways, the *Commands and Admonitions* represents the struggle of Celestial Master communities in the North from about 250 to 350 CE. However, we know that its reformist program was not completely followed because a great Daoist master stepped forward to offer a 'New Code' for following the *dao* and structuring the life of the community.

Kou Qianzhi's New Code for a Daoist Theocracy

Kou Qianzhi (365–448 CE) was born into a Celestial Master family in Northern China near Chang'an (Xi'an). As was the case with the other Celestial Master libationers we have discussed thus far, Kou was committed to the search for a form of government that would bring a new age of Great Peace. He followed the way of a master of the *dao* as it had been done for centuries before by going to live on a sacred mountain, taking up residence on Songshan Mountain in Henan Province (the central of the five sacred peaks of Daoism). According to the *History of the Wei Dynasty*, Kou practiced visualization of spirits and learned from immortals and numinal beings the methods for nourishing *qi* and practicing *daoyin* (*qigong*) exercises. He was reported to have transformed his body into light in order to 'disappear in broad daylight', changing his phases to become numinous. The accounts of his life say that his complexion changed through diet and alchemy and became radiant (Kohn 2004c: 301). Kou's quest was rewarded by a visitation from the Highest Lord Lao. Upon the basis of the revelations he received, Kou reformulated Celestial Masters' doctrines and practices and created what we now know as the Northern Celestial Masters' lineage.

The text *Precepts of the New Code Recited in the Clouds* was revealed to Kou in 415 CE, and it contained a set of 36 precepts for a new type of Celestial Masters' community. The original of this text is now lost, but it partially survives in the *Classic of Recited Precepts of Lord Lao*. Each precept is introduced with the phrase 'Lord Lao said'. Kou took this New Code to the royal court of the Northern Wei dynasty, where he was welcomed by Emperor Taiwu and Prime Minister Cui Hao because of his reputation for knowing the methods for longevity and immortality. The emperor gave Kou the authority to implement his New Code. Kou even ascended to head a department of the Northern Wei government specifically dedicated to the quest for immortality through alchemy and laboratory elixirs. Under his influence, Taiwu named Daoism the official state ideology and dedicated himself to ruling as a libationer should. Because of his influence on Taiwu and the spread of the New Code, Kou is now known as the founder of the Daoist theocracy in the North.

According to the New Code, the ruling Celestial Master need not be a direct descendant of Zhang Daoling, as was the practice among Celestial Masters in the South. The new Celestial Master need only stand in the line of those receiving a revelation from Lord Lao. On practical matters, the New Code replaced the old 24 centers of the Celestial Masters' structure in Sichuan. Kou followed the revelations he recorded as the *Perfect Classic of Registers and Charts* in 423 CE to implement a new administrative structure and standardize a new understanding of Registers. Kou's new numinal chart established 28 centers that mirrored the 'Twenty-eight Stellar Mansions' (*ershiba xiu*), abandoning the old 24-center model of Zhang Daoling. Since this text is now lost, a great number of the details are unknown, but many new Daoist institutions and sites were established in the provinces of the Wei based upon it.

The high point of Kou's theocracy came in 440 CE when the emperor himself underwent Daoist investiture rites and became a libationer, changing his reign title to 'Perfect Lord of Great Peace' (*Taiping Zhenjun*) (Kohn 2004c: 285). The Prime Minister, Cui Hao, showed his commitment to the theocracy by launching a persecution of practitioners who did not conform to Kou's program and also targeting the foreign religion of Buddhism. After Kou's death, Cui Hao became a megalomaniac usurping power everywhere, forcing the rulers of the Wei to take action against him. In the aftermath, the Daoist theocracy was dissolved. By 450 CE, Daoists in the North faced persecution and had to flee to other areas, including the Daoist center that had been established at Louguan Tai.

The Daoists of Louguan Tai

Daoists became objects of persecution after the end of the theocracy in the North, and many took refuge in a Daoist center called 'Tower Observatory' or *Louguan Tai* on Zhongnan Mountain (*Zhongnan shan*) in Shaanxi Province, not far from Chang'an (Xi'an). It is not clear when Louguan was first settled or even how it came to be used as a center for Daoism, although we do know that Kou Qianzhi received support from the Northern Wei court to build structures at Louguan Tai for the many Daoists already living in the area. Probably the most familiar narrative about its founding is that Louguan became a Daoist observatory on land near Zhongnan Mountain, owned by a Daoist master named Yin Tong (398–499? CE). Yin Tong obtained a reputation as a great master, skilled in the arts of dietetics, herbal medicine, elixir alchemy and petitions to the stars. He drew a number of disciples to him. In order to justify imperial expenditures at Louguan Tai, Kou convinced the officials that Sima Qian's tale of Laozi transmitting the *Daodejing* to Yin Xi, the Keeper of the Pass, in *Records of the Historian* was true. He told the emperor that this pass was precisely at the site of the Louguan observatory. By the late 400s CE, a large group of Daoist masters and adepts lived at Louguan Tai and an early collection of Daoist texts was made at the center, including those of the later Shangqing and Lingbao lineage traditions (see pages 120ff. and 127ff.).

The Origin of Louguan Tai

In addition to the tradition in the *Records of the Historian* that Louguan Tai was the residence of Yin Xi, who was the first recipient of the *Daodejing* (see 'Early Shaping of the Trunk: The *Daodejing*' in Chapter II on page 9), there were other accounts of its origin. An alternative story explaining the choice and ascendancy of Louguan Tai is related to the use of the term *guan*, meaning 'observatory'. This term became widely used for Daoist sacred temples and sites on mountains. The most common explanation for calling a Daoist mountain temple an 'observatory' is that Daoist lineages placed great importance on the stars. They thought the Big Dipper was the residence of the Three Offices and the Supreme One (Taiyi). Thus there is a tradition that Daoists watched the stars from this mountain. A third account, which brings the previous two versions together, is also interesting. According to it, Yin Xi ascended the 'tower observatory' and saw a purple numinal ether (purple is the color of the *qi* breath of *dao*) rising from Laozi as he approached the path to leave for the West (Schipper 1985). It is little wonder, then, that Louguan is still known as 'The Observatory (*Guan*) of the Ancestral Sage'.

Several Daoist texts produced at Louguan Tai stand out as important. The *Precepts of the Highest Lord Lao* was a Louguan text dating from around 500 CE and based on Kou's New Code. The book has as its setting an exchange between Yin Xi and Laozi concerning the proper conduct of a Daoist. It sets out what became known as the 'Five Rules' for Daoist moral life, and these are identical to the five rules in Buddhism: abstain from killing, stealing, lying, sexual misconduct and intoxication. Instead of justifying these five rules by an appeal to revelation or tracing their derivation from contact with Buddhism, the text says there are the five essential precepts because they are correlated in the process of the *dao* with the Five Phases, the five sacred mountains and the five organs in the body. Indeed, in each explanation of the five precepts in the text, Lord Lao shows its connection to everything from the greater cosmos, to the health and prosperity of a single individual:

Lord Lao said,

… The five precepts in heaven are represented by the five planets [Jupiter, Venus, Mars, Mercury, and Saturn]. They rule the energies of the five directions [north, south, east, west, centre], making sure they remain in harmony and maintain their constancy. As soon as the Dao of heaven loses its precepts, there are natural catastrophes.

… On earth, they are represented by the five sacred mountains [Mts. Tai, Heng, Hua, Heng, and Song]. They govern the energies of the earth and rule the weather, gathering and dispelling the clouds. As soon as the Dao of earth loses its precepts, the hundred grains can no longer grow.

… Among the seasonal patterns, they are represented by the five phases. As soon as the five cycles lose their precepts, fire and water fight each other, and metal and wood do each other harm.

… In government, the five precepts are represented by the five emperors. As soon as rulers lose their precepts, dynasties topple and rulers perish.

… In human beings, they are represented by the five inner organs. As soon as people lose their precepts, their health and inner nature goes astray. (Kohn 1994: 203)

The Contests with Buddhism

Buddhists and Daoists presented themselves at the Tang court to debate which tradition could provide greatest stability for the empire and offer the most benefit to the emperor and his people. In 520 CE, the Daoist, Jiang Bin and the Buddhist, Tanmuzui, debated over two principal issues: which tradition was older and whether Laozi converted the Buddha. In 570 CE, another court debate was more extensive and also more serious philosophically and spiritually. To aid in these debates, Louguan Tai masters created the first Daoist encyclopedia, entitled *Esoteric Essentials of the Most High*, in 574 CE. However, the encyclopedia left out some key Louguan Tai teachings, such as the deity of Laozi and his conversion of the barbarians. These ideas seemed not to carry much weight against the Buddhists by the late 500s CE. In the newly founded Temple of the Pervasive Way (Tongdao Guan) in Chang'an, Daoist masters formulated more powerful criticisms of Buddhism. In the early 620s CE, Tongdao master Fu Yi proposed to the Tang court that all Buddhist institutions be abolished and the monks and nuns returned to laity. Li Zhongqing argued that Buddhism was inferior to Daoism by writing a tract to show Buddhism's principal faults. It was entitled *The Ten Differences and Nine Errors* (c. 626 CE). Clearly, in radical contrast to the Lingbao lineage in the South (see pages 127ff.), which imitated Buddhist rituals and copied their scriptures rather indiscriminately, the Northern Celestial Masters were much more intent on maintaining the integrity and uniqueness of Daoism in this period.

The Southern Celestial Masters

Unlike their Northern counterparts, the Southern Celestial Masters were never able to regain a centralized theocracy after the dissolution of the Hanzhong kingdom of Zhang Lu (Nickerson 2004: 256). Members of the movement diffused into the South by multiple routes and for many reasons. They always had to struggle in order to distinguish themselves from folk practices, and actually there was a great deal of overlapping and syncretism between the lineages of the Southern Celestial Masters and traditional beliefs and practices. Nevertheless, the southern tradition survives today in the lineages of Zhengyi *daoshi* in South China and Taiwan that still look to the descendants of Zhang Daoling as the authorized Celestial Master transmission. One way in which the Southern Celestial Masters defined themselves without an elaborate political organization was by the use of moral texts.

The Code of Nuqing for Controlling Ghosts
The *Code of Nuqing for Controlling Ghosts* is probably the oldest extant Celestial Master text (Schipper 1994: 69, n.20). The text claims that it was revealed in 143 CE to Zhang Daoling by the numinous being Nuqing, who lives in the Big Dipper (Schipper and Verellen 2004: 1, 127). However, some scholars date the *Code of Nuqing* into the period of Zhang Lu's leadership of the community. A later Lingbao lineage text, entitled *Scripture of Great and Minor Merits, and the Classified Rules of the Three Principles*, names Nuqing as the one who established the invisible spirit offices that keep records on good and evil behavior.

In spite of the ongoing controversy about its date, the *Code of Nuqing* may be regarded as an inside look at the practices of the earliest Celestial Masters in the South of China. It describes ways to identify 320 ghost spirits and provides spells for how to bind and neutralize them. Such practices were traceable to the lineage teachings transmitted to Zhang Daoling and apparent in his mother's practice of Daoist arts. As we saw in the *Zhuangzi* with respect to the mountain spirits (*shenxiao*), each of these spirits had a name and their appearance could be described (19h, 203–4). These are spirits of the mountains and seas, plague, wind and water and so forth. According to the *Code of Nuqing*, when people ceased following the *dao*, evil ghosts, pestilences and dangerous beasts appeared. The text teaches that these forces are aroused by immoral actions, so it provides 22 rules of conduct (*daolu jinji*) for the 'seed people' of the *dao* designed to bring harmony and prevent the ghost spirits from being stirred up. The work also discloses the names of the ghost soldiers in the earth prisons of Fengdu who are in charge of processing the newly deceased and of punishing them for their misdeeds. By learning the names of these ghosts, people may bind them and receive protection both for themselves and for their deceased relatives. However, the overriding intention of this work is not to teach spellbinding, but to offer the moral statutes that, if followed, will keep the forces of *dao* in balance.

The 22 statutes of Nuqing teach that one should not denigrate the spirits, travel without permission, discuss one's teacher's teachings, gossip, lie, murder, use curses to cause bad fortune, be unfilial, quarrel, get drunk or be unchaste. Each rule is followed by a number of years that will be subtracted from a person's lifespan by the numinal powers of the Three Offices of Heaven in case of infringement. Here are some examples:

3. Do not drink wine, eat meat, or revile and curse *dao*. For this Heaven will subtract 1,300 days [from your life].

6. Do not slight or despise the old, or yell and curse your in-laws and woman folk. Curses and harsh words cause mutual killing and harm, poison the heart, and create bad fortune. They lead to lack of filial piety and the five adverse forms of conduct. For this Heaven will subtract 180 days [from your life].

9. Do not wander about east and west, mingling freely with men and women, promising to dissolve disasters you cannot in fact prevent and thus causing disruption and confusion. For this Heaven will subtract 3,000 days [from your life] and haunt your descendants for seven generations.

17. Do not destroy any being given life by Heaven, wantonly kill running beasts, or with pellets shoot down flying birds. Do not point south and say it is north, just following your whim. This is not obeying the ghost statutes. For this, Heaven will subtract 3,000 days [from your life]. (Kohn 2004d: 6–9)

One Hundred and Eighty Rules of Lord Lao

Another work of moral instruction used by Celestial Masters in the South was the *One Hundred and Eighty Rules of Lord Lao*, one of three moral codes collected in the Ming dynasty canon under the title *Canonical Rules of the Most High Lord Lao*. Almost all of the actual precepts themselves date into the 200s CE, perhaps to the time of Zhang Lu, although their formal listing in the 180-form is not confirmed before the mid-400s CE. Some precepts seem to repeat the essential teachings of others, for example, #22, 'Do not covet or begrudge material goods', and #106, 'Do not covet or hanker after a nice residence'. The presence of these kinds of repetitions in an ethical text may indicate that the collection has been increased through time without harmonizing or deleting earlier rules. Some moral rules seem to be influenced by Buddhist practices, such as the prohibition of fishing and hunting (#79). Such a rule was not a restriction in Daoism prior to this text. Moreover, both #176 and #177 require vegetarianism that was not a part of classical Daoist practice either. One Lingbao text (Schipper 2001: 89) says libationers should respectfully abide by the Laojun's *One Hundred and Eighty Rules of Lord Lao*, and that if a libationer has not received these rules, such a master should not be honored by the people. During the Six Dynasties period, this text continued to be the most commonly used moral text in all of Southern Celestial Masters Daoism, and it remained the standard code of conduct until the collection of texts by Lu Xiujing (406–77 CE).

The *One Hundred and Eighty Rules of Lord Lao* contain guidance for an extreme range of normal human life. They contain expected prohibitions against stealing (#3), adultery (#2), killing or harming another human (#4), coveting others goods (#22), owing or selling slaves (#27), slandering (#48) and (#50) deceiving others. A substantial number of moral rules have to do with the community members' relationships to nature and animals: 'Do not raise pigs or sheep' (#8); 'Do not burn fields, wild lands, mountains, or forests' (#14); 'Do not wantonly cut down trees' (#18). Quite a number of ethical rules are designed to address one's attitude, inner character or moral psychology: 'Do not claim to be skilled' (#44), 'noble' (#45) or 'prideful' (#46); 'Do not give rise to anger or rage from others' (#64); 'Do not delight in other people's death or failure' (#69).[10]

Many of the rules of Lord Lao are designed to make the community run harmoniously and smoothly: 'Do not praise other people to their face yet in a different place discuss their faults' (#34); 'Do not use your connections with district officials to harm other people' (#92); 'Always diligently avoid being cruel to others, do not abandon or turn your back on your friends' (#150).

Some of the precepts have to do expressly with spiritual practices: 'Do not slight or be rude to other people's worthies' (#38); 'Do not practice astrology, star divination, or analyze the cycles of Heaven' (#78); 'Do not sacrifice to the ghosts and spirits in search of good fortune' (#118); 'Do not concoct poisonous drugs and keep them in vessels' (#125); 'Do not advertise yourself as a healer of the sick, only go if invited by the family' (#135); 'Always be true to Orthodox Unity (*Zhengyi*) and do not get involved in worldly practices' (#144); 'Every time people address you as libationer, take care to establish awe in them, do not act lightly or hastily and become their laughing stock' (#153).

Finally, several precepts conclude the work with words that underwrite its importance to the followers of the *dao*: 'If you are able to honor the wise, give importance to the sages, and practice wisdom, I [i.e., Lord Lao] will take you beyond to where you will encounter *zhenren* and immortals' (#178). Some passages show the power of the text: 'During travels, if you do not have proper lodging or family, you can take shelter under trees and rocks; then recite the 180 precepts, and the spirits will come to stand guard over you, three layers deep. No soldier, brigand, demon, or tiger will dare to come close' (#179). Then, Lord Lao told all the followers of the *dao*: 'In the old days, all the wise ones, immortals, and sages attained the *dao* following these 180 precepts' (see Kohn 2004a for text).

Essential Precepts of Master Redpine
Some time during the late 200s CE, two moral texts appeared that were attributed to the Daoist immortal Master Redpine (Chisongzi, see page 78). In Liu Xiang's *Biographies of the Immortals*, Master Redpine was reported to have lived in the age of Shennong and to have

possessed the powers of an immortal, including the ability to control the rain and wind, and to pass unharmed through fire. The work entitled *Essential Precepts of Master Redpine*, which now exists only in a Song dynasty edition, is a classic on the connection of moral behavior and the universe that contains materials that are probably traceable into the late 200s CE. It was cited in Ge Hong's *The Master Who Embraces Simplicity, Outer Chapters* (c. 316 CE), indicating that the original text dates very early. It is also quoted as an authority by the most famous of all Daoist morality books, the tenth-century work entitled *Tract of the Most Exalted on Action and Response*. The *Essential Precepts of Master Redpine* is a treasure house of Southern Celestial Master belief because it lays out a system of moral retribution overseen by a celestial administration based in the Three Offices. It also gives an early view of the realm of the underworld earth prisons of Fengdu, where people pay for their moral wrongs in various judicial courts.

The text is set up as a dialogue consisting of nine questions directed by the Yellow Emperor to Master Redpine. The questions are:

1. Why are people different in their fortunes?
2. How long is a typical human life?
3. Why are there miscarriages and the deaths of infants?
4. How can one improve one's situation in life?
5. Which moral wrongs are punished by subtractions from life expectancy?
6. Do moral wrongs and punishments match one another?
7. How can one dissolve immoral acts already accumulated?
8. Can one find the *dao* even in ordinary human life?
9. What types and ranks of masters are there? (Kohn 2004b: 155)

In brief, the answers to these questions are that the Celestial Officers of the Stars (i.e., the Big Dipper) and lesser officials such as the Arbiter of Fate (see *Zhuangzi* 18d, 193–4) govern human life by recording deeds and issuing cosmic responses to them. Officials who examine the moral life of persons apply the perfected talisman of the Great One (the numinal being, Taiyi) to the forehead of a person to reveal their transgressions. In this way, people cannot lie about their deeds. Moral and immoral deeds, like good and bad fortune, are inherited within families and the actions of one's ancestors influence following generations. Good deeds bring results in health, fortune and length of life. Moral rectitude will alleviate harm and bad fortune and lead to oneness with the *dao*. As the text says: 'fortune follows the person like a shadow' (Kohn 2004b: 159). Master Redpine tells the Yellow Emperor that there are over 800 transgressions, but he mentions only about 100. In his final response, the Yellow Emperor says: 'I will diligently follow what you have explained, and show its record to the multitude of people, thus creating a great passage [to transformation] for all living beings.'

Another text associated with Master Redpine and also important to a comprehensive view of the Southern Celestial Masters is *Master Redpine's Almanac of Petitions* that survives now only in a late Tang dynasty version. It is a composite and heavily edited work that contains some information about the practices of Celestial Master libationers, dating much earlier than the Tang, probably from the latter part of the Hanzhong period (c. 215–20 CE). This work demonstrates well the importance of talismanic petitions in the Southern Celestial Masters' communities. It contains instructions and rules for the writing of talismans and sending of petitions, originally indexing 134 different petitions, of which 68 have been lost. What remains are petitions having to do with ending drought, infestation of families or villages by ghosts, propitiating deceased ancestors and gaining release from punishment for the living or dead (Schipper and Verellen 2004: 134). The work includes several actual petitions that can be used as templates, with spaces for names, occasions and requests left blank to be filled in by the master.

Daoist Celestial Masters' Calligraphers and Painters

Two of the most famous names in the history of Chinese calligraphy and painting were affiliated with the Southern Celestial Masters movement, as is shown by their use of the character *zhi* in their names. Use of this character was a custom in the renaming of a master that came with ordination. Wang Xizhi (303–61 CE), referred to as 'the sage of calligraphy', lived in present-day Shaoxing in Zhejiang Province, not far from current Hangzhou. He was a follower of the Celestial Masters (Legeza 1975). His *Preface to the Poems Composed at the Orchid Pavilion*, dated to 353 CE, is regarded as one of the finest examples of calligraphy in Chinese history. Only three known copies of this work are in existence. There are 324 characters in this text: the character *zhi* appears 17 times, but it is never written in the same way twice. Largely because of what is said in this work, calligraphy became closely associated with *daoyin* (*qigong*), the physical exercises for concentrating *qi*. Writing in a Daoist way is allowing the *dao* to express *qi* energy through one's brush. The remarkable calligraphy of someone like Wang Xizhi is done spontaneously, without reflection or deliberation. Wang's most famous Daoist text is the *Inner Classic of the Yellow Court*. Although the original of this work is lost, copies in the form of ink rubbings are in the Palace Museum, Beijing, and the National Palace Museum, Taipei.

Gu Kaizhi (344–406 CE) lived near present-day Nanjing and is called 'the Father of Chinese Landscape Painting'. His essay 'On Painting the Cloud Terrace Mountain' is the earliest known reference to a painting of Zhang Daoling, and it provides a great deal of understanding about the way Daoists saw landscapes as mirrors of *dao* and *yin* and *yang* (Little 2004: 717). Xie He's 'Six Laws of Painting' (c. 550 CE) contains as its first law that an artist must be energized by concentrated *qi* in order to paint and that the *qi* vitality of any landscape must be sensed when approaching the work. Law 1 says a painting must have '*Qi* resonance and movement of *qi*' (*qiyun shengdong*). An excellent treatment of Daoist landscape painting is by Munakara (1991).

Chapter VIII

New Vines and the Masters Who Began Them

Ge Hong's Atrophied Lineage Vine

Ge Hong (283–343 CE) was the third son of a modestly aristocratic family living in Jurong, near present-day Nanjing. Like other southern gentry young men of promise, Ge Hong studied the Five Confucian Classics, until age 12, when his father died. Afterwards, from age 14 to 19, he learned under Zheng Yin. Master Zheng was himself formerly a student of Ge Hong's grand-uncle Ge Xuan (164–244 CE) and often referred to the teachings of Master Redpine. Ge Xuan had himself been an adept of the great Zuo Ci (155–220 CE).

> Zuo Ci is a mysterious figure about whom we know little authoritatively. Tradition says he lived in the Tianzhu mountains and practiced the Daoist arts of alchemical elixir, strengthening *qi* by breathing, *daoyin* (*qigong*) exercises, and conserving *qi* by never ejaculating in sex. Descriptions of his work say that he could ascend to the clouds, pass through rocks, change his shape to resemble any person or animal, hear at great distance, travel miles in one stride, deflect weapons without being injured, strike enemies with a wave of a force coming from his hand, and cause his numinal sword to decapitate enemies miles away. The *Romance of the Three Kingdoms* provides several narratives about his stormy relationship with Cao Cao, who was sometimes his patron but more often was trying to kill him. Zuo Ci often questioned the warlord's actions and decisions. The stories say that although Cao Cao tried to kill Zuo Ci several times, he was always frustrated because Zuo Ci's powers and abilities were unmatched.

Ge Hong's teacher, Zheng Yin, was classically educated. However, he had received various alchemical and other esoteric instructions and texts from Ge Xuan, and he in turn transmitted these to Ge Hong. Three of these are referred to in Ge Hong's *The Master Who Embraces Simplicity Inner Chapters*: the *Classic of Great Clarity*, the *Classic of the Nine Elixirs* and the *Classic of the Golden Elixir*.

Around 302 CE, Master Zheng and a number of disciples moved to Huoshan Mountain in Fujian province, but Ge Hong did not go with them. He took up a period of military service and later agreed to be military advisor to Ji Han, the newly appointed governor of Guangzhou (Canton) in far Southern China. Unfortunately, Ji Han was killed en route to take his new post, and Ge Hong was left without a position. He decided to remain in the Guangzhou area to pursue the techniques Zheng Yin had taught him. From an official named Bao Jing (260–327 CE), who later became his father-in-law, Ge Hong learned of Daoist masters who lived on nearby Luofu Mountain (Luofushan). Bao was an adept in the arts of the *dao*, and he often traveled to Luofu Mountain to visit the masters there, gather herbs and participate in their practices. Years before, Bao lived on Songshan Mountain (near Luoyang in Henan province); Ge Hong tells us that while Bao was residing in a cave on that mountain he witnessed the spontaneous carving of the text *The Writings of the Three Sovereigns* on the walls of the cave in March of 292 CE (*The Master Who Embraces Simplicity Inner Chapters* 19.8b; 20.9b).

In about 306 CE, Ge Hong took up an eight-year residence at Luofu Mountain. During that time, he wrote a number of poems and other important Daoist texts, including *The Master Who Embraces Simplicity Inner Chapters*, *The Master Who Embraces Simplicity Outer Chapters* and *Biographies of Shen Immortals*. By means of these works, Ge intended to establish his own Daoist lineage, extending the vine from his teacher Bao Jing, to Zheng Yin, to Ge Xuan, to Zuo Ci and to Master Redpine. Ge Hong provides a catalog of a library of the texts he received from Zheng Yin and Bao Jing as a part of his plan to construct a history of the lineage the growth of which he wished to foster. Unfortunately, virtually all the works on the catalog have disappeared (Robinet 1997: 79–80).

Ge returned to his family home in Jurong around 314 CE and found that he had to take up several minor political appointments over the years that followed in order to support his family. Then in 328 CE, a rebellion broke out against the Eastern Jin led by Su Jun (d. 328 CE), and Ge Hong returned to far Southern China to escape the turmoil and renew his quest to follow the way of Master Redpine. After the rebellion, Ge sought and received an appointment as District Magistrate of Julou, which is located in modern-day Vietnam, but instead he settled once again on Luofu Mountain. The account of his transformation in his official biography in the *Book of the Jin* may be more hagiography than history. According to the account, those who discovered Ge Hong's body found it to be light and supple, as if alive, and his contemporaries all supposed that he had finally achieved the technique of transformation to numinosity called 'liberation from the corpse' (*shijie*). The year was 343 CE.

Ge Hong admired those *zhenren* immortals whom the *Zhuangzi* mentions, and whose hagiographies appear in Liu Xiang's *Biographies of Immortals* (see page 77). Many of the practices he describes as designed to increase the powers of a follower of the *dao* reach back into the Warring States period c. 300 BCE. In the *Master Who Embraces Simplicity Inner Chapters*, Ge Hong describes the practices essential to the development of the substances necessary for acquiring longevity and even immortality. Two chapters of the work are concerned with the explanations of alchemical techniques provided in three texts he received from Zheng Yin: *Classic of Great Clarity*, *Classic of the Nine Elixirs* and *Classic of the Golden Elixir*. Ge says that these three texts were first brought into his area by Zuo Ci, who received them while in a numinous state in the mountains of Shandong province at the end of the second century CE. They show detailed similarities with the teaching of Li Shaojun, the court master of the *dao* associated with Emperor Wu of the Han (see page 54).

Ge said 'Human beings live on *qi* and *qi* fills human beings. From Heaven and Earth to the myriad beings, all need *qi* to live. Whoever can guide the *qi* will nourish his body on the inside and protect himself against harmful influences on the outside' (*The Master Who Embraces Simplicity Inner Chapters* 5.96). The unity with the *dao* that is the power of the Great One could be preserved by refining one's *qi*. Ge thought that each person had a finite amount of *qi* at birth: techniques to *preserve* it, such as sexual arts, and the skills of *concentrating* it through breathing exercises, calisthenics, dietary restrictions and the ingestion of herbal medicines, and the arts of *strengthening* it through elixirs, were fundamental to gaining immortality. Ge taught that all of these techniques had value and should be used in conjunction with each other. He said: 'Even if one performs breathing exercises and *daoyin*, as well as ingests herbal medicines, this can only extend the years of your lifespan, but it will not save you from death. Ingesting divine cinnabar will make your lifespan inexhaustible. You will last as long as Heaven and Earth, be able to travel on clouds and ride dragons, and ascend at will to the Heaven of Highest Clarity.'

The *Classic of the Nine Elixirs* was well known to Ge Hong and he accepted it as the guide for making the elixir of immortality. The text leaves no doubt that the making of elixir was a ritual act. It provides an account of the ritual process, including the purification of the master and the assistants, the gathering of all necessary ingredients and the choice of an auspicious place for the burner. Once all these components are in place, a sacred covenant is made and sealed between the master and his adepts to ensure that neither will retire from the process nor share the procedures and recipes.

Before the actual burning begins, a laboratory is constructed. When doing this, both the participants and the space around them must be protected from intervention of any kind, so talismans are composed and hung at all the cardinal directions. Registers and talismans are worn on the clothing of those participating. A mirror and sword are hung over the entrance as defenses against evil and unwanted *shen*. The auspicious day and time for beginning the process are determined. The fire is kindled while the master offers food and drink to the *shen*, who attend bringing their power. The compounding of the ingredients begins and the assistants attend the cooking process. Once the elixir is in liquid or mash form, able to be drunk or shaped into a pill or dried as a power, some of it is offered to the numinal beings of the Big Dipper and the Great Taiyi. A portion is taken into the village marketplace for those who cannot devote themselves to compounding. This elixir may bring health and longevity, even if it does not bring immortality. Finally, the elixir is ingested at dawn, while facing the rising sun. As one begins to transform, the result is that the person would become a *zhenren* and *xian* who could overcome illness, control ghost spirits, tame beasts, avoid weapons, raise the dead, see the future, appear and disappear at will, and live without food.

According to Ge Hong: 'As for the burning of gold and cinnabar, the longer one burns them, the more marvelous will be their transformations. When gold enters the flames, even after one hundred firings, it will not disappear. If you bury it forever, it will never decay. If one ingests these two substances, they will refine that person's body, and make it so that the person will neither age nor die.' The theory behind Ge Hong's explanation of the materials he used seems pretty clear. A person may make his body imperishable by ingesting imperishable things. So plants, herbs and medicinals, however valuable for one's overall health and energy, are inferior to gold and cinnabar for the acquisition of immortality because they are perishable. Materials used could vary, however, because there were at least nine types of elixirs and, depending on which was used, results other than immortality could follow (Pregadio 2004: 182; see also the *Canon and Instruction for the Divine Alchemy of the Nine Cauldrons of the Yellow Emperor*).

Choosing the proper location for the making of elixir was important, and it was a by-product of several techniques having to do with the planning of residences (*tuzhai shu*) that was extended into the arts of 'wind and water' (*fengshui*). The use of sacred charts such as that contained in *True Diagram of the Five Peaks*, which was collected in its present form about the time of Ge Hong and contained incantations and prayers of Zheng Yin and Bao Jing, was essential to the masters who wanted to develop the alchemy of immorality (Schipper and Verellen 2004: 265). In Daoism, such chart diagrams are almost always called 'the true form' of something whether the object is one's body or a place (see Talismans, Registers and Diagrams on pages 56ff.). A numinal diagram of a place is much more than a map. It is a geomantic chart, showing how and where the cosmic energies of a place are concentrated. We have seen how these diagrams were connected with the Five Phase system in identifying five sacred mountains in Daoism and in establishing first the 24 centres of the Celestial Masters, and later the 28 administrative centers identified by Kou Qianzhi. Some diagrams represent the geography of numinal places such as the abode of the Queen Mother of the West (*Xiwangmu*) on Kunlun Mountain and her garden of the peaches of immortality, or the underworld dwelling of ghost spirits and the courts of punishment called Fengdu.

Ge Hong also used the *Writings of the Three Sovereigns* obtained from Bao Jing that provided secret names, words and talismanic formulas for commanding the numinal *shen* of the sky and earth, including the *shen* of the Big Dipper or Highest Heaven (*Gaotian*). Putting together his training about sacred locations and secret names and talismans, Ge Hong wrote:

> When you are going into the mountains, choose a *jiayin* day on which to write the talismans on plain silk, place them at night on a table, and

as you face the Big Dipper (*beidou*) offer them [the numinal spirits of the Dipper] sacrifices of wine and salted meat. To each of them introduce yourself briefly by name, bow twice, and then place them [the talismans] in the neck of your garment. This will drive from you the many ghosts and powers, tigers, wolves, insects and poisons from the mountains and rivers. (*Master Who Embraces Simplicity Inner Chapters*, 17)

In Ge Hong's system, an adept carrying such a talisman will be free from all illness, pestilences and calamities. Persons without such talismans will be wasting their time in the mountains and might find the trek to be a dangerous one.

Ge Hong believed that anyone could obtain immortality. Wealth and position, and even education, were not relevant. One's moral life was, however, quite important. In effect, Ge added morality to the techniques necessary for immortality. Through this, we probably see the influence of his teachers upon him, particularly that of Master Redpine, as his teachings were transmitted to Ge probably through Zheng Yin. Ge Hong taught that good deeds are assigned merits and 300 merits will make one what he called an 'earthbound immortal', while 1,200 merits will make one a 'celestial immortal' capable of ascending to Heaven. He made a distinction among three different types of immortals: heavenly-celestial, earth-bound and corpse-liberated

- Celestial immortals are beings who have transmorphed their bodies into numinal energy and course through the universe of 'Great Clarity' (*Taiqing*).

- Earth-bound immortals Ge Hong mentions, such as Master Whitestone (Baishi Gong), have achieved an indefinite longevity on earth, exhibit extraordinary powers, and can appear and disappear at will.

- Corpse-liberated immortals have lesser powers and must undergo an escape, leaving behind a body. His followers believed that Ge Hong made use of a secret technique for 'deliverance from the corpse' in his own transformation.

Ge Hong is bringing together a number of traditions rather than announcing a single universal Daoist point of view on how to obtain immortality. He has no doubt that immortals exist, even if they are most often not visible to the vulgar herd who do not believe in them. And he intends to retell the extraordinary marvels of which immortals are capable as evidence of this belief. His *Biographies of Shen Immortals* is much longer than Liu Xiang's *Biographies of the Immortals*. Present versions of Ge Hong's work contain over 90 biographies, some of which are extensive. Unfortunately, none of our extant versions of the *Biographies of Shen Immortals* is the original text composed by Ge Hong. The Tang Buddhist scholar Liang Su (753–93 CE) claimed to have had a version of Ge Hong's work with accounts of 190 biographies.[11]

Symbols of Immortals

As Chinese artists began to portray immortals based on the various biographies that emerged, certain objects and animals became associated with them or came to symbolize immortality.

Gourd: Immortals are often portrayed as carrying bottle gourds (not melon gourds). This association had its origin in the practice of masters to carry gourds over their shoulders or tied to their waists. The gourds contained medicinal herbs, powerful substances to be burned in alchemical furnaces and even immortality pills.

Cinnabar: Cinnabar is a red ore that contains mercuric sulfide. It was valued by Daoist alchemists both for its red color and for the precious product that comes from it after heating. The red color was considered auspicious and even referred to as 'dragon's blood' (*longxue*). When heated intensely, mercury is separated from the ore into a liquid form. The properties of mercury appeared mysterious to the ancients. Accordingly, it became associated with possessing the pure energy (*qi*) that empowers and animates transformation of the Five Phases.

Pine or Cypress: Evergreens, such as pine and cypress, are associated with longevity, even immortality. No matter the changes of the seasons, they continue to be green. Pine needles and nuts are very common in the pharmacology of masters, and they were used for healing and thought to prolong life. In rural China, a family may still plant a pine tree near a grave.

Peaches: Many Daoist texts report the tales of the immortal Queen Mother of the West who presented peaches and 'numinous fungus' to those who aspired to become immortal. So peaches are thought to possess the power of longevity and even immortality. At present, peaches are served on birthdays as a wish for long life.

Dragons, Cranes, Birds: Dragons were believed to have within them the sort of blood that makes them immortal. In the tales of the immortals and the visions of many Daoist masters, dragons come to pick up *zhenren* and take them away into reaches of the celestial beings. Likewise, in the accounts of immortals making appearances, cranes also are often the mode of transportation they use. Birds have the ability to fly and, because of their transformation, immortals also were believed to be able to fly. A popular belief in Chinese history is that the spirits of ancestors return to their homes or to their lineage temples on the seventh day of the seventh month on cranes or other birds.

The Highest Clarity Vine of Daoism

One of the most important developments in the Daoist kudzu came with the emergence of the lineage of Highest Clarity (*Shangqing*). The name *Shangqing* was a way of referring to the supremely high level of numinosity obtained by the beings from whom the knowledge of the masters of this lineage was derived. The *zhenren* of Highest Clarity were believed by the masters who transmitted their teachings to be superior to all other numinal beings. While the Highest Clarity masters continued the longevity techniques first used in the late Zhou and the Han dynasties, through the Celestial Masters and the Ge family, they laid more stress on meditation and spiritual visualization performed within 'meditation chambers' (*jingshi*).

This new vine on the Daoist kudzu owes its origin to knowledge received by Yang Xi (330–86 CE) from the numinal being 'Lady' Wei Huacun (251–334 CE). Beginning in 363 CE and lasting until 370 CE, the story goes that Yang received visits from a series of numinal personages called the Perfected Persons (*zhenren*). Lady Wei was believed to be one of these Perfected *shen* who communicated through Yang Xi as her medium. Although Lady Wei communicated through Yang Xi, the teachings themselves were meant to be transmitted through Yang to the Xu brothers: Xu Mi (303–73 CE) and Xu Hui (341–c. 370 CE). Yang was an official in the Xu household, that was related to Ge Hong's, a family by marriage.

'Lady' Wei Huacun

Wei Huacun was a female master who according to the *Declarations of the Perfected Persons* (c. 499 CE) became the spirit guide for Yang Xi. Her hagiography says she came originally from Jinning in the southwestern part of Shandong Province. In her early years, Wei Huacun read the Daoist and Confucian classics, used elixirs of immortality, and practiced breathing techniques to refine her *qi*. Her parents arranged a marriage for her to an official whom she did not want to marry. She later bore him two sons. All the while, she did not cease to follow the *dao*, and she became a libationer in the Celestial Masters lineage. She received visits from two immortals who transmitted to her techniques that eventually became the basic teachings of the Highest Clarity lineage, including how to visualize numinal forces in the body, a new method for Pacing the Dipper in rituals and unique instructions about how to prepare various elixir recipes. According to the account, Zhang Daoling himself transmitted to her the proper way to enter a meditation chamber and to write petitions to the numinous powers. She represents a living embodiment of the growing of a new vine in Daoism. In her, the Highest Clarity vine sprouted from the Celestial Masters, and this is why she is considered the First Patriarch of that lineage. In later Shangqing history, Wei Huacun was honored with the title Grand Sovereign of the Purple Vacuity Upper Perfected Director of Destinies Lady [Wei] of the Southern Mount [Hengshan].

In the seventh century, Huang Lingwei (c. 640–721) devoted herself to a quest for the location of the lost shrine of Lady Wei. According to the only extant accounts of her life, Huang was ordained as a *daogu* (female Daoist master) at the age of 12. When she discovered the shrine of Lady Wei, she restored it and began to practice regular rituals there. She attracted a number of disciples, apparently all female, and they continued her legacy for several decades after she transformed into a numinal being by following Lady Wei's techniques of liberation from the corpse (*shijie*) (Kirkland 2004: 140).

The teachings Yang Xi received from Lady Wei are embodied in the *Perfect Classic of Great Profundity* that exists in the Daoist canon under several titles. It is the most important Highest Clarity lineage text. We are told by Highest Clarity masters that this is not merely a book to be read. It is a talismanic work of power that holds the secrets to the transformation of the adept's body into a numinal form that may be delivered from its remains (i.e., the corpse).

Accordingly, there is an entire ritual for its recitation within a meditation chamber.[12] Before reciting the text, the master must call up a number of numinal beings whose protection and aid he seeks. As one chants the text's invocations, the numinal spirits draw near and take their places in the meditation chamber. One must visualize oneself in glory, seated on lions and wearing a feathered robe, flanked by the green dragon and the white tiger. Of course, all of this is very symbolic. Feathers, for example, are associated with birds, which are reminders of the perfected *zhenren* who can fly. The green dragon and white tiger are tropes for *yin* and *yang*. Surrounded by this crowd of attending powers, the person recites the text. Each of the central 39 stanzas is addressed to a celestial spirit associated with the visualization of the *shen* of the adept's body's organs, creating a unity between the body and the universe. For example, the brain is Kunlun Mountain, with nine inner connected palaces and compartments to be visited and into which one may bring 'the purple breath of power', signifying oneness with the *shen* who reside there. James Miller has translated a beautiful passage describing one report of this experience. It is taken from the *Central Classic of the Nine Perfected Persons* that is attributed to Master Redpine, who was adopted by the Highest Clarity tradition as one of its lineage forebearers.

Visualization of the Shen of the Body

In the first month, on your birthday, the *jiazi* day, or that *jiaxu* day, at dawn, the five spirits and the Imperial Lord of Great Unity merge together into one Great Spirit which rests in your heart. The spirit is called the Lord of Celestial Essence, his style is Highest Hero of Soaring birth, his appearance is like an infant immediately after birth. On that day at dawn, enter your oratory [chamber], place your hands on your knees, control your breathing, close your eyes. Look inside and visualize the Lord of Celestial Essence sitting in your heart. His name is called Great Spirit. Imagine him spewing forth purple energy to coil thickly around your heart in nine layers. Let the energy rush up into the brain palaces (*niwan*). Inner and outer are as one. When this is done, clench your teeth nine times, swallow saliva nine times, then recite this:

Great Lord of Celestial Essence,
Highest Hero of Soaring Birth,
Imperial Lord, transform inside me,
Come into vision in my heart.
★★★★

Your mouth spews out purple florescence,
To nourish my heart and concentrate my spirit.
As my crimson organ spontaneously becomes alive,
May I become a soaring immortal. (Miller 2003: 102–3)

The Highest Clarity lineage teaches a number of practices.[13] For example, there is the 'Method of the Whirling Wind' (*huifeng*), a technique for fusing numinal power with one's own body. The adept visualizes a 'white breath' (the color of light) entering the mouth and traveling through the body and turning purple inside of the body (the color of the *qi* at the center of the Big Dipper), activating the ability to control transformation and power.[14]

A second practice is 'Untying the Embryonic Knots'. At conception, the Five Phases coming into form as a body form 12 knots. These are the roots that make our physicality possible, but they are also responsible for aging, maladies of illness and mortality. In *The Embryonic Essence from Superior Transmutation of the Ninefold Elixir*, we read the following:

> When a man is born [i.e., conceived], there form in him while in the womb twelve knots which keep the five viscera tightly twisted together. The five viscera are hindered and obstructed. When the knots are not untied, when the nodules do not disappear, this is the cause of human maladies; it is because the knots create obstacles; when human fate is cut off, it is because the knots are still tightened. (3a)

One who wishes to be a *zhenren* must untie these knots by receiving the *qi* from the Nine Primordial Heavens as the purple breath, then untying one knot at a time. The result is an immortal embryonic body 'of gold and jade'. Once the knots are untied, one will see in a kind of psychodrama of altered consciousness one's name being written on the Registers of immortals (Robinet 1997: 137). Afterwards, the adept may leave the body behind as a chrysalis and be 'liberated from the corpse'. As we can see, this is an interiorized version of the nine elixirs with which Ge Hong is acquainted and we may say, then, that Highest Clarity represents what can be called an 'inner alchemy' (*neidan*) of transformation.

Another practice taught by Highest Clarity masters is 'Uniting in the Heavenly Palace'. This technique consists of visualizing 'the nine true numinal beings' uniting with the *shen* of 'the nine organs of the body' in the Heavenly Palaces of the Brain. The aim of this practice is to regenerate the body and strengthen its ability to transform itself and make itself luminous. Perhaps no better description of this new luminous immortal body can be offered than that of Lady Wei's appearance in her hagiography in the text entitled *The Pearl Bag of the Three Caverns*:

> Empyreal phosphor, glistening high;
> Round eye-lenses doubly lit;
> Phoenix frame and dragon bone;
> Brain coloured as jewel-planetoids;
> Five viscera of purple webbings;
> Heart holding feathered scripts. (8.22b)

A fourth practice of Highest Clarity is the 'Ingestion of Cosmic Florescence'. This is a form of nourishment for immortality that replaces the eating of the five grains that nourish the physical body. The goal is to reduce one's dependence on gross forms of energy such as grains and convert one's body into an instrument for the refinement of *qi* and the creation of a celestial form. In Highest Clarity, the florescence of the stars was believed to be pure light and the adept could absorb it (*fuguang*). The experience itself was primarily a visualization, in which numinal beings nourished the adept by loving touch and cosmic effluvia called 'soul of the sun' (*rihun*) or 'flower of the moon' (*yuehua*). The belief is that the spiritual essence of the sun and moon may be absorbed in order to refine the body and make it ever more evanescent.

The practice of 'Liberation from the Corpse' (*shijie*) is likewise central to Highest Clarity. Highest Clarity lineage masters taught that the successful adept may come and go in a numinal form at will, appearing and disappearing, transforming and coursing through the cosmic reaches and the stars. When the adept leaves for good, the corpse is left behind. The power to liberate from the corpse is associated closely with the seven methods for transformation given in the work *Seven Recitations of the Divine Realm with Seven Transformations for Dancing in Heaven*. This text gives methods for transforming oneself into a cloud, a beam of light, fire, water, a dragon or a *shen* liberated from the corpse.

Finally, there is the practice of 'Cosmic Excursions'. In these experiences, Highest Clarity texts describe how the *zhenren* enters an ecstatic state and travels throughout the cosmos, although one's body does not leave the meditation chamber. The adept may 'fly through the heavens' (*feitian*), or travel to the lands mentioned in the *Classic of the Mountains and Seas* (see page 55). The adept may meet numinal spirits and walk the isles of immortality by using guides, diagrams and charts, and protecting talismans along the way. By Pacing the Dipper (see pages 61-62) the adept may present petitions to the numinal beings of the nine stars of the Big Dipper who govern the destinies of human beings and even enter the residence of The Great One (Taiyi), returning with power to withstand all malevolent forces. The Highest Clarity text, known as the *Classic on the Three Limits on the Passes of Heaven*, provides instructions for rituals necessary to open the three gates of entry to the Big Dipper and formulas for citing the names of the *shen* beings of the Dipper and of the underworld of Fengdu, all of which may be used on these cosmic excursions. According to Highest Clarity, a *zhenren* who is able to visit such places will have great power (Miller 2003: 100).

Perhaps the most important figure in the early formation of the Highest Clarity lineage outside of its founders was Tao Hongjing (456–536 CE). Tao was an alchemist, pharmacologist and master of Daoist arts. A relative of both the Xu and Ge families, he was the ninth patriarch of the Highest Clarity lineage vine and arguably its most important representative. He was familiar with Ge Hong's *Biographies of Shen Immortals*, and he wrote about pilgrimages he made to visit *zhenren* in the mountains when he was a youth. He was a student of Sun Youyue of Dongyong, who taught him talisman writing, ritual performance and other skills. After reading the Highest Clarity texts, he left a career as an official when he was 36 years of age to live high atop Maoshan near Nanjing. As the masters before him described in the *Zhuangzi* had done, he twice refused the summons to return to court and take an official position. On Maoshan, he gathered disciples and gained a reputation for healing. He sought out the records and teachings of 'Lady' Wei Huacun, Yang Xi and the Xu brothers, and used them to compile two texts called *Declarations of the Perfected Person* and *Secret Instructions for the Ascent as a Perfected Person*. These works, along with Yang Xi's *The Perfect Classic of Great Profoundity*, have become the major documents of the Highest Clarity lineage.

陶
弘
景

Tao Hongjing

The *Secret Instructions* is unlike the *Declarations of the Perfected Person*. Whereas the latter contains declared revelations from numinal beings, the former is a practical manual for the adept. The *Secret Instructions* contains a set of spiritual exercises, such as the technique for 'Uniting in the Heavenly Palace'. Methods for corpse liberation are described, and talismans and diagrams necessary to the celestial wanderings of the *zhenren* are provided. One chapter heading is 'Merits' (*Ligong pin*), and it continues Ge Hong's emphasis on the importance of morality to the ability to transform oneself into the most pure states of being and become an immortal.

In about 500 CE, Tao compiled fragments of earlier works into *Shennong's Materia Medica*, which is an important collected pharmacology in China. This work, transformative in intent, actually laid the foundation for all later Chinese developments in pharmacological therapy and became the model for many later collections. Tao identifies over 700 drugs and arranges them in three different classes.

The Numinous Treasure Vine of Daoism

The Numinous Treasure (*Lingbao*) lineage vine developed in the fourth and fifth centuries CE and found expression in a set of 40 texts. Numinous Treasure masters regarded the Highest Clarity texts as authentic and valuable, but they tried to enhance the importance of their lineage teachings by saying that the Highest Clarity texts came from numinal beings who were lower than those who provided the Numinous Treasure revelations. Unlike the Highest Clarity masters, Numinous Treasure masters borrowed heavily from Buddhism, which began to filter into China along the east–west Silk Roads as early as the first century CE. Whereas Highest Clarity focused on the transformation of the individual, Numinous Treasure adopted the Mahayana Buddhist ideal of universal salvation. Numinous Treasure masters spurned cultivation of the physical body through therapeutic regimens, *daoyin* exercises, alchemy and even meditation. Instead, they emphasized abstention from moral wrongdoing and stressed ritual performances, including recitation of sacred texts, in order to achieve salvation for all. Despite these differences in emphasis, Numinous Treasure was subsumed under the leadership of Highest Clarity patriarchs by the sixth century CE.

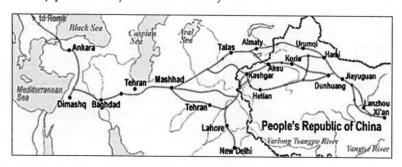

Buddhism Comes to China

Lingbao is also used for 'guardian of the numinous'. A *lingbao* refers to a person who was able to communicate with *shen*. The *lingbao* played a role in ancestor veneration as early as 700 BCE. *Lingbao* knew how to communicate with the spirits of one's ancestors and speak for them as a medium. They also served as guardians of these *shen* and made sure that during the ritual openings allowing them to communicate, other unwanted *shen* could not interfere or enter. In early China, when the *shen* of a grandparent was summoned, the grandchild (gender dependent on that of the relative to be summoned) would wear the skull of the deceased to provide the *shen* a place in which to focus its form. The child would speak as moved by the *shen* and was called the *lingbao*, and also sometimes called the 'representative of the corpse' or 'impersonator of the dead' (see *Zhuangzi* 13e, 32–3; Toshiaki 2004: 227). As the practice changed, some ritual masters dispensed with the skull and the child impersonated the deceased relative by wearing some clothes of the ancestor. In still other ritual traditions, wooden tablets inscribed with the name of the deceased became a substitute for the skull and the child. Both the *Master Who Embraces Simplicity Inner Chapters* and *The Later Han* confirm that these practices of the *lingbao* were ongoing. Information coming from the ancestors through the *lingbao* was expressed in a technique called 'investigating' (*he*), and it was always undertaken under the protection of talismans. Ge Hong is the first to mention what he calls the five *lingbao* talismans and a work called *The Classics of the Numinous Treasure* in his *Master Who Embraces Simplicity Inner Chapters.*

In the late fourth century, a Numinous Treasure text appeared called *Classic on the True Writings of the Five Ancients of the Primordial Beginning, Red Writings in Celestial Script on Jade Tablets.* The text was called 'red writing' because it was believed that the characters were created from cosmic fire in patterns of a celestial script that depended heavily on the use of the cosmology of the Five Phases, the five emperors, the five directions and the five sacred mountains. Numinous Treasure masters taught that the user who recited it possessed the ability to control the Registers of *shen* immortals, became endowed with power to take journeys into the cosmic regions, and gained control over the administrators of Fengdu, the abode of deceased *shen* who were undergoing punishment.

From the earliest days, masters of the *dao* were concerned with aiding the departed. The closer the connection between morality and transformation became, the more Daoists believed that those who lived immoral lives would be punished and even their family members might be affected. Moreover, as we have seen from the time of *Huainanzi*'s concept of 'action and response' (*ganying*), through the teachings of the Celestial Masters, to those of Ge Hong, morally warped lives were believed to affect the types of transformations possible under the Five Phase *qi* cosmology. Numinous Treasure masters saw a symmetry and connection between these ideas and the teachings in Buddhism called the 'Five Paths of Rebirth': reaching form in the earth prisons of Fengdu, becoming a hungry ghost, returning as an animal, coming back as a human again or transforming into a numinal being. The Numinous Treasure lineage's understanding of the reconstitution of a person's Five Phase form may be understood as a sinicization of Buddhism, mixing traditional Chinese concepts with newly arrived Buddhist ideas.

Without doubt, the most important text of the Numinous Treasure lineage vine is the *Most Excellent and Mysterious Book of the Marvelous Jewel That Saves Innumerable Human Beings*. Early in the Tang dynasty, this book was one of the three classics to be studied by Daoists for the official exam leading to investiture as a Daoist ritual master. According to Numinous Treasure belief, this text represented words actually spoken by the *Dao*. The work is divided into three parts. The first describes how the words of the text appeared in the celestial spheres at the beginning of the universe and how it was spoken by the Heavenly Worthy of Primordial Beginning (*Yuanshi tianzun*). The first part closes with instructions for the recitation of the text after Heaven's Gate is opened by a ritual master. The second part of the text is its core. It contains words that were thought to be the secret names of numinal beings; these make rhyming sounds when read by the trained master, who may then claim authority over these powers. The final part of the text is also made up of sounds of a secret language, the title of which shows the text's Buddhist linkage: 'Innumerable Sounds of the Secret Language of the Great Brahman Energies of the Heavens'.

The Numinous Treasure lineage ritual use of this text is fascinating. The text was not read to be understood cognitively or in any conscious way. The writing could be pronounced or chanted, but it was the ritual act of a master performing the reading that activated the numinal power of the text. The text itself taught that its recitation enabled the blind to see, the lame to walk and barren women to conceive (Robinet 1997: 164). After the *dao* delivered the text to the Heavenly Worthy of Primordial Beginning, the text says:

When he spoke the scripture through for the first time, all of the assembled great Sages voiced their approval. At once all those in the kingdom afflicted with deafness, both male and female, were able to hear again. When he expounded the scripture a second time, the eyes of the blind were opened to the light. When he expounded the scripture for the third time, the mute were able to speak. When he expounded the scripture for the fourth time, those long lame or paralytic were able to arise and walk. When he expounded the scripture for the fifth time, those with chronic illnesses or diseases were immediately made whole. When he expounded the scripture the sixth time, white hair turned black again and lost teeth were regrown. When he expounded the scripture for the seventh time, the aged were restored to youth and the young were made strong. When he expounded the scripture for the eighth time, wives became pregnant, while birds' and beasts' wombs were quickened. Not only were those already born made whole, but the unborn as well came whole into life. When he expounded the scripture for the ninth time, the stores of earth were leaded forth; gold and jade lay revealed. When he expounded the scripture for the tenth time, desiccated bones were revivified; all rose up to become human beings again. At once the whole kingdom, both male and female, inclined their hearts to the Dao. All received protection and salvation. All achieved long life. (Bokenkamp 1997c: 406–7).

Chapter IX

Daoism in the Tang: Robust Maturity of the Vine

Laozi, Protector of the Tang

The Tang dynasty (618–907 CE) is well known as the heyday of Chinese culture, especially in art and poetry. It is also one of the most intense periods of intercultural exchange between China and the lands to the west. Daoism flourished during this period. One reason for its success was the prophecy that a great ruler surnamed Li would arise and bring the Great Peace (*Taiping*) kingdom. The name Li came from one of the traditions that Laozi had the name Li Er. So, this prophecy was taken to mean that a descendant of Laozi would come to the throne and bring Great Peace. The family that came to rule the Tang dynasty also had this surname. Moreover, as we will remember, the declared intention of Daoists at Louguan Tai, and in the Northern Celestial Masters tradition in general, was to usher in a kingdom of Great Peace. Taken together these two factors provided Daoists the hope for which they were seeking, and it gave the Tang rulers powerful allies in their attempts to strengthen their imperial authority. When the founder of the Tang dynasty, Gaozu (r. 618–26 CE, birth name Li Yuan), came to power, the Highest Clarity Patriarch Wang Yuanzhi (528–635 CE) proclaimed that Li was chosen to establish the Great Peace Kingdom (Kohn and Kirkland 2004: 341). Many appearances of Laozi were reported during the ascendancy of Gaozu to power. The two most famous of these were when Laozi appeared to the mountain spirit of Huoshan Mountain (Huoshan) and then manifested himself to a commoner living on Yangjiao Mountain (*Yangjiao shan*) to transfer the news that Li Yuan (Gaozu) had been chosen to bring a new era of Great Peace. The result of such reports connecting the great vine of Daoism with the new rising power of the Tang dynasty was substantial imperial favor for the development of Daoist teaching, the building of its temples and support for the production of Daoist art.

As we have seen, Buddhism entered China in the late Han dynasty along the Silk Roads, and because of the proximity to western entrances into China, Dunhuang and Chang'an (Xian) were important sites of intercultural interactions between Daoism and Buddhism. In 637 CE, this new reality resulted in a special unified code that was issued by the state to govern both the lives of Daoist masters in temples and observatories sponsored by the government and Buddhist monks and nuns in monasteries, called *Rules for Daoists and Buddhists* (*Daoseng ke*).

Daoism Triumphant: Taizong (r. 627–50 CE) and Gaozong (r. 650–84 CE)

Tang rulers favored Daoism, and in 637 CE Emperor Taizong (r. 627–50, birth name Li Shimin) issued an edict that gave precedence to Daoism over Buddhism and Emperor Gaozong (r. 650–84 CE, birth name Li Zhi) continued to enforce it. One of the Louguan Tai masters, Yin Wencao (622–88 CE), moved to the capital and acted as a close counsel to Emperor Gaozong. Gaozong issued orders of importance to the history of Daoism:

1. In 666 CE, Gaozong established state supported Daoist *guan* in each of over 300 prefectures, with special dispensations for Maoshan, Bozhou and Louguan Tai. For centuries thereafter, these three mountain *guan* of Daoism became the principal centres for the flourishing of the Daoist kudzu.
2. Gaozong authorized the compilation of a Daoist canon in 675 CE.
3. In 677, Gaozong appointed Yin Wencao as head of Louguan Tai. The story goes that when Yin celebrated a Daoist ritual for the emperor in Luoyang, Lord Lao appeared and filled the court with clouds and drum sounds. Afterward, Yin received the title 'Great Officer of Silver-Green Radiance' (*Yinqing guanglu dafu*).
4. In 678 CE, Gaozong made the *Daodejing* a compulsory text in the imperial examination system for government service.
5. Under the patronage of Gaozong, Yin edited the first comprehensive history of Daoism.

Pan Shizheng (585–682 CE), the 11th Highest Clarity Patriarch, received visits from Emperor Gaozong at his mountain residence on Gaosong Mountain, and the emperor also sought the counsel of Ye Fashan (631–720 CE). Ye was believed to have the ability to communicate with the numinal spirits of the Big Dipper and possess the skill of 'tossing of the dragon' (*toulong*). This was a ritual in which a golden image of a dragon was cast into a waterway in order to take messages to the *shen* of the river (Kohn and Kirkland 2004: 433).

Xuanzong (r. 713–56 CE) and the Jixian Imperial College of Daoist Studies

The emperor Xuanzong (r. 713–56 CE, birth name Li Longji) was a committed student of Daoist texts. He wove Daoism and the imperial destiny closely together by launching a program of state-sponsored Daoist temples, having statues of Lord Lao and himself placed in each. He also decreed that the Li family ancestral temples in Chang'an (Taiqing Gong) and Luoyang (Taiwei Gong) must be reserved only for Daoist rituals. In 722 CE, he built what is now known as the White Cloud Temple (Baiyun Guan) in Beijing, the most famous Daoist temple in history.

Xuanzong nationalized Daoism by requiring registration of Daoist masters and putting its temples under direct imperial control through the office of 'Commissioner of Daoist Ritual' (*daomen weiyi shi*). This action may have been undertaken at the request of leading Daoists as an effort to control the eruption of new vines and stems from the tradition. Or it may have been more directly an attempt to distinguish approved Daoist practices and teachings from similar iterations in the popular culture. In any event, a number of new Daoist centers were created under Xuanzong as a part of this standardization process. A report dated 739 CE says that there were 550 *guan* for Daoist women, compared with 1,137 for men. Xuanzong also established the Jixian Imperial College of Daoist Studies to assemble Daoist masters to lecture and demonstrate their techniques. Beginning in 741 CE, Xuanzong inaugurated a program to place a 'College of Daoist Studies' in each prefecture and set up a new model of imperial examinations called the *Daoju*, which trained those unfamiliar with Daoist texts in the tradition so they could pass the exams necessary for holding bureaucratic office. He sought counsel and received lay ordination as a ritual master from the 12th Highest Clarity Patriarch, Sima Chengzhen (647–735 CE), a former disciple of Pao Shizheng on Gaosong Mountain.

Sima Chengzhen and Xuanzong became trusted friends. Xuanzong presented him with a stone inscribed with the entire *Daodejing* in three styles of Sima's calligraphy. He also built a temple for Sima on Wangwu Mountain (*Wangwu shan*), near the capital at Chang'an (Xi'an). In return, Sima presented the emperor with a numinous sword and mirror, together with a text illuminating their meaning and explaining how to use their power.

At the instigation of Daoist masters, the education of physicians was standardized during the Tang, creating an integration of Daoist and Chinese medical practices, especially in the area of longevity and the pharmacology related to it. Sima Chengzhen linked Chinese physical health techniques with Buddhist practices of insight meditation. According to Sima, the first step toward the transformation of the biospiritual form of the Five Phases is to ensure the body's health. Next, one has to cure all diseases and stop eating grains. Sima made use of the first systematic treatise on the etiology and pathology of illness collected by Chao Yuanfang in 610 CE and entitled *The Origins and Symptoms of Medical Disorders*. The work covers 1,739 specific diseases arranged according to their causes and symptoms. Finally, Sima regarded visualizations of spirits and deep immersions in the *dao* as necessary in the final stages of transformation.

With the increase in visibility and prestige of Daoism during the Tang, tales of immortals were no longer marginalized but took centre stage. A new *Biographies of the Immortals* (*Xuxian zhuan*) was compiled, and it was in many ways different from the earlier biographies of Liu Xiang and Ge Hong. In this work, immortals are not so often strange people who live on the fringes of society as in Liu Xiang, and they are more demonstrably historical figures rather than legendary ones as in Ge Hong. They are often associates of well-known people, hold responsible positions in society and are seldom portrayed as bizarre people who live in mountain hermitages or caves. While they make pilgrimages to the sacred mountains, they live in temples, visit court and show themselves to be well invested in Chinese society.

Alongside the interest in immortals during the Tang was the parallel preoccupation with alchemical elixirs that had not diminished appreciably in spite of Highest Clarity's interiorization of thought about alchemy. During the Tang dynasty, imperial fascination with and patronage of elixir alchemy resulted in the deaths of at least two emperors by elixir poisoning: Wu Zong (r. 840–6 CE, birth name Li Yan) and Xuanzong (r. 846–59 CE, birth name Li Chen). It is possible that a third emperor, Xianzong (r. 805–20 CE, birth name Li Chun), also died in this manner. While imperial interest in elixir alchemy continued after the Tang dynasty, perhaps as a result of these deaths Daoist lineages that emphasized inner alchemy and medita-tion such as the Highest Clarity vine began to enjoy a measure of popularity. Nonetheless, external alchemy's influence in Daoism was significant and did not die out completely, as is indicated by the fact that there are over 100 external alchemy (*waidan*) works in the Ming dynasty Daoist canon.

Shifts in Attainment of the *Dao* in the Tang Dynasty

Perhaps the most significant shift in becoming one with *dao* during the Tang was the development of Interior Meditation (*neiguan*). Under the influence of Buddhism, a collection of Daoist texts appeared and provided a new way of thinking about immortality as a state of mind, a developed level of consciousness that represented oneness with *dao* and not physical longevity or never dying. The technique for achieving immortality under this new definition was a form of silent meditation without visualization, making it distinct from what at first glance seems to be quite similar within the Highest Clarity masters' arts. In this rejection of visualization we see some marks of Buddhist influence. However, although both the *Daodejing* and *Zhuangzi* taught simplicity of life and the erasure of desire because the follower of the *dao* should set aside the distinctions that humans make, nevertheless the Daoist kudzu, even with all of its diversity, had not previously seen the human problem in the way Buddhists under-stood it. Historically, Daoist lineage masters did not teach cessation of desire in order to gain release from suffering. However, the new vine of Interior Meditation began to connect Buddhism and Daoism by reunderstanding Daoist philosophical language. For example, 'libera-tion from the corpse' came to mean 'freeing the mind from desires and attachments' (Robinet 1997: 202).

At the heart of the Interior Mediation vine of the Daoist kudzu lay texts such as Sima Chengzhen's *Essay on Sitting and Forgetting*.[15] The title of this work is a reference to *Zhuangzi* (Ch. 6) in which Yan

Hui tells Confucius that he has become identical with the Great Dao by sitting down and forgetting (distinctions such as benevolence and righteousness) (6g, 90–1). In Sima's reading, 'sitting and forgetting (*zuowang*)' is synonymous with meditation. He also calls for renunciation of the world, which heretofore was not a part of any Daoist lineage vine emphasis. Moreover, he interprets the *Zhuangzi*'s teachings about accepting change and transformation (e.g., 6c, 84–5; 18b, 191–2) as calling for the sort of placid stillness of mind that is prominent in Buddhism, being unaffected by change, never experiencing any turbulence, no matter what life offers. The longest section of Sima's work is on 'concentration of the heart' (*shouxin*). Sima says this kind of concentration leads to emptiness, which is understood by him to mean making the mind a void (compare this with the discussion on pages 18–19 of 'Emptiness, Stillness, and Femininity' in the *DDJ*).

Daoism in Tang Dynasty Poetry: Meng Haoran (691–740 CE), Li Bai (701–62 CE), Du Fu (712–70 CE) and Bai Juyi (772–846 CE)

The stability and affluence of the Tang dynasty created an environment in which the literary and visual arts could flourish. Some of China's greatest poets wrote during the Tang dynasty and a few of them used poetry to express Daoist sentiments and life.

Meng Haoran (691–740 CE) was a famous poet who was known for writing about mountain landscapes and Daoist cosmic excursions. Here are two of his poems:

> 'Returning at Night to Lumen Mountain'
>> A bell in the mountain-temple sounds the coming of night.
>> I hear people at the fishing-town stumble aboard the ferry,
>> While others follow the sand-bank to their homes along the river.
>> I also take a boat and am bound for Lumen Mountain –
>> And soon the Lumen moonlight is piercing misty trees.
>> I have come, before I know it, upon an ancient hermitage,
>> The thatch door, the piney path, the solitude, the quiet,
>> Where a hermit [*daoshi*] comes and goes.

'At a Banquet in the House of *Daoshi* Mei'
In my bed among the woods, grieving that spring must
end,
I lifted up the curtain on a pathway of flowers,
And a flashing bluebird bade me come
To the home of the Red Pine Immortal
The cinnabar elixir stove beginning to burn
Immortal peaches just beginning to flower
The countenance of boyhood in his face,
How intoxicating was the flow of the red clouds!

This second poem by Meng Haoran is written in honor of Master Redpine, the great immortal first mentioned in Liu Xiang's *Biographies of the Immortals* and also a prominent influence on Ge Hong's ideas about morality and immortality.

When he was a child, the poet Li Bai (701–62 CE) moved to Jiangyou, near modern Chengdu in Sichuan province, an area known for its prominent role in the Celestial Masters lineage. He was deeply influenced by Daoism. Although he married the daughter of a Tang official and settled for a while in Anlu, Hubei province, he took up the life of a wandering master on the model of the *zhenren* of the *Zhuangzi*. In fact, his poems were often based on his travels and friendships. He enjoyed a life of freedom motivated by his belief in constant transformation as taught by Zhuangzi. Li Bai lived for a while at Zhongnan Mountain near the Tang capital in Chang'an (Xi'an). He boated down the Yellow River and resided with Daoist friends in Luoyang and even with Buddhist monks at Wutai Mountain (Wutaishan) near Taiyuan. His poetry was so highly regarded that He Zhizhang called him 'a spirit emanating from Heaven'. Because of his famous poetry, he received a place among scholars at the court of the Emperor Xuanzong (Li Longji) sometime around 742 CE, where tradition says he composed poems to celebrate the romance between Xuanzong and his beautiful concubine Yang Guifei. He left court a few years later and traveled throughout China, striking up a friendship with another famous Tang poet, Du Fu. It seems that Li Bai committed suicide probably in 762 CE. The earliest introduction of his poems to Western readers was in Ezra Pound's *Cathay*, and in 1997 Simon Elegant novelized Li Bai's life in his work *A Floating Life*. Here are a few of Li Bai's works that have very direct connections to Daoism:

'Visiting the *Daoshi* [i.e., Daoist ritual master] Tianshan But
  Not Finding Him'
    A dog's bark amid the water's sound,
    Peach blossom that's made thicker by the rain.
    Deep in the trees, I sometimes see a deer,
    And at the stream, I hear no noonday bell.
    Wild bamboo divides the green mist,
    A flying spring hangs from the jasper peak.
    No-one knows the place to which he's gone,
    Sadly, I lean on two or three pines.

In this poem, Li Bai records a pilgrimage into the mountains to find
the Daoist master Tianshan. Its images give us a feeling for the life
of the master who lives in the mountains. Some of the things Li Bai
notices are more significant than others. For example, the peach blos-
som and the pines are both symbols of immortality, and we may take
it that Tianshan was likely thought to be an immortal.

'Staying the Night at a Mountain Temple'
    The high tower is a hundred feet tall,
    From here one's hand could pluck the stars.
    I do not dare to speak in a loud voice,
    I fear to disturb the people in Heaven.

As we know, Daoist masters performing rituals often 'Pace the Dipper'
and look to the numinal beings in the stars for power and guidance.[16]
Li Bai is well aware of this tradition, and even of the fact that Daoist
sacred sites on mountains were often observatories. We have already
seen that this is probably the origin of Louguan Tai. In the place
memorialized in this poem, Li Bai feels transparent and numinal. His
voice and vision can carry into the world of the *shen*.

Li Bai also wrote a poem of interest in the study of Daoism
addressed in honor of Meng Haoran:

'Meng Haoran' – Li Bai
    True-Daoist, good friend Meng,
    Your madness known to one and all,
    Young you laughed at rank and power.
    Now you sleep in pine-tree clouds.
    On moonlit nights floored by the Dragon.
    In magic blossom deaf to the World.

You rise above – a hill so high.
I drink the fragrance from afar.

The great Tang poet Du Fu was born near Luoyang in Henan province in 712 CE. He was the son of a minor Confucian scholar-
official, and he took the Civil Service Exam during the reign of
Xuanzong in 735 CE, although he failed it. After meeting Li Bai,
he wrote several poems in Li's honor. In the 750s, he married and
took a minor civil post until the An Lushan rebellion against the
Tang erupted in 755 CE. After the rebellion, he was able to attach
himself to the Tang imperial house, and when Chang'an (Xi'an)
was regained he was given a bureaucratic appointment, although the
work was boring and he soon left it behind. He settled in Chengdu
and lived there with his family in near poverty, following the way of
Zhuangzi by wearing coarse cloth with patches and shoes of hemp.
But, as Zhuangzi, Du Fu also thought of himself as poor 'but not in
distress!' because he possessed the *dao* (see *Zhuangzi* 20g, 216). His
home life in Chengdu is the setting for the poem 'I Know Well My
Thatched Hut':

> I know well that my thatched hut is very low and small,
> Because of that, the swallows on the river often come.
> The bits of mud they bring in their mouths get into my zither
> and books,
> And while they are catching flying insects, they often bump
> into me.

In the middle 760s, Du Fu and his family journeyed down the *Chang
Jiang (Yangzi)* river, but his poor health required them to settle near
the Three Gorges area in Kuizhou (modern Baidi) for almost two
years. These years were his most prolific as a writer. He wrote over
400 poems from 765 to 766 CE. In time, he formed the intention
to return to his home in Luoyang, but died in Tanzhou (modern
Changsha) in Henan province before he could reach home.

The poet Bai Juyi was educated near Chang'an (Xi'an), and he
passed the distinguished level of the Civil Service Exam, being named
a 'Presented Scholar' (*jinshi*). Unlike Li Bai, who became a member
of the elite Hanlin Academy (Hanlin Yuan) on the basis of his writings and service to the imperial court, Bai Juyi was given member-
ship because of his performance on the examinations. Bai later served

as the Prefect of Hangzhou and then of Suzhou. During his career he wrote almost 3,000 poems. His two most famous works are the long narrative poems *Song of Eternal Sorrow*, which tells the story of Yang Guifei, and *Song of the Pipa Player*. Some of his poems have Daoist themes and interests. We can look at this example:

'Reading Laozi'
   Those who speak do not know, those who know are silent,
   I heard this saying from the old gentleman.
   If the old gentleman was one who knew the way,
   Why did he feel able to write five thousand words?

In this poem, Bai Juyi is alluding to the beginning of the *Daodejing* and the 'old gentleman' is, of course, Laozi. The poem expresses an often heard objection to Daoism. If those who experience the *dao* cannot put their awareness into words, then why do they write and teach? As we have seen, Zhuangzi also talks about the 'wordless teaching' (14c, 156–8). There is more than the knowledge that can be expressed in words gained in an experience with *dao*. There is encounter and relationship with an unformed presence that we are unable to perceive as we go our way in the restricted limits of our pitiful senses.[17]

The Twilight of the Tang

In the twilight years of the Tang dynasty, the imperial Commissioner of Daoist Ritual was Du Guangting (850–933 CE), who was born near Chang'an (Xi'an) and lived on Tiantai Mountain (Tiantaishan). Du wrote a great number of works during the turbulent period of the collapsing Tang dynasty. For example, seeing the troubles of the Tang and their efforts to restore the greatness of their empire, he wrote *Reverence for the Dao over Successive Generations* in 885 CE. This work provides a history of Daoist miracles and signs in Chinese history meant to legitimate the attempted Tang restoration under Emperor Xizong (r. 862–88 CE, birth name Li Xuan). In 901 CE he gathered about 200 additional miracle stories into a *Record of Daoist Miracles*. In the following year (902 CE), Du recorded a set of tales about common people who met immortals, entitled *Accounts of Encounters with Spirit Immortals*. Many later tropes of this 'encountering immortals' genre deriving from Du's text are found in Chinese novels, plays, short stories and even modern film.

Women and Daoism in the Tang

The third-century Daoist master Lady Wei Huacun, who was honored as the founder of the Highest Clarity lineage, was not the only famous woman associated with Daoism. Although Tang dynasty Empress Dowager Wu Zetian (625–705 CE) removed the edict of Daoist precedence in 674 CE and lessened the support of Daoism for political reasons, she became more open to Daoism after she believed she witnessed an appearance of Lord Lao surrounded by immortals, riding in a cloudy chariot at the Dragon Terrace Guan (Longtai Guan) in Haozhou. Her attention may have turned sometimes to Daoism for two other reasons as well: (1) she became the trusted guardian of relics from the tomb of Lady Wei at Linchuan (Jiangxi Province) after receiving them as a gift from Huang Lingwei (see page 121); (2) she seems to have turned toward Daoism as a way of handling her guilty conscience.

> Empress Dowager (*Huang Taihou*) was the position of power imperial women achieved when their sons ascended to the throne under-age or were unable to rule because of physical or mental disability. Indeed, many have called this position the pinnacle of power available to a woman in imperial China. Confucian advisors almost always objected to women taking on such power and even referred to it as a 'female disaster' (*nuhuo*) (Thompson 2001).

Wu Zetian had a well-deserved reputation for obsessively desiring power. Apparently, while a low-level concubine to Emperor Taizong, she also had an affair with his son, Gaozong. At Taizong's death, she may have been forced briefly to leave the palace for a Buddhist monastery since this was common practice for concubines whose emperor had died. But she returned to court in the early 650s CE and became one of Gaozong's most favored concubines. To secure her power, she had two other rival concubines executed in a cruel manner and may have even killed her own infant daughter. When Gaozong became ill and started to have debilitating seizures, Wu Zetian ruled the country as Empress Dowager. She formed a group of loyal supporters to control opposition and arranged for the crown prince to be humiliated and forced to commit suicide.

While Empress Wu often favored Buddhism, these past deeds may have begun to weigh upon her. The most famous incident in her spiritual life centers around Daoism, its holy mountain Songshan in

Henan Province and its great temple Zhongyue Miao. In the year 700 CE, perhaps overwhelmed with her Machiavellian abuses of power and disregard of morality, she commissioned a golden talisman to be taken to the temple. Wu Zetian wrote the talisman herself:

> I, the empress of the great Zhou country, Wu Zhao am speaking in humility. I am fond of the genuine dao (*zhen dao*), and immortal divine gods of immortality, therefore I come to the gate of Zhongyue Songshan to present (by throwing) a gold talisman to plead with all the Three Officials (*san guan*) to eradicate my immoral deeds.[18]

There were other famous female Daoist masters during the Tang dynasty as well. The story of Master Geng is one of the 25 given in Wu Shu's *Records about Extraordinary Persons in the Area along the Rivers Jiang and Huai*. Although the text was written in c. 975 CE, the story of Master Geng is set in the reign of Xuanzong (Li Chen):

> Master Geng was the daughter of Geng Qian. When she was young she was intelligent and beautiful and liked reading books. Fond of writing, she sometimes composed praiseworthy poetry, but she was also acquainted with Daoist techniques, and could control the spirits. She mastered the 'art of the yellow and the white' (i.e., alchemy), with many other strange transformations, mysterious and incomprehensible. No one knew how she acquired all this knowledge.

As the hagiography of Master Geng's life continues, we are told that all her divination predictions came true, and she knew how to turn mercury into silver. A famous painting done during the Ming dynasty, called 'The Alchemy of Master Geng', commemorates such powers and it can be seen in the National Palace Museum, Taipei (Little 2000: 284).

Chapter X

Scrambling and Overlapping Vines and Stems of Daoism in the Song and Yuan

Daoism in the Five Dynasties

While under the Tang rulers China had greatly increased in size; with the fall of the Tang the country was divided into a number of different kingdoms, known simply as the Five Dynasties Period (907–60 CE). This period was a very important one for the Daoism. Lineages became increasingly focused around their power centers: Dragon-Tiger Mountain (Celestial Masters), Maoshan (Shangqing) and Gezaoshan (Lingbao). However, across China, and at the local level, new Daoist stems emerged. Many of these absorbed local

Guanyin

Guanyin originated in India as Avalokiteśvara and in a male form. He was a 'Bodhisattva', a being who works for the enlightenment of all. Commonly known in China as the Goddess of Mercy, Avalokiteśvara became known as Guanyin, was reconceived as female, and offered help and mercy to anyone. The center figure above is an example of her depiction with a 'thousand arms', each hand holding an object symbolic of her ability to help in any situation. She is also revered by Daoists as an immortal numinal being portrayed on the right.

heroes and *shen* into their practices and beliefs. Included among these was Guangong, the figure who embodied martial virtue; Guanyin, the Buddhist *bodhisattva*, who became the Daoist goddess of mercy; Mazu, the fisherman's daughter in Fujian province, who became the protector of seafarers; and Xu Jingyang, who was associated with the power to heal diseases, stave off plagues and guard the successful harvest for villagers and farmers in the Nanchang region.

Official lineages tried to prune away stems that they considered deviations. But at the same time, the lineage stems absorbed, transformed, suppressed and redirected popular cults and movements. Some local and regional mediums, such as Chen Shouyuan, became Daoist masters (Skar 2004: 418).

One example of the process of absorption of local spirits and heroes is the legendary Xu Xun. According to the local tradition, Xu lived in the late 200s CE and was renowned for having cleansed the region of an evil dragon and for demonstrating exemplary filial piety. He was venerated at Jade Prosperity Palace (Yulong Guan), a temple located on Western Mountain (*Xishan*) in Jiangxi Province. This temple and its masters were patronized by Song dynasty Emperor Huizong (see pages 145ff.). Because of Xu's popularity, great processions of pilgrims made an annual journey to Western Mountain in the mid-autumn. *Daoshi* soon began to administrate this temple, and they associated the pilgrimage with the anniversary of the transformation of Xu into a numinal being. They taught that he not only was a filial son but also a loyal and respectful subject of the ruler. In this manner, the *daoshi* brought in a new *shen* spirit venerated by the local population and aligned themselves with practices that supported the social order of the Song rulers (Robinet 1997: 215; see also Hymes 2002).

Early Song emperors looked to Daoist masters for the legitimization and protection of their rule in ways not unlike those of the Tang emperors (Cahill 1980; Davis 1985 and 2001: 30–50). One of the most important of these protecting *shen* was the Dark Warrior, Xuanwu. In the 200s BCE, Xuanwu was associated with the symbol of a tortoise entwined by a snake, indicating his role in healing and exorcism of baneful *shen*. Song emperor Zhenzong built a temple to Xuanwu in the Song capital of Bianliang (current Kaifeng, Henan province), and in 1018 CE he gave Xuanwu the title 'Perfected Warrior' (Zhenwu) and charged him with using his powers over the spirits to protect the Song state. Zhenwu was primarily associated with his place of manifestation in the Wudang mountain range of Hubei province, a site listed in Du Guangting's 'Seventy-two Blessed Plots' (*Qishier fudi*) (Lagerwey 1992: 293–5).

Song Huizong and the Kaifeng Assembly

The influence of Daoism in the early twelfth century is well represented in the reign of Emperor Huizong (r. 1101–25 CE, born Zhao Ji). In 1106, Huizong began a decade-long search for leading Daoist masters, including the town and regional *daoshi* called High Masters (*gaoshi*), Masters of Techniques (*fangshi*) and Solitary Masters (*yinshi*). He issued a call in 1114 CE that every administrative circuit should send ten masters of great powers to assemble at court in the capital of Kaifeng. The group included the 25th Shangqing Patriarch, Liu Hunkang (1035–108 CE) and the 30th Celestial Master, Zhang Jixian (1092–1126 CE). One of their assignments was to assess, arrange and organize the massive diversity of rituals, teachings, beliefs in *shen*, lineage hierarchies and texts into an authoritative canon that was completed in 1119 CE. This Kaifeng assembly was more dramatic in its scope and influence than either the Jixia Academy or the Huainan Academy. Its magnificence is immortalized in a Yuan dynasty wall painting in plaster (dated 1358) on the west wall of the Hall of Purified Yang in the Eternal Joy Temple (*Yongle Gong*), Shanxi province. The painting depicts palaces in the clouds where officials mix with *daoshi* (Ebrey 2000: 95).

Huizong's promotion of Daoism is legendary. He wanted to make the Song capital of Kaifeng into a Daoist community. He created immense gardens in the city, modeled after his vision of the paradise of Daoist immortals on Kunlun (e.g., the Genyue imperial garden). He also built in the city the great Daoist Temple of the Five Peaks (*Wuyue Guan*). According to the chronicler Cai Tao, Huizong's support of Daoism was rooted in a dream in which Laozi told him that it was his destiny to promote Daoism (Ebrey 2000: 102). However, Huizong was not satisfied to be only a patron of Daoism. He also became a practitioner and had a number of significant personal experiences himself. For example, the Zhengyi *daoshi* Wang Laozhi was very close to Huizong, and when the emperor's favorite consort died Wang served as a medium to carry messages between Huizong and Consort Liu. In his correspondence with Shangqing Patriarch, Liu

Hunkang, Huizong asked for instructions about using talismans and sought guidance about rituals he could perform to bring good fortune to his people and heal diseases.

When the *daoshi* Lin Lingsu came to court, Huizong believed him to be the most powerful of all the Daoist masters he had ever known. Lin had a revelation in 1116 CE that Huizong was the incarnation of the elder son of the Jade Emperor. Huizong was so pleased to learn this that he not only had a great temple built in the city but also ordered temples to himself and the Jade Emperor to be built throughout the land. Existing Daoist temples were required to be remodeled on that order; if there was no Daoist temple in the town, the Buddhist temple was to be converted to this style.

Huizong's practice of Daoism was expressed through his talents and abilities. He was a famous painter of Daoist subjects, especially auspicious events that the *dao* wrought. Many of Huizong's own paintings with Daoist subjects are quite famous. Two examples are the handscroll 'Auspicious Dragon Rock', now in the Palace Museum, Beijing, and the 'Cranes of Good Omen' in the Lioning Provincial Museum, Shenyang. Huizong even painted the appearance of numinal beings, at least according to a story in the hagiography of Lin Lingsu. In that account, Huizong asked Lin to summon Zhenwu, the Perfected Warrior. After prayer and fasting, and at the hour of noon, the sun was obscured and Zhenwu appeared to Huizong accompanied by thunder and lightning. The emperor sketched the *shen's* likeness, but when he called for the court painter to help him finish the work Zhenwu disappeared.

Huizong created a network of state-sponsored temples called Temples of the Eastern Peak (Dongyue Miao). These were temples dedicated to the numinal *shen* of Taishan Mountain, the Eastern Peak of Daoism's five sacred mountains. The *shen* of this mountain, as we have noted before, controlled all the bureaucracy of numinal beings who administered death and the earth prisons and who judged each individual's moral life. While subordinate to the Dongyue Miao *shen*, Song emperors later established a set of City God temples (Chenghuang Miao) in each township to recognize the local spirits of each village and city. The Daoist *shen* of the Eastern Peak (Taishan) represented the emperor, the City God acted as his high official, and the small shrine to the Earth God in every town and village represented the wealthy peasants. Daoism had grafted itself into Chinese culture in a way that made the two virtually inseparable. Daoist themes, numinal beings and practices were wound into the calendar, cultural festivals, theater, literature and the management of birth and death.

Neither the administration of Daoism through the Temple of the Eastern Peak network nor the officials at the great lineage centers at Dragon–Tiger Mountain, Maoshan or Gezaoshan could stop the proliferation of localized vines and stems of Daoist teaching during the Song. These sprung up, each with its own techniques and emphases. The stems scrambled and overlapped, and Daoism wound itself around and together with Confucianism and Buddhism in many new ways to create what came to be called 'The Three Teachings' (*sanjiao*). All of this intertwining of practices and beliefs was even strengthened when, on January 9, 1127, Jurchen Jin forces from the region of Manchuria ransacked Kaifeng, capital of the Song Dynasty, capturing both Emperor Qinzong and his father, Emperor Huizong. The Song capital shifted to Hangzhou in the south, and a new energy was transmitted into Southern China.

Power of the Lord of the Eastern Peak

(Taishan)

An example of the power of the *shen* of the Eastern Peak is the story of Rao Dongtian (c. 994 CE) told by his disciple, Deng Yougong (1110–50 CE). Deng says that Rao discovered a secret writing on Huagai Mountain that gave him the powers to call upon the *shen* under the Lord of the Eastern Peak. The records of Rao's powers are in *Ghost Code of the Numinous Writ of Bone Marrow in the Supreme Purity Tradition*.

Morality Books and Ledgers

The morality books (*shanshu*) and ledgers of merit (*gongguo ge*) made their impact felt among the common people in Southern and Central China from the Song to the Ming (1368–1644 CE) (Sakai 1970: 341). These books provided moral instruction by use of a skillful syncreticism of teachings, precepts and folk stories. Early on, many of the morality books had appended to them ledgers of merit and demerit. The ledgers did more than list good and evil deeds, they prioritized them with a ranking system. For example, one ledger allots 100 merit points to a man who saves the life of another, but deducts 100 from the account of a man who hoards rice rather than distributing it to the needy in times of famine. Such quantifications were of ultimate importance because the duration of a person's life, together with his fortunes in this world and hereafter, depended on them.

We have seen that writers in the Han work *Huainanzi* used the term *ganying* for the 'action and response' dynamic of how one's deeds produced a result (see page 72). Likewise, in Ge Hong's writings during the fourth century CE, we noticed evidence of a numerical method of merit accumulation tied to good and evil deeds in his *Master Who Embraces Simplicity Inner Chapters*. By the time of the Tang dynasty, the major streams of Chinese moral culture – Daoism, Buddhism and Confucianism all shared, whatever their other philosophical and ethical differences, a basic belief in some form of cosmic retribution and reward tied to a defined set of good and evil deeds that should be taught to the ordinary person.

By the twelfth century, two landmark texts were in use and they may serve as examples of this way of thinking about the moral life in Chinese culture. The first of these is the *Tract of the Most Exalted on Action and Response*, a book of precepts on piety and ethics that carefully integrated the three teachings of Confucianism, Daoism and Buddhism. A second example of the morality book genre is *The Ledger of Merit and Demerit of the Taiwei Immortal*, which appeared after the *Tract* had been in use for some time. It offered precise guidelines for the practice of merit calculation, providing a means whereby users could keep their own moral accounts. Taken together, these two works formed the heart of the merit–demerit system in the late Song and early Yuan dynasties. They were even included in the Imperial-sponsored village lecture system designed to educate the population generally, and they were often paired with dramatic performances designed to transmit their moral teachings (Brokaw 1991: 222–3; Handlin 1987).

Tract of the Most Exalted on Action and Response
This work consists of only 1,277 characters, and it has appeared in numerous editions and formats down to the present day. It is written in an uncomplicated form of classical Chinese and perhaps by the late imperial period some commoners could read it. The 1794 version of this work contains a long commentary in which the author sought to prove the book was in agreement with the teaching of Confucius

(Eberhard 1967: 26). But the *Tract* itself claims support from Daoist and Buddhist sources as well (Carus and Suzuki 1973: 52–4).

The work attributes its own authorship to Taishang, which means 'The Most High', by which is meant Laozi. In the introductory remarks of the *Tract*, Taishang says that transgressions reduce a person's lifespan and poverty comes upon the immoral person; he meets with calamity and misery, and all men hate him. He tells of the numinal beings who are record keepers in charge of recording good and evil deeds, and says that moral offences may cause the loss of between 100 days and 12 years of life each. He says that those who wish to attain to celestial numinosity should perform 1,300 good deeds, and those who wish to attain an indefinite earthly life should perform 300.

The text next gives a description of the acts of the good person and the blessings that accompany them. In these precepts we can see a blend of the three teachings of Confucianism, Daoism and Buddhism. The moral acts that are good include the following: loyalty; filiality; friendliness; self-correction; compassion for orphans and widows; respecting authority, the elderly and one's ancestors; not injuring any life; grieving at the misfortunes of one's neighbors and rejoicing at their good luck; not calling attention to the faults of others; humility; renouncing desires; bearing no grudges; and generosity (Carus and Suzuki 1973: 52–4).

A much longer section on the misdeeds of the evil man and the punishments that result then follows (Carus and Suzuki 1973: 54–6). Some of the evil deeds noted are: being unfilial; treating one's ruler or parents with contempt; being disrespectful of one's elders and rebelling against those one should serve; being unkind and unfaithful to one's wife; lying; breaking promises; being cruel or inhumane; oppressing subordinates; bearing grudges and not forgiving; murdering; stealing; taking bribes and being unjust; not correcting mistakes; disrespect for the holy and the rituals; impropriety and disregard for the proper way to do things; not controlling desires; and not being content with one's status in life. Some evils are self-reflexive and internal: refusing to correct one's errors; wishing others to incur loss, cherishing thoughts of seduction; harboring greed; and covetousness.

The background of moral authority for the *Tract* may be found in many sources, including Ge Hong's merit system in *The Master Who Embraces Simplicity Inner Chapters*, used for distinguishing the types of immortals, and other Daoist moral codes we have noted before, including the *One Hundred and Eighty Rules of Lord Lao* and the *Essential Precepts of Master Redpine.*

Stories supplemented to the actual text of the *Tract* represent examples of those who follow the moral teachings in the book and those who do not. They are object lessons. 'Offence Against a *Shen*' is one story that illustrates how the 'action–response' system was believed to work.

Offence Against a *Shen*

The village of Qing Qi had a shrine dedicated to the Goddess of the Water Realm (a manifestation of the Queen Mother of the West) in which the statue of the goddess was so beautiful that she looked as if she were alive. The villagers made her the guardian of their district and paid her homage. In the second month of the year, a party of young students was passing by. One of them lifted the curtain hung in front of the image of the goddess and exclaimed: 'How beautiful she is! If she were alive I would make her my mistress!' His friends were shocked, but he laughed, saying; 'Gods and spirits are not real. People who believe in them are superstitious.' He then composed an offensive poem and wrote it on the wall. Later that year, they all went to take the civil service examinations. While staying at the dormitory named after Wenchang, Patron Spirit of the Arts and Literature, Wenchang himself appeared to them in his ethereal form in a dream. He took out a scroll, declaring: 'As you know, any student who is guilty of being disrespectful to women will be excluded from this list [of those who will pass the exam]. Even ordinary women should be respected, not to mention a goddess. It has come to my attention that one of you has insulted the Goddess of the Water Realm.' Naming the offender, he struck that student's name from the list. When the students awoke the next morning and discovered they had all had the same dream, the offender scoffed and said: 'What does Wenchang have to do with such trifles? What harm can a clay image do anyway?' He entered his examination room and wrote his essays with his usual brilliance, confident of his success. But that evening the Goddess appeared to him with her attendants. She rebuked him for his offence and ordered her maids to strike him until the student lost his mind and destroyed all of his writings. When he was carried out of the exam room in the morning, he was unconscious and died soon afterwards (see Wong 2003: 77–78; Carus and Suzuki 1973: 109–10).

The stories attached to the *Tract* invoke the threat of the Earth prisons of Fengdu, a series of ten judicial courts where persons are punished according to their immoral deeds and then released for an appropriate rebirth. While the idea of rebirth was Buddhist, it was easily accommodated into the Five Phase transformational cosmology of Daoism. There were many ancient Daoist traditions of people transformed into different phasal combinations so as to appear as animals, persons of other gender and spirits that were both independent of Buddhist influence and predated Buddhism's appearance in China (see page 106 on *shanxiao*, mountain spirits).

The Ledger of Merit and Demerit of the Taiwei Immortal
This work appeared very soon after the *Tract*. It offered precise guidelines for the practice of merit calculation, providing a means whereby men could keep their own moral accounts. The *Taiwei Immortal* represents not only a highly quantitative view of morality but also a more sophisticated calculation system than the one found in the *Tract*. Not all actions are equal in merit or demerit in this ledger, and the system for these fine discriminations is set out carefully. Here are some examples: failing to venerate one's elders, teachers or parents (30 demerits) and teaching others to be immodest, unfilial or uncompassionate (1 demerit each occasion). More positively, venerating an ancestor receives 10 merits per person venerated. Deeds that relieve the sufferings of people or show generosity are meritorious: paying for the burial of the dead, 50 merits per corpse; aiding widowers or widows, orphans or the poor, 1 merit per 100 cash; constructing ferries, repairing bridges and roads, 1 merit per 100 cash (Brokaw 1991: 48–9).

The ledgering system gives us an interesting look into the view the Chinese held on punishment and reward as moral controls. The 'action-response' system is a highly realistic one that recognizes that the evil we do in some very fundamental ways can never be erased. The removal of the impact of an evil deed depends not upon confession and gaining forgiveness from a *shen* or a neighbor, but from the restoration of balance done by the work of the ledger keeper himself. A person must make the ledger tally, and this means doing meritorious deeds that will counteract the evil ones. Evil deeds themselves are never removed, deleted, erased or absolved; they can only be overrun by meritorious ones. Indeed, an abacus was particularly common in the Dongyue Miao temple network first established by Emperor Huizong as a reminder that *shen* tally the deeds of the people.

When we look at the cases of those who believe they have been successful because they followed the ledger of merit's self-cultivation,

Abacus at Dongyue Miao, Beijing

we can only say there is nothing so surprising in it. By following the
way set out in the ledger, individuals became the sort of people who
could go on to be a success in their culture because others in the
community found them to be of worth and leadership quality.

The Complete Perfection Vine of Daoism

After the fall of the Song dynasty in the North (1126 CE) and the
transference of the court and capital to Hangzhou in the south, a
period of war and turmoil followed. In 1159 CE, Wang Chongyang
(1113–70 CE), a former military officer, left a marginal political
career behind and devoted himself to the practice of inner alchemy
(*neidan*). Wang was the son of a wealthy family in Xianyang, Shaanxi
province, and he became the founder of the lineage transmitting the
techniques called Complete Perfection (Quanzhen).

Wang was educated in the Confucian classics, as well as Buddhist
and Daoist texts. He went to live on Zhongnan Mountain in Shaanxi
province, where he made a dugout for himself for three years and
spent four more years in a mountain hut. One day, when he was 48
years old, he entered into an altered state of awareness. The immortals Zhongli Quan, Lu Dongbin and Liu Haichan appeared to him
and gave him a set of secret rituals and instructions.

After this, Wang considered that he had passed back and forth through the transformation called death and had returned to the living form that most people knew. To show he was a new person as a result of this encounter, he followed the Daoist custom of adopting a new name. He referred to his dugout as a grave and called it 'the Abode of the Living Dead'. In 1167 CE, he left Zhongnan Mountain and traveled to Shandong province in the east, where he accepted a number of adepts as students. They gathered around his modest hut, and he promised to instruct them in a method he called 'Complete Perfection'. Wang's hut was on the grounds of the estate of Ma Yu, one of his disciples. Wang established five communities (*hui*) in Shandong. Each community considered itself to be founded on a synthesis of the three teachings: Confucianism, Daoism and Buddhism. He was committed to the synergy of the three teachings in doctrine and practice, and he stands as one of the most important representatives of what is known in China as 'harmonizing the three teachings' (*sanjiao heyi*).

In his last years, Wang took his four favorite disciples, Ma Yu (Daoist name Danyang), Tan Chuduan, Liu Chuxuan and Qiu Chuji (Daoist name Changchun) back toward the site of his revelation on Zhongnan Mountain, but he died on the journey. These four disciples carried his remains onward to the Zhongnan mountains and buried them in Liujiang where he once lived. After the traditional three years of mourning for their master, the disciples departed to spread his teachings. Liujiang became the early center of the movement and Ma Yu its first Patriarch. The Complete Perfection technique became a lineage vine, and it grew largely because of the efforts of Wang's students, who are known simply as 'The Seven Perfected' (*Qizhen*). These individuals were Ma Yu, Sun Bu'er, Tan Chuduan, Liu Chuxuan, Qiu Chuji, Wang Chuyi and Hao Datong.

Ma Yu was with Wang Chongyang almost from the beginning of his work in Shandong province. Tan became a disciple after Wang cured his illness. Qiu is probably the best known of the seven because of his meeting with the Mongol ruler Chinggis (Genghis) Khan in Samarkland in 1222 CE. Two works in the Daoist canon provide descriptions of this meeting: *Record of the Perfected Changchun's Travel to the West* and *Record of the Celebrated Meetings on the Mysterious Winds*. Qiu impressed the Khan and obtained from him assurances that the Chinese people would be spared the slaughter typical of Mongol conquests. And indeed, when the Mongols entered China in the late 1220s and early 1230s CE, millions of lives were undoubtedly spared because of Qiu's visit. Each of the Seven Perfected disciples had a lineage of followers, but Qiu's became most famous and still has a following today. It is known as the Dragon Gate (Longmen) lineage because Qiu moved to the Longmen Mountains in 1180 CE and gathered his disciples there. Sun Bu'er is the only woman among Wang's Seven Perfected disciples. She was Ma Yu's wife. But her presence in the group of adepts demonstrates clearly that women were welcome and no distinction was made with regard to their worthiness or ability to gain the techniques of the *dao* (Yao 2004: 579).

Of the 30 anthologies of writings in the current Daoist canon, 23 of them are associated with Complete Perfection lineage teachings. This material is very different in form from the texts we associate with the Celestial Masters because it consists largely of refined poetry displaying the high education of Quanzhen masters. Wang Chongyang himself produced a massive body of poetry that was later collected and edited into a work of over 1,000 poems. In these poems, Wang often exhorts people to sever family ties and pursue the *dao*. In the collection of his poems entitled *Chongyang's Anthology of the Ten Transformations by Dividing Pears*, written for Ma Yu and Sun Bu'er, he tries to convince them to separate from their spousal bonds. According to the editor's 'Preface' to this work, Wang was living in his hut at Ma Yu's estate and every ten days he would divide a pear and offer the halves to Ma and Sun. The term *fenli* 分梨 ('to divide a pear') became his pun for the homophone, *fenli* 分離 ('to separate'). Showing his appreciation for Buddhism, he tells his readers that to obtain immortality a person must be rid of the four enemies: wine, sex, wealth and anger. Although Wang uses the term 'immortal' he explains it in terms similar to those used by Buddhism. Immortality means to escape the cycle of rebirth. Other works by Wang Chongyang in the Daoist canon include a handbook for followers on cultivating one's relationship with the *dao*, entitled *Oral Instructions on the Golden Passkey and Jade Lock by the Perfected Chongyang*.

Wang was a master of the inner alchemy method, and he taught that an immortal, 'a person of no death', was one who possessed a 'pure and tranquil' (*qingjing*) inner nature (see page 50 for 'inner

nature' in the *Zhuangzi*). The term *qingjing*, meaning 'pure and tranquil', is the most important single term in the Complete Perfection
technique. It describes a state of being in which the mind is calm and
not distracted by desires, questions and perplexities or machinations
to achieve ends. Complete Perfection methods required 'quiet sitting'
(*jingzuo*) and 'sitting in forgetfulness' (*zuowang*), both of which were
associated with inner alchemy.

While this practice of quiet sitting was compatible with Buddhist
meditation, we should not conclude that it was derived from Buddhism.
As far back as the *Neiye* and *Zhuangzi*, Daoist masters sat quietly
and in stillness for inner cultivation. The Zhuangzi speaks of 'sitting
and forgetting' (6g, 90–1). The Highest Clarity adepts had meditation chambers and their methods of 'Whirling Wind', 'Untying the
Embryonic Knots', 'Uniting in the Heavenly Palace' and 'Ingestion
of Cosmic Florescence' are forerunners of these Complete Perfection
practices (Robinet 1997: 222).

For Wang, the body counterparts to *qi* energy are in semen (*jing*)
and blood (*xue*). Male semen and female blood must be conserved
in order to nourish *qi* and achieve purity (*qing*). Some Complete
Perfection male adepts ceased ejaculation and female followers actually stopped their menstruation. Like Buddhists, Complete Perfection
devotees turned from sexual desire and practiced methods of intense
meditation and concentration. The idea is that if a person 'does not
leak' (i.e., semen or blood), then a wondrous inner elixir will form
internally in what Wang called the lower cinnabar field (*dantian*) of
the body. Actually, Wang used a Buddhist term to describe this new
reality. He called it a 'dharma body' (*fashen*), which is referred to in
other Daoist inner alchemy texts as the 'holy embryo' (*shengtai*) of
the new birth or new person. Complete Perfection masters, making
use of the inner alchemy methods of the Song period, conceive of
the body as the true laboratory, the crucible, the alchemical burner
itself. The elixir is no longer thought of as cinnabar, but it is *qi* energy
within the body. Meditation, breathing and rigid discipline of desires
are symbolically understood to represent the fiery burning process to
refine the inner elixir of *qi*. It is not surprising, then, that Complete
Perfection communities resembled Buddhist monasteries in requiring celibacy, practicing vegetarianism and having a daily calendar
of meditations. The guidebook for living in these communities is
entitled *Pure Rules of Complete Perfection*.

Ma Yu likewise composed a huge number of poems and over
1,300 have been collected into *An Anthology of the Gold and Jade on
Comprehending Mystery*. Most of these poems are focused on recom-
mendations for cultivating the Daoist life. The best known of his
teachings in these poems concerns how to control one's 'monkey
mind' (*xinyuan*) and 'horse will' (*yima*). As an example of how to discipline the monkey mind and the horse will, Ma taught that an adept
should not see his relatives because doing so would disquiet the mind.
In his *Recorded Sayings of the Perfected Danyang* (i.e., Ma Yu), Ma makes
it clear that an imbalance of physical being will make it impossible
for a person to do good deeds and act morally. In his *Straight Words
from the Perfected Danyang*, Ma Yu says that living morally would make
one healthy! Although this connection between physical health and
good deeds is an ancient one in Daoism, perhaps no lineage makes it
clearer than does Complete Perfection.

Complete Perfection was primarily a Daoist vine for the elite
and well-educated. It was patronized by the Yuan (Mongol) rulers.
However, this support did not long endure. Complete Perfection
teachings and practices were much criticized by the Buddhists, especially what the Buddhists felt to be speculations about the connections among *qi*, physicality and morality.

Conflicts with Buddhism in the Reign of Xianzong

In 1225 CE, the Buddhist monk Fuyu (1203–75 CE) appeared before
the Yuan dynasty Mongol court of Xianzong (r. 1251–59 CE, Khan
name: Monke Khan). He complained that the Complete Perfection
masters had seized Buddhist temples and were distributing a fraudu-
lent document entitled *Classic of Laozi's Conversion of the Barbarians*,
which taught that Laozi had converted the Buddha to Daoist teachings (Yao 2004: 572). As a result of these complaints, a series of
Buddhist–Daoist debates was ordered by the emperor and the outcome was a large number of restrictions on the practices and spread
of Complete Perfection Daoism. The *Classic of Laozi's Conversion
of the Barbarians* was ordered to be burned. And when the disputes
continued, an edict was issued in 1281 CE by Emperor Shizu (r.
1260–94 CE, Khan name: Khubilai Khan), ordering that all Daoist
books except the *Daodejing* should be collected and destroyed, and
that Daoist teachers and their disciples should follow Buddhist rules

for their communities. This was a great disaster – many Daoist texts were likely lost forever – and Complete Perfection centers came to resemble Buddhist monasteries.

Once it was clear that the Mongols would conquer not only northern China but also the south (which they did by 1275 CE), the Celestial Masters' Patriarch espoused the cause of accepting Mongol rule. In turn, this won his lineage the favor of the Yuan rulers. The Complete Perfection masters were replaced in the imperial favor by those of the Celestial Masters' Zhengyi lineage, based on Dragon-Tiger Mountain in the south. The representative of the Celestial Masters' Patriarch to Shizu (Khubilai Khan) was Zhang Liusun (1247–1322 CE). Zhang was an accomplished healer and made himself well liked in the Mongol court. Accordingly, he was provided with resources to found many new Zhengyi Daoist sites, including, in 1223 CE, the great Temple of the Eastern Peak (Dongyue Miao) in Beijing.

The Eight Immortals

We should not think that the Complete Perfection lineage's understanding of the quest of immortality displaced the belief among most Daoists in immortals with extraordinary powers, who could live a long time and phase in and out of our sensory awareness. From the Yuan dynasty onward, the 'Eight Immortals' (*Baxian*) have been the most famous group of Daoist adepts in Chinese history. This group is made up of six men, one woman and one person who appears to be a hermaphrodite. These immortals appear to have emerged as an identifiable group during the Jin dynasty, after the fall of Kaifeng, and the Song dynasty in the north, some time around 1115–34 CE. They are depicted in ceramic tomb sculptures decorating the Jin dynastic tombs near Pingyang, Shanxi province. During the Song dynasty, they showed up in theater performances. Three of the eight immortals figure in Wang Chongyang's spiritual story. They remain popular in Chinese literature and even today on contemporary postcards, in comic books and in movies.

The Eight Immortals

- Zhongli Quan is generally considered the leader of the Eight Immortals. He uses his fan to resurrect the dead and often shows his bare stomach. He is a master of elixir and was responsible for bringing Lu Dongbin to immorality.

- Lu Dongbin is the most well known of the Eight Immortals. He is always portrayed as a scholar with a fly-whisk and a demon-slaying sword. He is a specialist in inner alchemy, a calligrapher, poet, healer, exorcist and medium.

- Li Tieguai (Ironstaff Li) has a crippled leg, an iron crutch and carries a gourd (for his elixir and medicinals). He lives in the body of a beggar because his disciples mistakenly thought he was dead when his body was left behind on one of his spirit journeys. They burned it and when he returned, he had to acquire that of a beggar.

- Cao Guojiu is always dressed as an official and sometimes called 'Uncle Cao' because he was said to be the uncle of a Song emperor.

- He Xiangu is a young woman who carries a lotus flower or a ladle. A numinous being appeared to her and gave her medicine of immortality in order that she might become etherealized and immune from death. She swallowed it and also vowed to remain a virgin.

- Han Xiangzi carries a flute and is presented as the nephew of the Confucian scholar Han Yu, who was an important official in the Tang dynasty. Xiangzi gave up his life as a Confucian to follow the *dao*.

- Zhang Guolao is very old and rides a donkey, often facing backward. He is a shape changer and became an immortal because he ate the pill of immortality given to him by Li Tieguai.

- Lan Caihe, who is depicted as both a male and female, carries a basket of fruit or flowers and sometimes a flute (Penny 2004: 118).

Probably the best known story of the Eight Immortals is 'The Yellow-Millet Dream', which tells about the first meeting of the two best known immortals, Lu Dongbin and Zhongli Quan. The story was converted into a famous drama by the Yuan dynasty playwright Ma Zhiyuan (1260–1325 CE):

> Once he [Lu Dongbin] entered into a tavern in Chang'an (Xi'an) to see a *daoshi* dressed in a gray cap and white gown spirit write a poem on a wall … Impressed and attracted to the *daoshi*'s strange appearance and unusual old age, as well as to the grace and naturalness of his verse, Lu bowed to him and inquired his name.
>
> 'I am Master Cloudchamber (Zhongli Quan),' he answered. 'My home is the Crane Ridge on the Zhongnan Mountain. Would you like to join me in my wanderings?'
>
> Lu hesitated to agree to this proposal [because he had the ambition to be an official], so Master Cloudchamber took him to an inn. While

the *daoshi* attended to the preparation of a simple meal, Lu reclined on a pillow. Soon he became oblivious of his surroundings and fell asleep.

He dreamed that he went up to the capital as a candidate of the imperial examination and passed it at the top of the list. Starting his career as a junior secretary to one of the Boards, he rapidly rose in rank to positions at the Censorate and the Hanlin Academy.[19] Eventually he became a Privy Councillor after he had occupied, in the course of his unbroken success, all the most sought-after and important official posts.

In his dream, he was twice married and both wives belonged to families of wealth and position. Children were born to him. His sons soon took themselves wives, and his daughters left the paternal roof for their husbands' homes. All these events happened before he even reached the age of fifty.

Next he found himself Prime Minister for a period of ten years, wielding immense power. But this corrupted him. Then suddenly, without warning, he was accused of a grave crime. His home and all his possessions were confiscated; his wife and children were separated from him. He himself, a solitary outcast, was doomed to wander toward his place of banishment beyond the mountains. Suddenly, he found his horse brought to a standstill in a snowstorm and was no longer able to continue the journey.

At this juncture in his dream, Lu woke with a heavy sigh. Lo and behold! The meal was still being prepared. Laughing at his surprise, Master Cloudchamber intoned a verse:

'The yellow millet simmers yet uncooked,

A single dream and you have reached the world beyond!'

Lu Dongbin gaped in astonishment. 'Sir,' he stammered, 'how is it you know about my dream?'

'In the dream that just came to you,' Master Cloudchamber replied matter-of-factly, 'you not only scaled the dizziest height of splendor but also plumbed the uttermost depths of misery. Fifty years were past and gone in the twinkling of an eye. What you gained was not worth rejoicing over, what you lost was not worth grieving about. Only when people have a great awakening, do they know the world is but one big dream.'

Impressed by this incident, Lu received spiritual enlightenment. He fell to his knees before the master and entreated him for instruction in the arts of transcending the limitations of this world. (Kohn 1993: 126–9)

After the tremendous growth and assimilation of traditions of all sorts during the Song dynasty, Daoism faced new challenges when the Yuan rulers came to power. By adapting itself to the conquering Mongols, Daoism escaped destruction and was even able to exercise influence on the Yuan dynasty leaders.

Chapter XI

Daoism Overgrows Chinese Culture: The Ming and Qing Dynasties

Many scholars have interpreted the Ming dynasty as a period in which Daoism was in decline. However, such a characterization misses the mark. Actually, Daoist practices and beliefs continued to exert substantial influence both at elite levels in government and in the art and literature of the Ming (1368–1644 CE).

Daoism in the Ming Imperial Families

According to the *History of the Ming*, the first emperor of the Ming, Zhu Yuanzhang (r. 1368–99 CE, also known as Taizu), had a number of Daoist advisors and sought to use the great lineage masters for his political ends (DeBruyn 2004: 594). He appointed the 42nd Celestial Master Zhang Zhengchang (1335–77 CE) as administrator of all matters related to Daoism, giving clear precedence to the Zhengyi lineage of the Celestial Masters rather than the Complete Perfection lineage. Later, he created under the Board of Rites (*libu*) a ministry called the Bureau of Daoist Registration (*Daolu si*), charged with the responsibility of the independent management of all levels of Daoist activity in the empire. The masters who frequented his court were known for their healing and divination abilities, some also being skilled in calendrics and the alchemy of immortality.

The third Ming emperor, Zhu Di (r. 1403–25 CE), best known by his 'era name' as 'the Yongle Emperor', was the fourth son of Zhu Yuanzhang. Under his rule, Daoism grew significantly. He studied Daoist techniques, learning talisman-making from two *daoshi* masters, and also alchemical practices. Two of the Yongle emperor's connections with Daoism stand out above all the others.

1) He patronized the Dark Warrior (Xuanwu, who had been known as Zhenwu, the Perfected Warrior, since 1018 CE, see page 144), making the Ming dynasty the period of Zhenwu's greatest

popularity and influence. Upon Zhu Di's ascent to the throne, the great Daoist master Li Suxi (1329–1421 CE), respected for his reclusive lifestyle on Wudang, the holy mountain associated with Zhenwu, sent the emperor pieces of fruit from a sacred tree on Wudang that was supposedly created by the Zhenwu himself. So, Li's act of sending the fruit was seen as an auspicious sign for Zhu Di's upcoming reign and Zhenwu was promoted as the numinal protector of the empire.

The Yongle emperor required his sons to make offerings to Zhenwu at the northern gate of Nanjing whenever they visited the capital, and he believed the teachings of the *Revelation Record of the Emperor of Dark Heaven* that Zhenwu was actually the 82nd transformation of Laozi. The emperor built many temples to Zhenwu, and the complex built in 1412 and 1413 CE on Wudang Mountain was called 'The Purple Forbidden City' (*Zijincheng*). The *Illustrated Album on the Auspicious Miracles Performed by the Supreme Emperor of the Dark Heaven* reproduces the decrees ordering the rebuilding of sanctuaries on Wudang, and records a number of apparitions and manifestations of Zhenwu on the mountain between 1412 and 1413 CE.[20] Moreover, when the capital was moved from Nanjing to Beijing in 1421 and the Imperial Palace (The Purple Forbidden City) was rebuilt there, the hall to Zhenwu was prominently placed in the Northernmost place directly on the north–south axis of the footprint of the city.

The Dark Warrior: Xuanwu (aka, the Perfected Warrior: Zhenwu)

By the mid-1400s CE, Zhenwu was the most important numinal power in Daoism, and his veneration extended to all levels of Chinese society. A Ming dynasty ink rubbing (dated 1586) of the image of Zhenwu survives in The Nelson-Atkins Museum of Art in Kansas City and bears an inscription from one Zhong Yin of Qiantang (Hangzhou), telling that he saw the stele and that the pilgrims to that place had rubbed the image in veneration so frequently that it was smoothed out to ruin (Little 2000: 310). Having Zhenwu on one's Register ensured an unparalleled power (Little 2000: 306). The magnificent Qing dynasty hanging scroll of the Register of Zhenwu in the Art Institute of Chicago portrays him as having command over 72 talismans of power.

---

2) A second important connection of the Yongle emperor Zhu Di, to Daoism was his authorization of the formation of a new Daoist canon of writings. Since the Yuan dynasty ruler Shizu (Khubilai Khan) had ordered the burning of all Daoist books in 1281, there was no longer a comprehensive Daoist canon. The Yongle emperor gave

an order to have a new canon compiled, and it was printed in 1445 CE during the reign of Zhu Qizhen (r. 1435–49 CE, also known by his era rule name of Zhengtong).

Daoist Canon of the Zhengtong Era

(Zhengtong daozang)

The canon divides its materials into Three Caverns and Four Supplements. The texts largely represent the lineages of Highest Clarity (Shangqing), Numinous Treasure (Lingbao), Three Sovereigns and Orthodox Unity (Zhengyi). Within each of the groups, there are subdivisions according to 12 categories: Fundamental Texts, Divine Talismans, Secret Instructions, Numinous Charts, Genealogies and Registers, Precepts and Regulations, Rituals and Observances, Techniques and Methods, Various Arts, Records and Biographies, Eulogies and Encomia, and Lists and Memoranda (DeBruyn 2004: 604). In 1598, a *Supplement to the Daoist Canon* was added.

The Daoist lineage vine that was most influential in the Ming dynasty was that of Zhengyi, and many masters from Dragon-Tiger mountain (Longhushan) married women of the imperial family. Their influence may be seen in many ways. Zhu Gaozhi (r. 1425–26 CE, temple name Renzong), the Yongle emperor's eldest son, who was infamous for canceling the expeditions of the great Chinese maritime master, Zheng He, died after only one year of rule because he ingested a Daoist elixir of immortality. Zhu Jianshen (r. 1465–88, temple name Xianzong) was manipulated by *daoshi* claiming extraordinary powers, and so when his son Zhu Youtang (r. 1488–1506 CE) came to power, he tried to rid his court of all Daoist influences. And yet, Zhu Houcong (r. 1521–66 CE, temple name Shizong) was known as 'The Daoist Emperor'. Zhu Houcong was an adept of several Daoist masters during his reign. Even the Confucian officials who worked in various bureaucratic offices were required to study Daoist techniques and teachings in order to be promoted.

But after Zhu Houcong, the official status of Daoism was reduced in favor of a syncretism of the three teachings of Daoism, Confucianism and Buddhism. We have seen this emphasis emerge from the Complete Perfection lineage, but now it was expressed in Lin Zhao'en's (1517–98 CE) Three-in-One Teaching (*sanyi jiao*) centered in Putian in Fujian province.

Women and Daoism in the Ming

Empress Zhang (1470–1541 CE) was an important force in Ming political history because her influence at court extended for 50 years, over three emperors' reigns. She was the sole consort of the Hongzhi Emperor, Zhu Youtang (r. 1488–1505); mother of the Zhengde emperor, Zhu Houzhao (r. 1506–21); and 'Imperial Aunt' of the Jiajing emperor, Zhu Houcong (r. 1522–66). When Zhu Youtang died, she became Empress Dowager. Zhu Houcong was Empress Zhang's nephew, who had to be appointed because Zhu Houzhao died at the age of 29, without an heir. Although she wanted Zhu Houcong to continue to allow her the title of Empress Dowager, he turned instead to his own mother for that honor and called Empress Zhang 'Imperial Aunt', but she remained quite powerful.

Empress Zhang was associated specifically with 'Protecting the Ming Temple' (Baoming Si). Although originally a Buddhist site, it was the principal place of practice for a *daogu* (i.e., a female *daoshi*) named Yang. Yang was so close to Empress Zhang that at some point the Empress changed the nature of this Buddhist temple by bestowing on it the title 'Daoist premises'. Fearing the growing power of the *daogu* because of her association with Empress Zhang, Emperor Zhu Houcong tried to close the site, but was unsuccessful because of Empress Zhang's opposition. Empress Zhang believed, much to the chagrin of her nephew, that Yang had protected the Ming dynasty by means of her *daogu* powers (Thompson 2001).

Empress Zhang was an ordained *daogu* herself. Daoist ordination (*chuanshou* or *shoudu*) was the liturgical confirmation of the transmission of texts and the recognition of the Register and mastery of rituals and techniques of a Daoist master. The 85-foot hand scroll commemorating her ordination is dated 1493 CE and can now be seen in the San Diego Museum of Art in the USA (Thompson 2001; Little 2000: 208–13). Although no mention is made of her ordination in the official biography of the Empress, the hand scroll contains her ordination certificate and documents the rituals by which she was authorized to prepare ritual documents to be sent to numinal beings, providing them with an announcement of the ritual (*biao*); offering them an invitation to manifest themselves and/or inhabit ritual images and vessels (*tie*); giving them talismanic orders they must perform (*fuming*), and making petitions of them (*zhang*) (Little 2000: 213).

Daoism in Ming Dynasty Literature: The *Peony Pavilion* and *Journey to the West*

Daoism was expressed in the Ming in ways other than its influence at court. Literature was one of the most important of these. The theater grew in popular appeal from the Song, through the Yuan, and into the Ming. One of the most famous of Ming dynasty playwrights was Tang Xianzu (1550–1616 CE). He wrote four 'dream plays', each with a central Daoist character. A great deal of the action in these plays required for understanding quite a good background in the rituals and teachings of Daoism, showing that these details must have been very familiar to Ming dynasty audiences. One of the most interesting of these four plays is the *Peony Pavilion*.

The *Peony Pavilion* is called *Mudan Ting* in Chinese. It was first performed in 1598 as an opera within a year or two of William Shakespeare's *Romeo and Juliet*. The *Peony Pavilion* is written in a beautifully poetic style. It is the love story of Liu Mengmei, a young scholar, and Du Liniang, the daughter of a high official in Nan'an in Southern China. Liniang is a filial daughter who is trained in the Confucian classics and teachings for women. One day, while she is in the family garden, she falls asleep and is approached in a dream by Mengmei, with whom she then has a romantic affair in the Peony Pavilion. Awakening from her dream, she becomes lovesick (*xiangsi bing*) and inconsolable and eventually pines away and dies of a broken heart.

After her death, Mengmei comes into the foreground of the play. We see him on his way to the imperial examination in Hangzhou. But he falls ill at Nan'an and is given a resting-place in the Du family garden. Walking in the garden, he happens to discover Liniang's portrait and he spends many hours longingly and fondly gazing at her lovely form. He develops a deep feeling that he knows the woman in the portrait from a dream in his past. While his feelings for her are coming to the surface, the author shifts the scene to the Earth prisons of Daoist belief. In that dreadful place, Liniang appears before Judge Hu, master of the hells. Judge Hu checks to see if her death was at the correct time and in the proper manner and discovers that she has died before her time because of her lovesickness. He confirms that she was destined by Heaven to marry Mengmei. So, he sends her back to find her lover a full three years after her death. They meet and later marry.

One of the central figures in this extraordinary play is Shi Daogu (i.e., Shi the *daogu* master). The writer's portrayal of her work in the play tells us a great deal about Daoist practice during the Ming period and especially about the role of female Daoist practitioners. Shi Daogu is an earthy and somewhat bawdy woman, not some holy nun defined by living a pure celibate life.[21] When her marriage dissolved because of a physical deformity in her female organs making her very hard and impenetrable, she became a *daogu* and she became master at the Purple Light Temple (Ziyang gong) dedicated to the Daoist Three Pure Ones. She tells us that upon arriving at the temple, she hung up portraits of the guardian *shen* and started 'Pacing the Dipper' (Tang 2002: 79).

When Liniang becomes lovesick, her mother sends for Shi Daogu and asks her to invoke the power of the Dipper stars to restore her daughter's health. The household fears that Liniang is under the control of a ghost spirit and they want the *daogu* to bind the ghost. Shi Daogu uses a little talisman (*xiao fu er*), but it fails and Liniang dies. The author's literary point is that if her condition had been caused by a ghost spirit or if it could have been controlled by the powers of the Dipper gods, she would have been saved. But her illness is one of lovesickness and not curable by Daoist arts.

Scene 27 in the play is important. It is set three years after Liniang's death. In the play, Shi Daogu conducts a ritual to summon Liniang's spirit into the sacred space she has created near Liniang's burial place. Shi Daogu's task is to call Liniang's spirit and then to send it either on to Heaven or to release her back to Earth. In the sequence of time, this would be occurring at the same point Judge Hu sends Liniang back from the Earth prison hells. Shi Daogu says: 'This burial shrine of Bridal Du has been in my charge for over three years now. Today is an auspicious day, which I have selected for a ritual to secure her rebirth in the Realm of Jade' (Tang 2002: 148). Here we see that again Tang is true to what we know about the work of Daoist masters in what is called the soul-summoning ritual (*zhaohun*). We may also recall the famous Warring States' tale of a man named Dan who returned three years after his passing and took up an earthly life again (see page 57).

Tang tells us little about the actual ritual or about Shi Daogu's preparation of the ritual space, but he reveals a few details that probably were rather well known in the popular culture of the Ming dynasty.[22] Among the first of her acts, Shi Daogu sets up a summoning banner (*zhaofan*) to attract the attention of the departed spirit of Liniang and summon it to that place. She invokes the *shen* of the First Consort of the Southern Dipper, who is charged with mortal matters; and the Lady of the Eastern Peak, who is charged with reincarnations. Next, Shi Daogu makes obeisance before Liniang's wooden spirit tablet and provides a vase of flowering apricot.

The ritual progresses until it is time for the evening meal. Then the author tells us that when the celebrants go to eat, Liniang in an ethereal form (i.e., as a ghost spirit) enters the pavilion area of the ritual from the 'Home-gazing Terrace' in the tenth court of the Earth prison hells of the ghost world of Fengdu.[23] She is drawn back into this specific place by the sweet scent of the incense and the vase of apricot sprig blossoms. Just then a female disciple, present to help with the ritual and who has stayed behind to see whether Liniang will appear, calls for Shi Daogu to return in a hurry:

> Shi Daogu: What's all this fuss?
>
> Disciple: I was hiding in the lantern shadows to see who it was, when I saw this goddess or fairy maid. She shook her sleeve and the banner fluttered, and then she vanished! (Tang 2002: 154)

A little further questioning about the appearance of the apparition and Shi Daogu is convinced that the disciple has seen the *shen* form of Liniang. Shi Daogu wastes no time in having everyone repeat an incantation command designed to send Liniang on to Heaven, saying 'Speedily may you ascend to Heaven, ascend to Heaven: linger no longer where you have no home' (Tang 2002: 155). But Liniang instead seeks Liu Mengmei, who is staying in her family's home recuperating from his illness.

Scene 35 of the *Peony Pavilion* is the long-hoped-for return to life (*hui sheng*) of Liniang. Having been set free from the hells and allowed to return to Earth, and having been summoned back to the proper place by the ritual of Shi Daogu, Liniang visits Mengmei as a ghost spirit. He seeks out Shi Daogu to assist him in bringing Liniang back to life. Shi Daogu consents and identifies the auspicious day for opening the grave. She also procures the proper kinds of medicinal herbs and restoratives needed to nourish Liniang's revived body (Tang 2002: 199).

When the grave is opened, we see that Liniang's body was protected from corruption by a spiritually activated ball of mercury
Shi Daogu put into Liniang's mouth when she was buried. After
securing help to bring Liniang from the coffin, the *daogu* says to Liu
Mengmei:'Lay her in this peony pavilion while we administer drugs
to restore her.' And later, the revived Liniang says to Shi *daogu*: 'I lay
dead for three years, but love's devotion brought a secret pact to new
fulfillment. I owe my rescue to Master Liu [Mengmei] and yourself
for your faithfulness. Now you restore me hour by hour with wine
and health-giving tonics, and over these past days I have felt a gradual
revival of vigor' (Tang 2002: 205).

We have taken such a detailed look at a literary work in order to
stress that canonical philosophical texts and historical records are not
our only sources for an understanding of Daoist belief and practice.
We have many times through the course of telling Daoism's story
seen the value of material culture shown in art and archeology. But
now we see the way in which literature also may reveal what the people of the Ming dynasty thought to be in the range of *daoshi* powers
and what kinds of practices they could perform.

Other literary works from the Ming period also reveal a great deal
about how Daoism was understood. *Journey to the West* is one of 'the
four great classical novels' of Chinese literature.[24] It was published
anonymously in the 1590s, but has been generally accepted in its final
form to be the work of Wu Chengen. This novel is a 'journey narrative', retelling in a fictionalized form the actual historical travel of a
Buddhist monk associated with Chang'an (Xi'an) named Xuanzang
(602–64 CE) who returned to India for the purpose of retrieving
Buddhist sutras, some of which he later translated (Wiggins 2004).
It is filled with trials and tribulations, mingled with folk tales and
popular Daoist beliefs. It contains the sort of syncreticism of the three
teachings that formed the vernacular belief system of the people of
Ming China. There are Confucian values, Buddhist *bodhisattvas* and
monks, and Daoist immortals and *zhenren*.

The *Journey to the West* has 100 chapters, and arguably the best
translation into English of the entire work is that done by Anthony
Yu in four volumes (1977–83). The first seven chapters are regarded
as a preamble introducing the figure that in many ways is the
most memorable and popular character in the book: Sun Wukong,
also known as the Monkey King. It is likely that this material

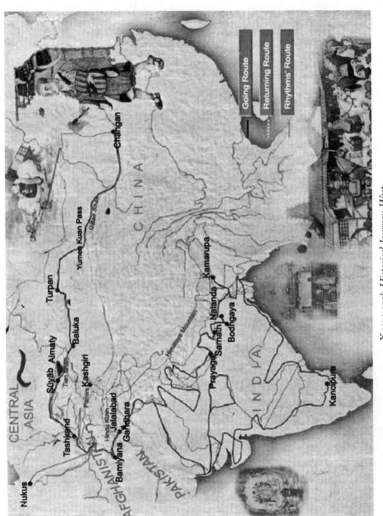

Xuanzang's Historical Journey West

circulated in an earlier fashion and was adapted and modified by Wu
Chengen. Then Chapters 8–12 introduce the reader to Xuanzang,
providing the background to his great journey West. Chapters 13–22
introduce Xuanzang's traveling companions. There is another intro
for Sun Wukong, followed by those of Zhu Bajie and Sha Wujing.

Taking the background material on Sun Wukong from Chapters
1–7 and 13, we can reconstruct his history in this way. He lived on
Monkey Island, where he was born from a stone by spinning out a
marvelous combination of the Five Phases. Sun Wukong's powers
in this fantasy are modeled on those of Daoist immortals we have
learned about from Liu Xiang's *Biographies of the Immortals* (*Liexian
zhuan*), Ge Hong's *Biographies of Shen Immortals* and the Tang dynasty
Biographies of the Immortals (*Xuxian zhuan*). He can travel vast distances
with ease, such as 108,000 li in one somersault. He has powers over
his Five Phases to express 72 transformation powers that allow him to
become various animals and objects. He can clone himself, as well as
weapons and other objects. He knows spells to command the wind,
bind ghosts and freeze humans. So, to be sure that Sun Wukong
would behave in his assigned task to aid Xuanzang, Guanyin fash-
ioned a numinal headband for him that Xuanzang could, by means
of a special chant, tighten it and cause Sun Wukong great pain if he
became unruly.

Xuanzang and His Companions

Zhu Bajie, whose name literally means 'Eight Rules Pig', is simply known as 'Pigsy'. According to the text, he was originally a
commander of celestial naval forces named Marshall Tian Peng, but
because he flirted with the Goddess of the Moon, Cheng'e, he was
sent back to the physical world through the wheel of reincarnation.

Although he was supposed to emerge as a human, his inability to control his appetites and passions made him come back as a half-pig and half-man. So, in his 'biography', we see the merger of traditions from Buddhism and Daoism, blended with Chinese folk tales about Cheng'e.

Sha Wujing, most often called 'Sandy', was also formerly a celestial being and general. Unfortunately, he shattered a goblet belonging to the Heavenly Queen Mother, and he was punished by the Jade Emperor by being reincarnated as a river *shen* doomed to live in the sands of the river and devour unsuspecting men. However, since the Buddha gave Guanyin the responsibility to oversee the protection of Xuanzang in his quest to return to India, she sought out Sandy as a powerful bodyguard for Xuanzang and converted him to Buddhism. He became a part of the entourage accompanying Xuanzang, wearing a monk's rope and being renamed Sha Wujing (i.e., 'the sandy one awakened to purity').

After introducing the journey companions, Chapters 23–86 of *Journey to the West* form the meat of the novel. There are 24 episodes of varying length, all of which pose challenges and threats to Xuanzang and that depend largely on Sun Wukong's great powers to ensure success. Chapters 87–99 concern adventures in India and culminate in Xuanzang's receiving the Buddhist texts from a living Buddha. Chapter 100 is the summary of the return journey to the Tang capital in Chang'an (Xi'an) and the rewards given to the participants. More reliable historical versions of Xuanzang's success during Emperor Taizong's reign attribute to him the building of what is the Big Wild Goose Pagoda (Dayan Ta) in Chang'an (Xi'an), for the storage of the texts and icons he brought back from India.

In both the *Peony Pavilion* and *Journey to the West*, we see the authors' skillful ability to intertwine Daoism, Confucianism and Buddhism with Chinese culture, imagination and folk belief. These two literary works provide us with a window into the ongoing beliefs of the Chinese about Daoist teachings and practices during the Ming period. They also are excellent further examples of the syncretic work that we see in Wang Chongyang's Southern Song Daoist vine of Complete Perfection, the morality book *Tract of the Most Exalted on Action and Response* and the Ming dynasty Daoist stem of the Three-in-One Teaching of Lin Zhao'en.

Pruning and Controlling Daoism in the Qing Dynasty

The rulers of the Qing dynasty sought to establish a rigid state control over all spiritual and religious organizations, and Daoism was included in their program. They limited the number of officially ordained *daoshi*, restricted the number of state-sanctioned Daoist study and ritual sites (*guan* and *miao*), and controlled the range of rituals that were approved as well as their scheduling (Smith 1990: 293). In the Qing bureaucracy, just as we have seen in the Ming, Daoism was governed by the Bureau of Daoist Registration. This agency certified and monitored all aspects of officially recognized Daoism all the way down to the prefectural and county levels. The Qing officials, as did those in the Ming before them, recognized only two approved schools of Daoism: Celestial Masters (*Zhengyi*) and Complete Perfection (*Quanzhen*). Complete Perfection had standardized its training in its Dragon Gate (Longmen) branch in Beijing at the White Cloud Temple (Baiyun Guan), and integrated so much of Zhengyi teaching and practice that it became difficult to tell the two great lineage vines apart. Since the Qing rulers gave all formal ritual and talismanic privileges to the Zhengyi lineages, and the followers of Complete Perfection lived in ascetic and well-regulated monasteries, the officials of both lineage vines were easily brought into conformity.

The Qing rulers officially followed Tibetan Buddhism and the Emperor Kangxi (r. 1654–1722 CE) openly ridiculed the quest for a medicine of immortality. During the era of the Qianlong emperor (r. 1735–96 CE), the Gelugpa school of Tibetan Buddhism became the state religion (Esposito 2004: 623). The educational doctrine under the Qianlong emperor was called Neo-Confucianism, and it was endorsed as the basis of the official exam system, much as the Tang emperors Gaozang and Xuanzong had done for Daoism. Daoist practitioners were increasingly marginalized and the number of *daoshi* declined. Their official involvement in Chinese political and elite society greatly diminished. *Daoshi* status was lowered, deterring many of the best and brightest from seeking out a *daoshi* master to follow and from whom to learn the arts of transformation. However, this decline in sanctioned *daoshi* paralleled an increase in the number of *daoshi* practitioners closer to the grass roots and ordinary life of the people. Although the Qing emperors did little to encourage Daoism, they did not try to destroy it. That effort came from a very different and unexpected direction, but it almost succeeded, especially in southern China.

An Attempt to Exterminate Daoism: The Great Taiping Rebellion of God's Chinese Son

Hong Xiuquan (1812–64 CE) was a Hakka Chinese Christian who led the Taiping Rebellion (1851–64 CE) and established the Heavenly Kingdom of Great Peace (Taiping) in Nanjing. The Taiping Rebellion during the Qing dynasty was one of the bloodiest conflicts in history. At least 20 million Chinese perished as a result of it. One of the best overviews of this turbulent period is Jonathan Spence's *God's Chinese Son* (1996).

Hong had dreams that convinced him he was the Son of God, the younger brother of Jesus, and that his mission on Earth was to rid China of evil influences, such as the Qing (Manchu) rulers, Daoists, Buddhists and Confucians. He taught his followers that the worship of the constellations (as in Daoism's idea of the Big Dipper) was superstitious and that veneration of the Daoist *shen* represented idolatry and emptiness. He was convinced that Buddhists prayed to a man long dead and Daoist masters practiced the sort of magic the Christian Bible's apostle Paul required Simon Magus to give up in order to be saved (*Acts of the Apostles* 8: 9–24).

In the late 1840s, Hong struck out at the 'idols' of the Buddhists, as well as the City God (Chenghuang) and Daoist temples. Hong began to write his own tracts in 1845 and to lay out moral commandments for the heavenly kingdom he felt called to usher in – never to lust, always to obey parents, never to kill people, not to steal, to stay away from witchcraft and magic, and not to gamble. As his influence grew, he garnered enough power to officially change the name of the Nine Immortals Temple (*Jiuxian Miao*) in Wuxuan District to Nine Demons Temple (*Jiuyao Miao*), and his forces destroyed hundreds of Buddhist and Daoist temples and forced many monks and *daoshi* out of their callings.

By December 1850, Hong had amassed such a large and formidable army that the Qing could not control Southern China. On March 19, 1853, the Taiping army breached the walls of Nanjing, and on March 29, 1853, Hong was named ruler of the Kingdom of

Great Peace. On January 26, 1862, the Taiping launched an ill-fated winter attack on Shanghai, asking foreigners to withdraw. But the snow began to fall and the resistance was heavy. The Qing forces were well prepared, but, more than that, the military commanders defending the city were taking orders from Charles Gordon of the British Royal Engineers. The entire area from Nanjing to Shanghai was in desolation; refugees were everywhere, seeking shelter wherever they could find it. The Taiping were defeated. By 1863, Qing forces were finally able to mount a siege of Nanjing. By the spring of 1864, starvation was rampant in Nanjing. And then, on June 1, 1864, Hong died of an unknown illness. Although his son took over the leadership, the Qing seized the city on July 19, 1864 and ended the Taiping rule. Nevertheless, the effects of the Taiping Rebellion on Daoism were dramatic and debilitating, reaching not only to the visible and official *daoshi* and their temples and teaching sites but also the common and ordinary practices of Daoism.

Making Daoism Ready for the West: Early Translations of Daoist Texts

While Hong sought to destroy Daoism in the name of Christianity, the Christian missionary James Legge (1815–97 CE) wanted to translate Daoist texts in order to make them available to the people of the West. Legge accepted an appointment by the London Missionary Society to work in the outpost at Malacca near Hong Kong, to assist in the Anglo-Chinese College there. Reflecting on this period in his life, Legge later wrote that his 'grand object' in preparation for his mission work was to speak and write as a Chinaman (Legge 1897: 102–3). His motivation for this endeavor was the feeling that the missionary should know his field of possible converts; this required a close examination of their history, philosophy, religion, poetry, customs and manners. In this, Legge was unique as a missionary because a prolonged linguistic and cultural translation of the literature and character of the so-called 'heathen' was not generally characteristic of missionaries at the time (Girardot 2002: 35).

Legge arrived in Malacca in 1824, but he did not produce his first translation of a Chinese work until 1843. Another 18 years passed before he would even begin to try to translate the Chinese classics. The first volume of the *Chinese Classics* published in 1861 included the Confucian texts of the *Analects, The Great Learning* and the *Doctrine of the Mean* (Legge 1861a). The initial volume was followed by a translation of *The Mencius* (1861b), reflecting Legge's belief that this structure comported well with the New Testament pattern of the Gospels and then the Pauline material. In the late 1860s, the magnitude of Legge's impact was already being felt. With the death of Stanislas Julien in 1873, Legge became 'the single most influential translator-interpreter of China for the Western world' (Girardot 2002: 67).

On June 4, 1873, when he was 58 years old, Legge left China never to return. From late 1873 to 1875, Legge lived a life of semi-retirement and completed his translations of the last of the Five Classics. The retirement was soon abandoned in favor of Legge's new collaboration with Max Muller, holder of the Chair of Comparative Philosophy at Oxford, in the project called the *Sacred Books of the East*. In 1875, Legge was appointed to the first Oxford professorship of Chinese Studies, and from 1879 to 1893 was prolific. In 1880, Legge published *The Religions of China: Confucianism and Taoism Described and Compared with Christianity* (Legge 1880). Then, in 1891, he published Volumes 39 and 40 in the *Sacred Books of the East* series entitled *The Texts of Taoism*, containing *The Book of the Way and Its Power (Daodejing)*, the *Zhuangzi* and *Tract of the Most Exalted on Action and Response*.

Legge's work on Daoist thought was more substantial and impor-tant in institutionalizing a discourse about Daoism than was his work on either Confucianism or Buddhism. Basically, his view was that there was an originally pure philosophical Daoism contained in the *Daodejing* and *Zhuangzi* and called *daojia*. However, this pure phil-osophical tradition declined into alchemical practices, idolatry and superstitious magic, expressed in what he called the 'repellent' exter-nal rituals of the second-century Daoist religion *daojiao* and its later sects (the Celestial Masters and others). Thus, Daoism was divided for the purposes of scholarly study by Legge into 'philosophical Daoism' and 'religious Daoism'. This division had a dramatic effect on schol-arship in the West. Translators and interpreters accepted it without question.

In *The Religions of China*, Legge takes up *daojiao* and its 'gross' religious forms, calling them 'repugnant superstitions'. Speaking of the leaders of Celestial Masters' Daoism, including Zhang Daoling, as 'popes', he likens their system of administration to that of the Catholic Church, with which he very much disagreed. He says that the emergence of Daoist religious practices represented a further corruption of a pre-Confucian primordial monotheism that was God's witness to the Chinese. He claims that Daoist religion grew because the people were 'debarred from communion' with God. He concludes that the beliefs in immortality and alchemy crept in along with the popes, priests, iconography, liturgy and scriptures of religious Daoism after the Han (Legge 1880: 160–202).

In contrast, Legge associates pure Daoism with the *Daodejing*. He says that its teachings encourage humility and loss of self in ways that made its readers better prepared to receive the message of the gospel than were the Confucian literati (Legge 1880: 275–6). Legge compares the text to the Sermon on the Mount because it seemed to him that the two works share a broad trajectory of moral vision (especially humility) and style (the parabolic or aphoristic form).

It was not until 1968 that Western scholars began to point out that an important dimension of the historical context of the *Daodejing* was being neglected because connections between the text and Warring States' religious beliefs and practices had been overlooked by Legge and those under his influence. Kristofer Schipper was the first to call scholars' attention to the problems in dividing Daoism into a pure philosophy and a degenerate religion. In his paper entitled 'Taoism: the Liturgical Tradition', delivered to the First International Conference on Taoism in 1968, Schipper argued that Legge's division of Daoism was an artificial construct and that there was never any form of purely philosophical Daoism existing apart from its religious context and expression.[25] Since then, scholars such as Livia Kohn, Harold Roth, James Miller, Terry Kleeman, Norman Girardot, Russell Kirkland, Michael LaFargue and others have recognized the fundamental flaws in Legge's narrative of Daoism's history.

Chapter XII
Spreading the Daoist Vine at Home and Abroad

Daoism's Survival of the Great Cultural Revolution

With the end of the Qing dynasty, the split between the bureaucracy of China and Daoism was greater than it had ever been. The Qing blamed Daoism for a great deal of the ruin of the nation that they inherited. They wanted to return to Confucian orthodoxy. Indeed, at the beginning of the twentieth century, the great Daoist canon made during the Ming survived in only one complete copy![26] The progressive disestablishment of official recognition and influence put a cap on the centuries-long bubbling up of Daoism from the popular and ordinary life of China into the elite intellectual and official structures of the culture. Many Daoist sanctuaries were destroyed in the Taiping Rebellion in the name of Christianity in order to combat 'superstition'. Hundreds of magnificent complexes were devastated, including the Dragon and Tiger mountain (Longhushan) structures. Kristofer Schipper has reminded us that these structures were as old as the gothic cathedrals of Europe (1994: 18).

After the collapse of the Qing dynasty, the Republican government of 1912 in China sought to confiscate Daoist temples and turn them into public buildings, schools, hospitals and senior citizen centers. The May Fourth Movement continued this program. In the 1920s, the New Life Movement encouraged students to destroy Daoist statues and icons throughout the country. During the Anti-Japanese War (i.e., World War II), many Daoist temples were requisitioned as army barracks either by Chinese forces or Japanese ones. By the time of the establishment of the New China in October of 1949, there were only about 300 Daoist temples in Beijing, where a century before there had been 1,000, and only around 50 in Shanghai, where before there were 200. Only the most prestigious Daoist temples were maintained at all and then only as historical monuments, not as places of spiritual practice.

Then came the Great Proletarian Cultural Revolution (1966–76). During this period *daoshi* throughout the country had a very hard time. The temples with which some of them were associated were closed, and they were officially required to cease practicing rituals. Many textual and ritual manuscripts in their possession were confiscated and destroyed. Some *daoshi* hid their lineage texts at great risk to themselves. Numerous *daoshi* were 'struggled against'. The more prominent a *daoshi* was, the less likely it was that he could escape notice. However, since Zhengyi Daoism was centered then as now on 'hearth-dwelling' *daoshi*, who worked out of their homes more than at temples, they were able to continue performing rituals and training acolytes, although these activities had to be done in secret. Deng Xiaoping is credited with restoring some religious tolerance beginning in 1982 and *daoshi* could slowly return to public work.

Leaders of the People's Republic of China have recognized Daoism as an important traditional religion of China and a potential focus for tourism, so many of the more scenic temples and monasteries have been repaired and reopened. Daoism is one of the five religions recognized by the People's Republic (Daoism, Buddhist, Islam, Catholicism and Protestantism). It is controlled through a state bureaucracy and the China Daoist Association, but, as we have seen, this is not something new or exclusively Communist. Imperial ministries were designed to control and administrate Daoism as long ago as the Tang dynasty. It is difficult to know how many Daoist masters there are in the People's Republic of China because quite a number of Zhengyi *daoshi* are unregistered and deliberately avoid the training and official certification procedures of the Chinese Daoist Association. Some estimates are that there are over 25,000 Daoist masters in China of both the Complete Perfection and Zhengyi lineages. There are somewhat more than 2,000 temples in mainland China that are specifically identified as Daoist, but many Zhengyi masters do their work through associations with sites such as City God (Chenghuang) temples and even through individual contact with Chinese citizens apart from any official institution. The Chinese Daoist Association, through its Daoist Research Office, has encouraged study of Daoist history and methods both generally and in many of the major universities in the People's Republic.

Contemporary Daoist Practice and Practitioners in China

Unknown to most outside observers of contemporary China who wrongly believe the current culture to be atheistic and materialistic, there has been occurring in China since 1979 a resurgence of traditional rituals, local Daoist practice and an appreciation for the role of *daoshi* Masters in the community, especially in some provinces, such as Fujian, where several recent scholars such as Kenneth Dean (1993), Erin Cline and the author of this text have all done field work with contemporary Daoist masters and their lineages.

The Daoist masters in the Putian area are generally part of hereditary family lineages of the Zhengyi vine, in which each *daoshi* is trained by his grandfather or sometimes his father. They work within a kin network. The *daoshi* are highly autonomous. Indeed, they resist instruction or interference from outside of their own lineage. Few are members of the Daoist Association of Fujian, which tends to be more closely associated with Complete Perfection Daoism and with the National Daoist Association of China.

At first sight, a visitor would notice nothing to distinguish a Zhengyi master from an ordinary person. He does not dress as a monk, as a Complete Perfection master might. He does not live a monastic life. Yet masters have investiture ceremonies after long years of apprenticeship. Today, hereditary *daoshi* in the tradition are always men, but this situation does not derive from Daoist principle. Quite to the contrary, the liturgical pattern of the early Celestial Masters, the group most often associated with the founding of Daoist religion, admitted both men and women to the role of a master without prejudice. Although the lineage is hereditary, ascendancy to the position of Master of High Merit definitely is not. As Daoists say, one must have 'the bones of an Immortal' to occupy such a role. The majority of descendants in a lineage are never ordained and perform only small rites and act as acolytes and minor officiants at major rituals. On the other hand, a Master of High Merit not only has exclusive right to perform certain rites but also is the keeper of the ritual and scriptural texts of the family lineage. He makes hand copies of these and transmits them to the next generation.

Currently, the people in the towns and villages can reach *daoshi* on their cellular phones. But the *daoshi* are not leaders of congregations, and in the place of the community roster we now have simply the free self-selection of the people. In this sense, one understanding of what it means to be a Daoist in contemporary China is that it means a person who makes use of a *daoshi*.

The people of contemporary China seek *daoshi* for a wide range of needs. They ask for protection from bad fortune or ill health. They seek assistance in acquiring justice when they have been wronged. They ask *daoshi* to perform rites for the dead. They also schedule individual, family and communal rituals. The common people who ask *daoshi* to lead rituals for them believe the master's actions will change their future in this life, help them obtain justice and protect their family both living and dead.

The selection of a Daoist ritual master to lead a ritual is a very important decision. People are well acquainted with the principal *daoshi* and they have watched the masters work at various rituals because they attend ceremonies in villages and cities other than their own. A master, by virtue of the powers at his disposal, has a certain realm of expertise and he may refer an inquiry to another *daoshi* if that person is better able to help with the request. A *daoshi* also has a general geographical area of practice, but the people need not observe any rigid boundaries in their search for a master.

While common people discuss the components and size of a ritual with the master, and even help prepare various elements to be used in it, they do not know what parts of the ritual actually correspond to the spiritual processes the *daoshi* explains to them. The people follow the instructions given to them by the *daoshi* during the actual per-formance of the ritual. They would not know what to do otherwise. They do not understand the words the *daoshi* sings or the texts and talismans he reads, or even the formulas he says. The people simply trust the *daoshi* to know what to do. Indeed, such confidence is evi-dent not only with regard to the performance of the ritual itself but also with respect to the trust they invest in the *daoshi* to summon and control the spiritual forces. It is their role as ritual masters and not because they have knowledge of Daoist doctrines that is important to the *daoshi*'s authority.

In addition to these field-work findings, there are other fascinat-ing entries into contemporary Daoist practice in China. One such source is the striking and overwhelming work about Daoists in China by Bill Porter, entitled *The Road to Heaven: Encounters with Chinese*

Hermits (1991). This work is based on Porter's visits with Daoist mountain recluses, mostly in Western China. Anyone interested in the current training, belief and practice of a Daoist master may profit from reading the authorized biography of Wang Liping (1949–), an 18th Generation Complete Perfection Master in the Dragon Gate (Longmen) branch of Daoism, as told to his students Chen Kaiguo and Zheng Shunchao. Translated under the title *Opening the Dragon Gate: The Making of a Taoist Wizard*, this work tells the 15-year story of Wang's training, which began in 1962. The work anchors Wang Liping to his three teachers and gives us an inside look at the development of a Daoist master, revealing that much remains unchanged since the time of Zhuangzi.

Can Daoism Be for the World?

It is fair to ask whether a tradition so rooted in China, as is Daoism ,can ever find the right kind of soil to grow in other cultures and parts of the world. At first glance, it may seem impossible. However. perhaps the spread of Daoism to other global communities is not as unthinkable as it might first appear. After all, Anglo-Europe and even the Americas became fertile soil for beliefs and practices attached to a Jewish prophet from Nazareth and an Arab seer from Mecca.

Daoism has spread to other East Asian countries at several points in its history, and yet it did not do so because of its evangelistic fervor. Most often the Daoist vine grew because it was so intertwined with the transmission of other parts of Chinese culture. During the Tang dynasty, an initial extension of Daoism into Korea and Japan occurred because these cultures were interested in all things Chinese (Kohn 2001: 205). In both cases, Daoism was confronted with a full set of well-established indigenous beliefs and practices. In response, many of the same philosophical and social dynamics operated in these new cultures as they had during the period of the Song, when Daoism grew over, grafted onto and became hybrid with a wide range of popular beliefs. Daoism's cosmology of *yin* and *yang*, and its traditions about immortals and *shen* beings, as well as its techniques of exercise, meditation, medicinals and diet, all took hold in East Asia with varying levels of strength. A second extension of Daoist influence in Korea about the 1500s CE and in Japan under the Tokugawas (1600–1868 CE) carried the techniques of inner alchemy and the use of the morality books to those cultures. In Vietnam during the early twentieth century (1920s CE), Daoist ritual practices, talismans and petitions were grafted into the Caodai tradition by Ngo Minh Chien, its founder.

However, the situation with Daoism's growth in the West has been different. Edward Said has made us well aware of the problematic nature of the early constructions of the 'Orient' as Westerners began to contact Chinese and other Asian worldviews. Orientalism was a way in which the West gained strength and identity by setting itself off against the dreamy and romantic Orient. It fed the imperialism and colonial domination of the West (Said 1985). And yet, the Western attitude toward Daoism may not best be characterized under the rubric of Orientalism. Although the early exposure to Daoism in the West was shaped greatly by figures associated with Anglo-European missionary expansionism, Daoism featured only marginally in the Western consciousness during the colonial epoch. It came into view only at the end of that period (Clarke 2000: 7). In his work *The Tao of the West: Western Transformations of Taoist Thought*, J.J. Clarke explores the rich diversity of the ways in which Daoism has been appropriated and engaged in the cultures of the West.[27]

W.T. de Bary insists, and rightly so, that 'no tradition ... can survive untransformed in the crucible of global struggle' (1988: 138). We have been witnesses to such transformations of Daoism in films such as *Crouching Tiger, Hidden Dragon* (*Wohu canlong*, dir. Ang Lee, 2000) and *Hero* (*Ying xiong*, dir. Zhang Yimou, 2002), and in the fiction of such Western writers as the American novelist Ursula Le Guin. Le Guin has done her own translation of the *Daodejing* and she has allowed Daoism to graft itself into most of her fiction, especially *Books of the Earthsea*[28] and the novel *The Dispossessed*. These works represent the hybridization of Daoism into Germanic and Anglo-European contexts and narrative frames in highly creative ways.

Some recent attempts to understand the historical interaction between Daoism and its new Western soil have been written. With respect to America, Elijah Siegler's *The Dao of America: The History and Practice of American Daoism* (2003) is a thorough work that provides an historical frame, a very complete list of Daoist organizations in the USA and a chart of North American Daoist lineages. There are Daoist temples in Arizona, New York, Hawaii and a number of other places in the USA. The Penglai temple in Toronto is perhaps the best known Canadian site of Daoist influence in that culture. In the UK, the British Daoist Association was founded in 1996 and there is likewise a Daoist Association in France. Daoism was first established by immigrants to Sydney, Australia and there is also a community in New South Wales.

The living vine of Daoism will continue to grow and transform, as we have seen it do in each new era and change in culture during its past. The new hybrid that is produced may have stems and shoots that are short lived, but other vines may wrap themselves around new global challenges and realities and transform them and the people involved, just as the *zhenren* have been made and remade for well over 2,000 years.

A Quick Guide to Pronunciation

Adapted from Terry Kleeman and Tracy Barrett,
The Ancient Chinese World, p. 171

ai	the y in fry	hai	is pronounced hi
an	the on in on	fan	is pronounced fahn
ang	the ong in gong	fang	is pronounced fahng
ao	the ow in cow	gao	is pronounced gaow
c	the ts in fits	cao	is pronounced tsaow
e	the oo in foot	se	is pronounced suh
ei	the ay in bay	fei	is pronounced fay
en	the un in fun	men	is pronounced muhn
eng	the ung in fungus	meng	is pronounced muhng
er	the are in are	mu'er	is pronounced moo-er
g	the g in girl	gao	is pronounced gaow
i	the ee in glee	qi	is pronounced chee
ia	ee, plus ah	xia	is pronounced sheeah
iang	ee, plus the yang in yang	chiang	is pronounced cheeahng
ie	ee, plus the yeah in yeah	qie	is pronounced cheeyeh
in	the ee in been	xin	is pronounced sheen
iu	ee, plus oh	jiu	is pronounced jeeoh
ou	oh	mou	is pronounced mwho
q	the ch in child	qin	is pronounced cheen
u	the ew in few	yu	is pronounced yew
u	the oo in boo	gu	is pronounced goo
ua	the wa in water	hua	is pronounced hwah
uan	the wan in wander	huan	is pronounced hwahn
uang	the wan in wander plus ng	huang	is pronounced hwahng
ue	oo, plus the e in went	que	is pronounced chooeh
un	the won in won	sun	is pronounced swun
uo	the awe in awful	guo	is pronounced gwoh
x	the sh in should	xing	is pronounced shing
yuan	oo, plus the en in went	yuan	is pronounced yuwen
z	the ds in yards	zeng	is pronounced dzeng
zh	the j in juice	zhou	is pronounced jo

Glossary of Titles

Accounts of Encounters with Spirit Immortals (DZ 592) (*Shenxian ganyu zhuan* 神仙感遇傳)

Analects (*Lun yu* 論語)

Annotated Explanation of the Transmission Formalities of Scriptures and Precepts (DZ1238) (*Chuanshou jingjie yi zhujue* 傳授經戒儀註訣)

An Anthology of the Gold and Jade on Comprehending Mystery (DZ 1149) (*Dongxuan jinyu ji* 洞玄金玉集)

Bamboo Laozi (*Zhujian Laozi* 竹簡老子)

Biographies of the Immortals (DZ 294) (*Liexian zhuan* 列仙傳)

Biographies of the Immortals (DZ 295) (*Xuxian zhuan* 續仙傳)

Biographies of Shen Immortals (*Shenxian zhuan* 神仙傳)

Book of Changes (*Yijing* 易經)

Book of the Early (Former) Han (*Hanshu* 漢書)

Book of the Jin (*Jin shu* 晉書)

Book of Odes (*Shijing* 詩經)

Book of Rites (*Liji* 禮記)

Canon and Instruction for the Divine Alchemy of the Nine Cauldrons of the Yellow Emperor (DZ 885) (*Huangdi jiuding shendan jingjue* 黃帝九鼎神丹經訣)

Canonical Rules of the Most High Lord Lao (DZ 786) (*Taishang laojun jinglu* 太上老君經律)

Catalog of the Scriptures and Writings of the Three Caverns (*Sandong jingshu mulu* 三洞 經書目錄)

Central Classic of the Nine Perfected Persons (DZ 1376) (*Shangqing taishang dijun jiuzhen zhongjing* 上清太上帝君九真中經)

The Chart of the True Shape of the Five Sacred Mountains (DZ 1281) (*Wuyue zhenxing tu* 五嶽真形圖)

Chart of United Energy (*Yiqi tu* 一氣圖)

Chongyang's Anthology of the Ten Transformations by Dividing Pears (DZ 1155) (*Chongyang fenli shihua ji* 重陽分梨十化集)

Classic of Concentration and Meditation (DZ 400) (*Dongxuan lingbao dingguan jing zhu* 洞玄靈寶定觀經諸)

Classic of the Golden Elixir (*Jinye jing* 金液經)

Classic of Great Clarity (*Taiqingjing* 太清經)

Classic of Laozi's Conversion of the Barbarians (*Laojun bashiyi huahu jing* 老君八十一化胡經)

Classic of Laozi's Transformations (*Laozi bianhua jing* 老子變化經)

Classic of the Mountains and Seas (*Shanhai jing* 山海經)

Classic of the Nine Elixirs (*Jiudan jing* 九丹經)

The Classic of the Numinous Treasure (*Lingbao jing* 靈寶經)

Classic of Recited Precepts of Lord Lao (DZ 785) (*Laojun yinsong jiejing* 老君音誦戒經)

Classic on the Three Limits on the Passes of Heaven (DZ 1366) (*Shangqing tianguan santu jing* 上清天關三圖經)

Classic on the True Writings of the Five Ancients of the Primordial Beginnning, Red Writings in Celestial Script on Jade Tablets (DZ 22) (*Yuanshi wulao chishu yupian zhenwen tianshu jing* 元始五老赤書玉篇真文天書經)

Code of Nuqing for Controlling Ghosts (DZ 790) (*Nuqing guilu* 女青鬼律)

Commandments of the Celestial Master from the One and Orthodox Canon (DZ 789) (*Zhengyi fawen tianshi jiaojie kejing* 正一法文天師教戒科經)

Commands and Admonitions for the Families of the Great Dao (*Dadao jialing jie* 大道家令戒)

Comprehensive Mirror of the Immortals Who Embodied the Dao Through the Ages (DZ 296) (*Lishi zhenxian tidao tongjian* 歷世真仙體道通薦)

Daodejing 道德經

Daoist Methods, United in Principle (DZ 1220) (*Daofa huiyuan* 道法會元)

Day Book (*Ri Shu* 日書)

Declarations of the Perfected Person (DZ 1016) (*Zhengao* 真誥)

Dietary Proscriptions of the Divine Agriculturist (Shennong) the Yellow Emperor (*Shennong huangdi shijin* 神農黃帝食禁)

Doctrine of the Mean (*Zhongyong* 中庸)

Dream of the Red Mansions (*Hongluo meng* 紅樓夢)

The Embryonic Essence from Superior Transmutation of the Ninefold Elixir (DZ 1382) (*Shangqing jiudan shanghua taijing zhongji jing* 上清九丹上化胎精中記經)

Esoteric Essentials of the Most High (DZ 1138) (*Wushang biyao* 無上祕要)

Essay on Sitting and Forgetting (DZ 1036) (*Zuowang lun* 坐忘論)

Essential Precepts of Master Redpine (DZ 185) (*Chisongzi zhongjie jing* 赤松子中戒經)

Fifty-two Healing Methods (*Wushi'er bingfang* 五十二病方)

Formal Registers of the Awesome Covenant of Orthodox Unity (CT 1209) (*Zhengyi mengwei falu* 正一盟威法籙)

Ghost Code of the Numinous Writ of Bone Marrow in the Supreme Purity Tradition (DZ 461) (*Shangqing gusui lingwen guilu* 上清骨髓靈文鬼律)

The Great Brilliance of Huainan (*Huainan honglie* 淮南鴻烈)

The Great Learning (*Da xue* 大學)

Great Peace Classic (DZ 1101.a) (*Taipingjing* 太平經)

Guanzi 管子

Gymnastic Chart (*Daoyin tu* 導引圖)

Han Dynasty Tombs at Mawangdui Silk Texts Naming Catalog (*Mawangdui Hanmu boshu zhengli xiaozu* 馬王堆漢墓帛書整理小組)

Hanfeizi 韓非子

Heshanggong 河上公

History of the Ming Dynasty (*Ming shi* 明史)

History of the Wei Dynasty (*Wei shu* 魏書)

Illustrated Album on the Auspicious Miracles Performed by the Supreme Emperor of the Dark Heaven (DZ 659) (*Da Ming xuantian shangdi ruiying tulu* 大明玄天上帝瑞應圖錄)

Imperial Encyclopedia of the Taiping Era (DZ 1230) (*Taiping yulan* 太平御覽)

Inner Classic of the Yellow Court (*Huangting neijing jing* 黃庭內景經)

Innumerable Sounds of the Secret Language of the Great Brahman Energies of the Heavens (*Zhutian zhong dafan yinyu wuliang yin* 諸天中大梵隱語無量音)

Inward Training (*Neiye* 內業)

Journey to the North (*Beiyou ji* 北遊記)

Journey to the West (*Xiyou ji* 西遊記)

The Later Han (*Hou hanshu* 候漢書)

The Ledger of Merit and Demerit of the Taiwei Immortal (DZ 186) (*Taiwei xianjun gongguo ge* 太微仙君且L格)

Master of Huainan (*Huainanzi* 淮南子)

Master Redpine's Almanac of Petitions (DZ 615) (*Chisongzi zhangli* 赤松子章曆)

The Master Who Embraces Simplicity Inner Chapters (DZ 1185) (*Baopuzi Neipian* 抱朴子內篇)

The Master Who Embraces Simplicity Outer Chapters (DZ 1187) (*Baopuzi Waipian* 抱朴子外篇)

The Mencius (*Mengzi* 孟子)

Mister Lu's Spring and Autumn Annals (*Lushi Chunqiu* 呂氏春秋)

Most Excellent and Mysterious Book of the Marvelous Jewel That Saves Innumerable Human Beings (DZ 1) (*Duren jing* 度人經) (*Lingbao wuliang duren shangpin miaojing* 靈寶無量度人上品妙經)

Nine Cauldron Elixir Formula of the Yellow Emperor (*Huangdi jiuding dan fa* 黃帝九鼎丹法)

On Nourishing Life (*Yangshen lun* 養生論)

On Painting the Cloud Terrace Mountain (*Hua yuntai shan ji* 畫雲台山記)

One Hundred and Eighty Rules of Lord Lao (*Laojun shuo yibaibashi jie* 老君說一百八十戒) in *Canonical Rules of the Most High Lord Lao* (DZ 786) (*Taishang laojun jinglu*太上老君經 律)

Oral Instructions on the Golden Passkey and Jade Lock by the Perfected Chongyang (DZ 1156) (*Chongyang zhenren jinguan yusuo jue* 重陽真人金關玉鎖訣)

The Origins and Symptoms of Medical Disorders (*Zhubing yuanhou lun* 諸病源侯論)

Outlaws of the Marsh, a.k.a., Water Margin (*Shuihu zhuan* 水滸傳)

The Pearl Bag of the Three Caverns (DZ 1139) (*Sandong zhunang* 三洞珠囊)

Peony Pavilion (*Mudan Ting* 牡丹亭)

Perfect Classic of Great Profundity (in CT 5, 103, 6 and 7) (*Dadong zhenjing* 大洞真經)

Perfect Classic of Registers and Charts (*Lutu zhenjing* 錄圖真經)

Poems of Chu (*Chuci* 楚辭)

Precepts of the Highest Lord Lao (DZ 784) (*Taishang laojun jiejing* 太上老君戒經)

Precepts of the New Code Recited in the Clouds (*Congyunzhong yinsong xinke jiejing* 從雲中音誦新科戒經)

Preface to the Poems Composed at the Orchid Pavilion (*Lantingji xu* 蘭亭集序)

Purple Texts Inscribed by the Spirits, a.k.a, The Upper Scripture of Purple Texts Inscribed by the Spirits (*Lingshu ziwen shangjing* 靈書紫文上經)

Pure Rules of Complete Perfection (DZ 1235) (*Quanzhen qinggui* 全真清規)

Record of the Celebrated Meetings on the Mysterious Winds (DZ 176) (*Xuanfeng qinghui lu* 旋風慶會錄)

Record of Daoist Miracles (DZ 590) (*Daojiao lingyan ji* 道教靈驗記)

Record of the Perfected Changchun's Travel to the West (DZ 1429) (*Changchun zhenren xiyou ji* 長春真人西遊記)

Recorded Sayings of the Perfected Danyang (DZ 1057) (*Danyang zhenren yulu* 丹陽真人語錄)

Records about Extraordinary Persons in the Area along the Rivers Jiang and Huai (DZ 595) (*Jiang-Huai yiren lu* 江淮異人錄)

Records of the Historian (*Shi ji* 史记)

The Rejection of Grains and Absorption of Qi (*Quegu shiqi* 卻穀食氣)

Revelation Record of the Emperor of Dark Heaven (CT 958) (*Xuantian shangdi qishi lu* 玄天上帝啟示錄)

Reverence for the Dao over Successive Generations (DZ 593) (*Lidai chongdao ji* 歷代崇道記)

Rites of Zhou (*Zhouli* 周禮)

Romance of the Three Kingdoms (*Sanguo zhi* 三國誌)

Rules for Daoists and Buddhists (*Daoseng ke* 道僧科)

Rules and Precepts on Worshiping the Dao (CT 1125) (*Fengdao kejie* 奉道科戒)

Scripture of Great and Minor Merits, and the Classified Rules of the Three Principles (DZ 456) (*Taishang dongxuan lingbao sanyuan pinjie gongde qingzhong jing* 太上洞玄靈寶三元品戒功德輕重經)

Secret Instructions for the Ascent as a Perfected Person (DZ 421) (*Dengzhen yinjue* 登真隱訣)

Seven Recitations of the Divine Realm with Seven Transformations for Dancing in Heaven (DZ 1331) (*Dongzhen shangqing shenzhou qizhuan qibian wutian jing* 洞真上清神州七專七變舞天經)

Shennong's Materia Medica (*Shennong bencao jing* 神農本草經)

Song of Eternal Sorrow (*Chang hen ge* 長恨歌)

Song of the Pipa Player (*Pipa xing* 琵琶行)

Straight Words from the Perfected Danyang (DZ 1234) (*Danyang zhenren zhiyan* 丹陽真人直言)

Supplement to the Daoist Canon (*Xu daozang* 續道藏)

Techniques for Fifty-Two Ailments (*Wushier bingfang* 五十二病方)

Techniques of the Heart (*Xinshu* 心術)

The Ten Differences and Nine Errors (*Shiyi jiumi lun* 十異九迷論)

Tract of the Most Exalted on Action and Response (DZ 1167) (*Taishang ganying pian* 太上感應篇)

True Diagram of the Five Peaks (DZ 1281) (*Wuyue zhenxing tu* 五嶽真形圖)

Wondrous Mushrooms of the Yellow Emperor and His Various Disciples
  (*Huangdi zazi zhijun* 黃帝雜子芝菌)

The Writings of the Three Sovereigns (*Sanhuang wen* 三皇文)

Xiang'er Commentary on the Daodejing (S. 6825) (*Laozi xiang'er zhu* 老
  子想爾注)

Yellow Emperor's and Three Kings' Techniques for Nourishing (*Yang
  Huangdi sanwang yangyang fang* 黃帝三王養陽方)

Yellow Emperor's Classic of the Golden Bookcase and Jade Scales (DZ 284)
  (*Huangdi jinkui yuheng jing* 黃帝金匱玉衡經)

Yellow Emperor's Inner Classic (*Huangdi neijing* 黃帝內經)

Yellow Emperor's Old Willow Divination by Dreams (*Huangdi changliu
  zhanmeng* 黃帝長柳占夢)

The Yellow Millet Dream (*Huangliang meng* 黃粱夢)

Zhengtong daozang 正統道藏

Zhuangzi 莊子

Glossary of Names and Terms

ao 奧
Ao Guang 敖广
bagong 八公
Bagua 八卦
baijia 百家
Bai Juyi 白居易
Baishi Gong 白石公
Baiyun Guan 白雲觀
Bao Jing 鮑靚
Baoming Si 保明寺
Baxian 八仙
bei-a 倍阿
beidou 北斗
benming 本命
bianhua 變化
bianhua ruo shen 變化若神
Bianliang 汴梁 *or* 汴樑
biao 表
bigu 辟穀
boshan lu 博山爐
boshu 帛書
Boyang 伯陽
Bozhou 亳州
busi 不死
Cai Tao 蔡條
Cao Cao 曹操
Cao Guojiu 曹國舅
Chang Jiang 長江
Chang'an 長安
Changchun 長春
Chang'e 嫦娥

changsheng 長生
Chao Yuanfang 巢元方
Chen Shouyuan 陳守元
Chen Tuan 陳摶
chengfu 承負
Chenghuang 城隍
Chenghuang Miao 城隍廟
chengxian 成仙
Chisongzi 赤松子
Chong'er 重耳
Chongxu Si 崇虛寺
chuanshou 傳授
ci 慈
Cui Hao 崔浩
da dao 大道
Da Ming huanghou santian jinque yufu shangxian hongci puhui tidao xuanjun 大明皇后三天金闕玉輔上仙宏慈溥惠體道玄君
Dan 丹 (person)
dan 丹
dantian 丹田
Danyang 丹陽
dao 道
Dao Xi 道覡
daode 道德
daogu 道姑
daojia 道家
daojiao 道教
daojing 道經
Daoju 道聚

Daojun 道君
daolu jinji 道律禁忌
Daolu si 道錄司
daomen weiyi shi 道門威儀使
daomin 道民
daoshi 道士
daoyin 導引
Daoyuan 道院
Daxian Liangshi 大賢良師
Dayan Ta 大雁塔
de 德 (virtue, power)
De 杜 (family)
dejing 德經
Deng Yougong 鄧有功
difei 地肥
diwen 地文
Dong Zhongshu 董仲舒
Dongfang Shuo 東方朔
donggong zhi shi 東宮之師
Donghua Dijun 東華帝君
dongtian 洞天
Dongyue Miao 東嶽廟
dou 斗
Du Fu 杜甫
Du Guangting 杜光庭
Du Liniang 杜麗娘
duan chang 斷腸
dui 兌 (trigram)
dunjia 遁甲
Emperor Wudi 武帝
ershiba xiu 二十八宿
fan xing 反性
fangshi 方士
Fangzhangshan 方丈山
fashen 法身
Fei Zhi 肥致
feitian 飛天
Fengdu 酆都
fengshui 風水

fenli 分梨, (divide)
fenli 分離, (separate)
fu 符
Fu Xi 伏羲
Fu Yi 傅奕
fuguang 服光
fuming 符命
fushui 符水
Fuyu 福裕
gang 綱
ganying 感應
gaoshi 高士
Gaosong shan 高嵩山
Gaotian 高天
Gaoxuan fashi 高玄法師
Gaozong 高宗
Gaozu 高祖
Ge Chaofu 葛巢甫
Ge Hong 葛洪
Ge Xuan 葛玄
Gengsang Chu 庚桑楚
Genyue 艮煨
Gezaoshan 閣皂山
gongguo ge 功過格
Gongsun Qiang 公孫強
Gu Kaizhi 顧愷之
Guan 觀 (observatory)
guan 館
Guangong 關公
guanling 關令
Guanyin 觀音
gui 鬼
guibing 鬼兵
guidao 鬼道
guili 鬼吏
guishen 鬼神
Gushe 姑射
Guo Xiang 郭象
Guodian 郭店

Han Xiangzi 翰湘子
Han Yu 翰愈
Hanlin Yuan 翰林院
Hanzi 漢字
Hao Datong 郝大通
Haozhou 郝州
he 劾 (investigate)
he 和 (harmony)
He Xiangu 何仙姑
He Zhizhang 賀知章
Hemingshan 鶴鳴山
Hengshan 恒山 (northern sacred mt)
Hengshan 衡山 (southern sacred mt)
Hongzhi弘治
Hong Xiuquan 洪秀全
hua 化
Huainan 淮南
Huang He 黃河
huang hu 恍惚
Huang Taihou 皇太后
huangbai 黃白
Huangdi 黃帝
Huangjin 黃巾
Huang-Lao Daoism 黃老道
Huang-Lao 黃老
huanjing bunao 還精補腦
Huashan 華山
hui sheng 回生
Hui Shi 惠施
hui 會
huifeng 回風
Huizi 惠子
Huizong 徽宗
Huoshan 霍山
hu 虎
Ji Kang 稽康
jia gu 甲骨

jiang 降
Jiang Bin 姜斌
Jianling Jijiu 奸令祭酒
jiao 郊
jiao 醮
jiazi 甲子
jijiu 祭酒
Jin Chang 晉昌
jing 精 (numinal essence, energy)
jing 經 (text, scripture)
jingmo 經脈
jingqi 精氣
jingshi 靜室
jingzuo 靜坐
Jinning 济宁
jinshi 進士
jiu jie zhang 九節杖
Jiuxian Miao 九仙廟
Jiuyao Miao 九妖廟
Jixia 稷下
Jixian 集賢 (Jixian yuan 集賢院, Jixian academy)
jueqi 決氣
Jurong 句容
Kaifeng 開封
kaishan 開山
Kangxi 康熙
kanyu jia 堪與家
King Hui of Liang 梁惠王
King Wei 威王
King Xuan 宣王
Kong Miao 孔廟
kongde 孔德
Kongtong 崆峒
kongxue 孔穴
Kou Qianzhi 寇謙之
Kuang 曠
Kunlun Mountain 崑崙山
Kunqu 崑曲

Lan Caihe 藍采和
Langmei 桹梅
Lao Dan 老聃
Laozi 老子
Lei Bei 雷被
Li 李 (surname of Laozi; Tang emperors)
Li Bai 李白
Li Changling 李昌齡
Li Chen 李忱
Li Chun 李純
Li Er 李耳
Li Longji 李隆基
Li Qingjun 李庆军
Li Shang 李尚
Li Shaojun 李少君
Li Shimin 李世民
Li Suxi 李素希
Li Tieguai 李鐵拐
Li Xuan 李儇
Li Yan 李炎
Li Yuan 李淵
Li Zhi 李治
Li Zhongqing 李仲卿
Liang Su 梁肅
libu 禮部
Liezi 列子
Ligong pin 立功品
Lin Lingsu 林靈素
Lin Zhao'en 林兆恩
Linchuan 臨川
ling 靈
Lingbao 靈寶
lingfu 靈府
lingjue 領決
Liu An 劉安
Liu Chuxuan 劉處玄
Liu Haichan 劉海襜
Liu Hunkang 劉混康

Liu Mengmei 柳薲梅
Liu Sheng 劉勝
Liu Xiang 劉向
Liujiang 劉蔣
long 龍
Longhushan 龍虎山
Longmen 龍門
Longtai Guan 龍台觀
longxue 龍血
Louguan Tai 樓觀台
lu 錄
Lu Dongbin 呂洞賓
Lu Xiujing 陸修靜
Lunheng 論衡
lunhui 輪迴
Luofushan 羅浮山
Luoyang 洛陽
lusheng 錄生
Ma 馬
Ma Yu 馬鈺
Ma Zhiyuan 馬致遠
Mancheng 滿城
Mao Bei 毛被
Maoshan 茅山
Marshall Tianpeng Yuanshuai 天蓬元師
Mawangdui 馬王堆
Mazu 媽祖
Meng Haoran 孟浩然
Mengcheng 蒙城
Mengzi 孟子
miao 廟 (temple)
ming 明
mingqi 明器
Mo 鏌 (*Mo-ye*, the greatest magical sword)
nanwu 男巫
neidan 內丹
neiguan 內觀

Neijing tu 內經圖
neipian 內篇
niaoshen 鳥伸
niwan 泥丸
nuhuo 女禍
nuo 儺
Nuqing 女青
Pan Shizheng 潘師正
Penglai 蓬萊
Penglai shan 蓬萊山
Pengzu 彭祖
pian 篇
pu 扑
Putian 莆田
Puyang 濮陽
qi 氣
qian 鉛
Qianlong 乾隆
qigong 氣功
qing 清
qingjing 清靜
Qinshihuang 秦始皇
Qishier fudi 七十二福地
Qiu 丘 (Confucius' personal name)
Qiu Chuji 邱處機
qixue 氣穴
qiyun shengdong 氣韻生動
Qizhen 七真
qizheng 七政
Quanzhen 全真
quegu 卻穀
Quren 曲仁 (Laozi's village)
Rao Dongtian 饒洞天
ren 仁
Renzong 仁宗
Ri Shu 日書
rihun 日魂
Ruyi Jingu Bang 如意金箍棒

sanjiao 三教
sanjiao heyi 三教合一
sanyi jiao 三一教
sanyuan 三元
Sha Wujing 沙悟淨
shan 善
shanfa 山法
Shangqing 上清
Shanqing 山卿
shanshu 善書
shen 神
shen qi 神器
shen yi 神矣
shengren 聖人
shengtai 聖胎
shenhua 神化
Shennong 神農
shenren 神人
shenxian 神仙
shenxiao 神霄
shi 士, master, teacher
shi 尸, impersonator of the dead
Shi Daogu 石道姑
Shi Tanying 釋曇影
shijie 尸解
shizhan 筮占
Shizong 世宗
Shizu 世祖
shou 壽
shoudu 授度
shouxin 收心
shui yin 水銀
Shunu 庶女
si 寺
Sima Chengzhen 司馬承禎
Sima Qian 司馬遷
siming shi 司命史
Songshan 嵩山
su 俗

Su Fei 蘇非
Su Jun 蘇峻
Suixian 隨縣
Sun Bu'er 孫不二
Sun Wukong 孫悟空
Sun Youyue 孫遊嶽
taiji 太極
Taiji tu 太極圖
Taiping 太平
Taiping dao 太平道
Taiping Zhenjun 太平真君
Taiqing 太清
Taiqing Gong 太清宮
Taishan 泰山
Taishang 太上
Taishang fujun 太上府君
Taishang Laojun 太上老君
Taishang yuanshi tianzun 太上元始天尊
Taiwei 太威
Taiwei Gong 太微宮
Taiwu 太武
taixi 胎息
Taixuan dusheng 泰玄都箸
Taiyi 太一
Taizong 太宗
Taizu 太祖
tan 壇
Tan Chuduan 譚處端
Tang Xianzu 湯顯祖
Tao Hongjing 陶弘景
tian 天
tian wang 天網
Tian You 田由
tiandi 天帝
tianmen 天門
tianren 天人
Tianshi Dao 天師道
Tiantaishan 天台山

Tianxin 天心
tiaozhi 條制
tie 貼
ting 停
Tongdao Guan 通道觀
toulong 投龍
tu 圖
tugu naxin 吐古呐新
tuzhai shu 圖宅術
waidan 外丹
waipian 外篇
wang 望
Wang Bi 王弼
Wang Chong 王充
Wang Chongyang 王重陽
Wang Chuyi 王處一
Wang Laozhi 王老志
Wang Xizhi 王羲之
Wang Yuanzhi 王遠知
Wangwu shan 王屋山
Wei Huacun 魏華存
weijing 微經
Wenchang 文昌
Wenzhou 溫州
wu 巫
Wu Bei 伍被
Wu Chengen 吳承恩
Wu Shu 吳淑
Wu Zetian 武則天
Wu Zong 武宗
Wudi 武帝
Wudoumi Dao 五斗米道
Wuhan 武漢
wusi 無死
Wutaishan 五台山
wu-wei 無為
wu-xing 五行
wuyue 五嶽
Wuyue Guan 五煬觀

Xi Wu 席武

xian 仙 (immortal)

Xi'an 西安

xiangshu 相術

xiangsi bing 相思病

xianyao 仙藥

Xianzong 憲宗

xiao 孝

xiao fu er 小符儿

xiao zhoutian 小周天

Xie He 謝赫

xin 信 (sincere)

xin 心 (heart-mind)

Xinchu zhengyi mengwei zhi dao 新出正一盟威之道

xing 性

xingming 性命

xingqi 行氣

xinyuan 心猿

xiongjing 熊經

Xishan 西山

Xiwangmu 西王母

Xizong 僖宗

Xu Hui 許翽

Xu Jingyang 許旌陽

Xu Mi 許謐

Xu Xun 徐遜

xuan 玄

xuan pin 玄牝

xuan tong 玄同

xuan zhi you xuan 玄之又玄

xuande 玄德

Xuanwu 玄武

Xuanzang 玄奘

Xuanzong (r. 713–56 CE) 玄宗

Xuanzong (r. 846–59 CE) 宣宗

xue 血

xuejiu 血酒

xueshi 血食

xun 訓

Xunzi 荀子

ya mu 崖募

Yang Guifei 楊貴妃

Yang Xi 楊羲

Yangjiao shan 羊角山

yangsheng 養生

Yangzi 揚子

yannian shishi 延年石室

Yanqing Guan 延慶觀

Ye Fashan 葉法善

Yi 乙 (name)

yi 義 (righteousness)

yima 意馬

Yin Tong 尹通

Yin Wencao 尹文操

Yin Xi 尹喜

Yingzhou shan 瀛洲山

Yinqing guanglu dafu 銀青光錄大夫

yinshi 隱士

yishe 義舍

yishi guishen 役使鬼神

Yongle 永樂

Yongle Gong 永樂宮

yu 雩 (sacrifice)

Yu shan 玉山

yuan fen 緣份

Yuanshi tianzun 元始天尊

Yubu 禹步

yuehua 月華

Yuhuang Shangdi 玉皇上帝

Yulong Guan 玉隆宮

Yunu 玉女

Yunu Lingguan Tang 玉女靈觀堂

yuren 羽人

Yushi 雨師

zai pian 磠篇

zaohua 造化

Zeng 曾

zhang 章

Zhang 章 (Ming Empress)

Zhang Daoling 張道陵

Zhang Guolao 張果老

Zhang Heng 張衡

Zhang Jiao 張角

Zhang Jixian 張繼先

Zhang Liusun 張留孫

Zhang Lu 張魯

Zhang Xuanqing 張玄慶

Zhang Zhengchang 張正常

Zhang Zongyan 張宗演

Zhao Ji 趙佶

zhaofan 招幡

zhaohun 召魂

zhende 真德

zheng 正

Zheng He 鄭和

zheng qi 正氣

Zheng Yin 鄭隱.

zhengde 正德

Zhengtong 正統

Zhengyi daoshi 正一道士

Zhengyi nushi 正一女士

zhenmu wen 鎮墓文

zhenren 真人

Zhenwu 真武

Zhenzong 真宗

zhi 之 (centre and character in surname of Celestial Masters))

zhi 治 (regulated and ordered)

zhi jing wei shen 至精為神

zhitou dajijiu 治頭大祭酒

Zhongli Quan 鐘離權

zhongmin 種民

Zhongnan shan 终南山

Zhongshan 鍾山

zhongsong 冢訟

Zhongyue Miao 中岳廟

Zhou 周

Zhu Bajie 豬八戒

Zhu Di 朱棣

Zhu Gaozhi 朱高熾

Zhu Houcong 朱厚熜

Zhu Houzhao 朱厚照

Zhu Jianshen 朱見深

Zhu Qizhen 朱祁鎮

Zhu Youtang 朱祐樘

Zhu Yuanzhang 朱元璋

Zhu Ziying 朱自英

Zhuang Zhou 莊周

zi 子

Zijincheng 紫禁城

Zixiao Gong 紫霄宮

Ziyang Gong 紫阳宫

ziyin 自隱

Zongyong 中庸

zui 最

Zuo Ci 左慈

Zuo Wu 左吳

Zou Yan 鄒衍

zuowang 坐忘

Illustration, Map and Picture Credits

Notes

Prelims

1 See Anna Seidel's (1997) very fine discussion of all the ways we can become entangled in Western languages and preconceptions while trying to talk about Daoism. Michael Lowe and Edward Shaughnessy (1999) provide an excellent history of ancient China.

Chapter II

2 In the *Zhuangzi*, the names Lao Dan and Laozi are used interchangeably.

3 Julia Hardy (1998) provides a helpful overview of Western interpretations of the *Daodejing*. Judith Boltz (1987) provides us with a survey of Daoist literature.

4 This sort of appreciation for the aggregate character of the *Daodejing* is really not new. Among the earlier generation of translators, D.C. Lau goes so far as to call the *Daodejing* 'an anthology' (Lau 1963: xiii). He divides the chapters with section numbers to indicate where he thought the aphorisms had been independent originally, and he even makes a distinguishing mark on each passage that he believed was further exposition of an aphorism but added by yet another editor or source.

5 Another interesting feature of the *Daodejing* that also goes to support the view that there was no single author of the text is the frequent repetition of sayings. Lau has an excellent list comparing repetitions of phrases, concepts and images in the text. Although it relies on his section numbering system, it is still easy to use.

6 Cline (2004); Ivanhoe (1999); Ames (1989); Nivison (1996).

Chapter III

7 There are other newer translations of *Zhuangzi* that are also good. Mair (1997) is one of these. The Hyun and Yang version (2007)

uses pinyin names and terms and modernizes a great deal of the English. An exampe of an important recent study of *Zhuangzi* is Kjellberg and Ivanhoe (1996).

Chapter IV

8 Scholars such as Harold Roth believe that we should include the *Neiye* in the materials that formed the trunk of Daoism. Russell Kirkland (2001) thinks the *Neiye* has implications for an understanding of *wu-wei*.

9 See Kingsley (1999 and 2003).

Chapter VII

10 There are some fine discussions of Daoism's appreciation for nature and the environment such as Giradot, Miller and Liu (2001), and Schipper's specific essay in that work (2001).

Chapter VIII

11 A fine work on Ge Hong's writings about the immortals is Robert Campany (2002).

12 The ritual description offered in the text comes from Robinet (1997: 132–3). Peter Nickerson has translated a petition text used by Celestial Masters libationers that may be related to these practices

13 Isabelle Robinet provides a detailed exposition of these practices (Robinet 2004: 216–21).

14 *The Purple Texts Inscribed by the Spirits* (contained in DZ 639, 255, 442 and 179) amplifies on the Whirling Wind method of absorbing numinal essence for biospiritual transformation.

Chapter IX

15 The final section of the essay is a version of a Tang work entitled *Classic of Concentration and Meditation*.

16 For more on the approaches to the stars and their relationship to Daoism in the Tang, see Schafer (1977).

17 There are many fine collections of Tang dynasty poets, including those of Cooper (1973) and Rexroth (1971). Elegant (1999) has written an interesting historical novel about Li Bai.

18 This translation of the Wu Zetian talisman, discovered on the mountainside near Zhongyue Miao, was made by Li Qingjun.

Chapter X

19 The Hanlin Academy was a famous collection of scholars in
   Chang'an (Xi'an) during the Tang dynasty. Piet van der Loon gives
   us a survey of the libraries available to Song dynasty scholars.

Chapter XI

20 There is a Ming dynasty reprint dated 1598 CE of one of these
   apparitions in the Bibliothèque nationale de France and printed
   in Schipper and Verellen (2004: 1201).

21 Her description of her naked husband on their wedding night is
   quite explicit. (Tang 2002: 82). And her teasing of Teacher Chen
   shows a brazen and bold earthiness.

22 Tang is not trying to report the entire ritual that constitutes the
   rite of the summoning of the soul and its deliverance. Since the
   time of the Song this rite had an extended ritual sequence. The
   sequence begins with 'Lighting the Lamps and Destroying the
   Earth Prisons'; then the Daoist master transforms into the divine
   Heavenly Worthy 'Savior from Distress' and walks the Dipper.
   The master burns talismans in each direction and recites an
   incantation. The talismans break the locks of the earth prisons
   and release the soul. The first part of the ritual concludes with
   the lighting of incense and prayers. The second act of the ritual
   is the summoning of the soul into the ritual area (Davis 2001:
   233–4). The coming of the soul into the ritual area is often the
   context for some extraordinary reports of episodes of possession
   such as the common occurrence of the appearance of a ghost or
   the possession of one of the celebrants, especially younger girls
   and boys.

23 This terrace is the place from which spirits in the earth prisons
   would gaze back over their previous lives one last time. Then they
   would enter a wheel (symbolic of some transformational process)
   and be cast out of it in a new form of the Five Phases, returning
   to Earth. Buddhists had a slightly different version. There were
   18 hells, but still the wheel of 'reincarnation' as they called it,
   and they did not use the Five Phase cosmology to explain the
   process.

24 The other three great novels are *Romance of the Three Kingdoms*,
   written by Luo Quanzhong in the 1300s; *Outlaws of the Marsh*,
   originally a set of folktales that were finally brought into a novel

form perhaps in the 1400s CE; and the *Dream of the Red Mansions*, composed in the middle of the 1700s, during the Qing dynasty.

25 For another approach breaking down this distinction, see Strickman (1979).

Chapter XII

26 Fortunately, this copy, preserved at the White Cloud Temple (*Baiyan Guan*) in Beijing, was reproduced in 1926 by a photolithographic process.

27 Clarke's third chapter, entitled 'Cramped scholars', is a good introduction to the Western thinkers that engaged Daoism historically (2000: 37–63).

28 It is generally acknowledged that the Earthsea works go in this order: *A Wizard of Earthsea, The Tombs of Atuan, The Farthest Shore, Tehanu, Tales from Earthsea, The Other Wind*.

Works Cited

Allan, Sarah and Crispin Williams (eds) (2000). *The Guodian Laozi: Proceedings of the International Conference, Dartmouth College, May 1998* (Berkeley: University of California).

Ames, Roger T. (1989). 'Putting the *Te* Back into Taoism', in J. Baird Callicott and Roger T. Ames (eds), *Nature in Asian Traditions of Thought* (Albany, State University of New York Press), pp. 113–44.

Bokenkamp, Stephen (trans.) (1997a). *Commands and Admonitions for the Families of the Great Dao*, in Stephen Bokenkamp (ed.), *Early Daoist Scriptures* (Berkeley, University of California Press), pp. 149–85.

—— (1997b). *Xiang'er Commentary on the Daodejing*, in Stephen Bokenkamp (ed.), *Early Daoist Scriptures* (Berkeley, University of California Press), pp. 78–148.

—— (1997c). *The Wondrous Scripture of the Upper Chapters on Limitless Salvation*, in Stephen Bokenkamp (ed.), *Early Daoist Scriptures* (Berkeley, University of California Press), pp. 405–38.

Boltz, Judith (1987). *A Survey of Taoist Literature, Tenth to Seventeen Centuries* (Berkeley CA, Institute of East Asian Studies).

Brokaw, Cynthia (1991). *The Ledgers of Merit and Demerit: Social Change and Moral Order in Late Imperial China* (Princeton NJ, Princeton University Press).

Cahill, Suzanne (1980). 'Taoism at the Sung Court: The Heavenly Text Affair', *The Bulletin of Sung-Yuan Studies* 16, pp. 23–44.

Campany, Robert Ford (2002). *To Live As Long As Heaven and Earth: Ge Hong's Traditions of Divine Transcendents* (Berkeley, University of California Press).

Carus, Paul and D.T. Suzuki (trans) (1973). *Treatise on Response and Retribution* (Chicago, Open Court).

Cedzich, Angelika (1993). 'Ghosts and Demons – Law and Order: Grave Quelling Texts and Early Taoist Liturgy', *Taoist Resources* 4, pp. 23–51.

Clarke, J.J. (2000). *The Tao of the West: Western Transformations of Taoist Thought* (London, Routledge).

Cline, Erin M. (2004). 'Two Interpretations of *De* in the *Daodejing*', *Journal of Chinese Philosophy* 31, pp. 219–33.

Cooper, Arthur (1973). *Li Po and Tu Fu: Poems Selected and Translated with an Introduction and Notes* (New York, Penguin).

Csikszentmihalyi, Mark (2004). 'Han Cosmology and Mantic Practices', in Livia Kohn (ed.), *Daoism Handbook* (Boston, Brill), pp. 53–73.

Davis, Edward (1985). 'Arms and the Tao: Hero Cult and Empire in Traditional China', in Sodaishi Kenkyukai (ed.), *Sodao no shakai to shukyo* (Tokyo, Kyuko shoin).

—— (2001). *Society and the Supernatural in Song China* (Honolulu, University of Hawaii Press).

Dean, Kenneth (1993). *Taoist Ritual and Popular Cults of Southeast China* (Princeton NJ, Princeton University Press).

De Bary, W.T. (1988). *East Asian Civilization: A Dialogue in Five Stages* (Cambridge MA, Harvard University Press).

DeBruyn, Pierre-Henry (2004). 'Daoism in the Ming', in Livia Kohn (ed.), *Daoism Handbook* (Boston, Brill), pp. 594–622.

DeWoskin, Kenneth (1981). *Doctors, Diviners and Magicians of Ancient China: Biographies of the Fang-shih* (New York, Columbia University Press).

Despeux, Catherine (2004a). 'Talismans and Diagrams', in Livia Kohn (ed.), *Daoism Handbook* (Boston, Brill), pp. 498–540.

—— (2004b). 'Women in Daoism', in Livia Kohn (ed.), *Daoism Handbook* (Boston, Brill), pp. 384–412.

Eberhard, Wolfram (1967). *Guilt and Sin in Traditional China* (Berkeley, University of California Press).

Ebrey, Patricia (2000). 'Taoism and Art at the Court of Song Huizong', in Stephen Little (ed.), *Taoism and the Arts of China* (Chicago, The Art Institute of Chicago), pp. 95–111.

Elegant, Simon (1999). *A Floating Life: The Adventures of Li Po* (New York, Ecco).

Engelhardt, Ute (2004). 'Longevity Techniques and Chinese Medicine', in Livia Kohn (ed.), *Daoism Handbook* (Boston, Brill), pp. 74–108.

Esposito, Monica (2004). 'Daoism in the Qing', in Livia Kohn (ed.), *Daoism Handbook* (Boston, Brill), pp. 623–58.

Girardot, Norman J. (2002). *The Victorian Translation of China: James Legge's Oriental   Pilgrimage* (Berkeley, The University of California Press).

——, James Miller and Liu Xiaogan (eds) (2001). *Daoism and Ecology: Ways within a Cosmic Landscape* (Cambridge MA, Harvard University Press).

Graham, Angus (1986). 'How Much of *Chuang-tzu* Did Chuang-tzu Write?', in *Studies in Chinese Philosophy and Philosophical Literature* (Singapore, Institute of East Asian Philosophies).

Hahn, Thomas H. (2004). 'Daoist Sacred Sites', in Livia Kohn (ed.), *Daoism Handbook* (Boston, Brill), pp. 683–708.

Handlin, Joana (1987). 'Benevolent Societies: The Reshaping of Charity During the Late Ming and Early Ch'ing', *Journal of Asian Studies* 46, pp. 309–37.

Hardy, Julia (1998). 'Influential Western Interpretations of the *Tao-te-ching*', in Livia Kohn and Michael LaFargue (eds), *Lao-tzu and the Tao-te-ching* (Albany, State University of New York Press), pp. 165–88.

Harper, Donald (1994). 'Resurrection in Warring States Popular Religion', *Taoist Resources* 5, pp. 13–28.

—— (1999). *Early Chinese Medieval Manuscripts: The Mawangdui Medical Manuscripts* (London, Wellcome Asian Medical Monographs.

Henricks, Robert (1989). *Lao-Tzu: Te-Tao Ching* (New York, Ballantine Books).

Hymes, Robert (2002). *Way and By-Way: Taoism, Local Religion, and Models of Divinity in Sung and Modern China* (Berkeley, University of California Press).

Hyun, Hochsmann and Yang Guorong (trans.) (2007). *Zhuangzi* (New York, Pearson).

Ivanhoe, Philip J. (1999). 'The Concept of de ("Virtue") in the Laozi', in Mark Csikszentmihalyi and P.J. Ivanhoe (eds), *Religious and Philosophical Aspects of the Laozi* (Albany, State University of New York Press), pp. 239–55.

—— (trans) (2002). *The Daodejing of Laozi* (New York, Seven Bridges Press).

Kalinowski, Marc (1990). 'La Littérature divinatoire dans le *Daozang*', *Cahiers d'Extreme-Asie* 5, pp. 85–114.

Kingsley, Peter (1999). *In the Dark Places of Wisdom* (Inverness CA, Golden Sufi Centre).

—— (2003). *Reality* (Inverness CA, Golden Sufi Center).

Kirkland, Russell (2001). '"Responsible Non-Action" in a Natural World: Perspectives from the *Neiye, Zhuangzi,* and *Daodejing*', in Norman Giradot, James Miller and Liu Xiaogan (eds), *Daoism and Ecology* (Cambridge MA, Harvard University Press), pp. 283–305.

—— (2004). *Taoism: The Enduring Tradition* (New York, Routledge).

Kjellberg, Paul and Philip J. Ivanhoe (eds) (1996). *Essays on Skepticism, Relativism, and Ethics in the Zhuangzi* (Albany, State University of New York Press).

Kleeman, Terry (1998). *Great Perfection: Religion and Ethnicity in a Chinese Millenial Kingdom* (Honolulu, University of Hawaii Press).

—— (2007). '*Tianshi dao*', in Fabrizio Pregadio (ed.), *The Encyclopedia of Taoism* (London, Routledge), vol. 2, pp. 981–6.

—— and Tracy Barrett (2005). *The Ancient Chinese World* (Oxford: Oxford University Press).

Knaul, Livia (1982). 'Lost Chuang-tzu Passages', *Journal of Chinese Religions* 10, pp. 53–79.

Kohn, Livia (ed.) (1993). *The Taoist Experience: An Anthology* (Albany, State University of New York Press).

—— (1994). *The Five Precepts of the Venerable Lord, Monumenta Serica* 42, pp. 171–215.

—— (2001). *Daoism and Chinese Culture* (Cambridge MA, Three Pines Press).

—— (2004a). 'The 180 Precepts of Lord Lao', in Livia Kohn (ed.), *Cosmos and Community: The Ethical Dimension of Daoism* (Cambridge MA, Three Pines Press), pp. 136–44.

—— (2004b). 'The Essential Precepts of Master Redpine', in Livia Kohn (ed.), *Cosmos and Community: The Ethical Dimension of Daoism* (Cambridge MA, Three Pines Press), pp. 154–67.

—— (2004c). 'The Northern Celestial Masters', in Livia Kohn (ed.), *Daoism Handbook* (Boston, Brill), pp. 283–308.

—— (2004d). 'Rules from the Demon Statues of Nuqing', in Livia Kohn (ed.), *Supplement to Cosmos and Community* (Cambridge MA, Three Pines Press), pp. 6–9.

—— and Russell Kirkland (2004). 'Daoism in the Tang (618–907)', in Livia Kohn (ed.), *Daoism Handbook* (Boston, Brill), pp. 339–83.

—— and Harold Roth (eds) (2002). *Daoist Identity: History, Lineage, and Ritual* (Honolulu, University of Hawaii Press).

Komjathy, Louis (2003). *Title Index to Daoist Collections* (Cambridge MA, Three Pines).

LaFargue, Michael (1992). *The Tao of the Tao-te-ching* (Albany, State University of New York Press).

Lagerwey, John (1992). 'The Pilgrimage to Wu-tang Shan', in Susan Naquin and Chun-fang Yu (eds), *Pilgrims and Sacred Sites in China* (Berkeley, University of California Press), pp. 293–332.

Lau, D.C. (1963). *Tao Tê Ching* (Baltimore, Penguin Books).

—— and Roger Ames (trans.) (1998). *Yuan Dao: Tracing Dao to Its Source* (New York, Ballantine).

Legeza, Laszlo (1975). *Tao Magic: The Secret Language of Diagrams and Calligraphy* (London, Thames and Hudson).

Legge, James (1861a). *The Confucian Analects; The Great Learning; The Doctrine of the Mean, The Chinese Classics: with a Translation, Critical and Exegetical Notes, Prolegomena, and Copious Indexes,* vol. 1 (Hong Kong, At the Author's, London, Trubner & Co).

—— (1861b). *The Works of Mencius, The Chinese Classics: with a Translation, Critical and Exegetical Notes, Prolegomena, and Copious Indexes,* vol. 2 (Hong Kong, At the Author's, London, Trubner & Co).

—— (1880). *The Religions of China: Confucianism and Taoism Described and Compared with Christianity* (London, Hodder and Stoughton).

—— (1897). 'Notes of My Life'. Helen Edith Legge's 160-page typed and edited manuscript now in the Bodleian Library, Oxford University.

Little, Stephen (2000). *Taoism and the Arts of China* (Chicago, The Art Institute of Chicago).

—— (2004). 'Daoist Art', in Livia Kohn (ed.), *Daoism Handbook* (Boston, Brill), pp. 709–46.

Liu Xiaogan (1994). *Classifying the Chuang-tzu Chapters* (Ann Arbor, Center for Chinese Studies, University of Michigan).

Loewe, Michael and Edward L. Shaughnessy (eds) (1999). *The Cambridge History of Ancient China* (Cambridge: Cambridge University Press).

Loon, Piet van der (1984). *Taoist Books in the Libraries of the Sung Period* (London, Oxford Oriental Institute).

Mair, Victor (1997). *Wandering on the Way: Early Taoist Tales and Parables of Chuang Tzu* (New York, Bantam).

Miller, James (2003). *Daoism: A Short Introduction* (Oxford, One World Publications).

Moeller, Hans-Georg (2004). *Daoism Explained: From the Dream of the Butterfly to the Fishnet Allegory* (Chicago, Open Court).

Munakara Kiyohiko (1991). *Sacred Mountains in Chinese Art* (Urbana, University of Illinois Press).

Nickerson, Peter (1994). 'The Great Petition for Sepulchral Plaints', in Stephen Bokenkamp (ed.), *Early Daoist Scriptures* (Berkeley, University of California Press), pp. 230–74.

—— (2004). 'The Southern Celestial Masters', in Livia Kohn (ed.), *Daoism Handbook* (Boston, Brill), pp. 256–82.

Nivison, David (1996). '"Virtue" in Bone and Bronze', in David Nivison and Bryan Van Norden (eds), *The Ways of Confucianism: Investigations in Chinese Philosophy* (Chicago, Open Court), pp. 17–30.

Penny, Benjamin (2004). 'Immortality and Transcendence', in Livra Kohn (ed.), *Daoism Handbook* (Boston, Brill), pp. 109–33.

Porter, Bill (1991). *The Road to Heaven: Encounters with Chinese Hermits* (San Francisco, Mercury House).

Pound, Ezra (1915) *Cathay* (London, Elkins Mathews).

Pregadio, Fabrizio (2004). 'Elixirs and Alchemy', in Livia Kohn (ed.), *Daoism Handbook* (Boston, Brill), pp. 165–95.

—— (ed.) (2007). *Encyclopedia of Taoism*, vol. 1 (London, Routledge).

Rexroth, Kenneth (1971). *One Hundred Poems from the Chinese* (New York, New Directions).

Robinet, Isabelle (1997). *Taoism: Growth of a Religion*, trans. Phyllis Brooks (Stanford CA, Stanford University Press).

—— (2004). 'Shangqing – Highest Clarity', in Livia Kohn (ed.), *Daoism Handbook* (Boston, Brill), pp. 196–224.

Roth, Harold (1991). 'Who Compiled the Chuang-tzu?', in Henry Rosemont, Jr (ed.), *Chinese Texts and Philosophical Contexts* (La Salle IL, Open Court), pp. 79–128.

—— (1999). *Original Tao: Inward Training (Nei-yeh) and the Foundations of Taoist Mysticism* (New York, Columbia University Press).

Said, Edward (1985). *Orientalism* (Harmondsworth, Penguin).

Sakade Yoshinobu (2004). 'Divination as Daoist Practice', in Livia Kohn (ed.), *Daoism Handbook* (Boston, Brill), pp. 541–66.

Sakai, Tadao (1970). 'Confucianism and Popular Educational Works', in William Theodore de Bary (ed.), *Self and Society in Ming Thought* (New York, Columbia University Press).

Schafer, Edward (1977). *Pacing the Void: Tang Approaches to the Stars* (Berkeley, University of California Press).

Schipper, Kristofer (1985). 'Taoist Ritual and Local Cults of the T'ang Dynasty', in Michel Strickmann (ed.), *Tantric and Taoist Studies in Honour of R.A. Stein* (Brussels: Institut Belge des Hautes Etudes Chinoises), vol. 3, pp. 812–34.

—— (1994). *The Taoist Body* (Berkeley, University of California Press).

—— (2001). 'Daoist Ecology: The Inner Transformation. A Study of the Early Daoist Ecclesia', in Norman Giradot, James Miller and Liu Xiaogan (eds), *Daoism and Ecology* (Cambridge MA, Harvard University Press), pp. 79–93.

—— and Franciscus Verellen (eds) (2004). *The Taoist Canon: A Historical Companion to the Daozang*, 2 vols (Chicago, University of Chicago Press).

Seidel, Anna (1997). 'The Unofficial High Religion of China', *Taoist Resources* 7, pp. 39–72.

Siegler, Elijah (2003). *The Dao of America: The History and Practice of American Daoism*, PhD dissertation, University of California, Santa Barbara.

Skar, Lowell (2004). 'Ritual Movements, Deity Cults and the Transformation of Daoism in Song and Yuan Times', in Livia Kohn (ed.), *Daoism Handbook* (Boston, Brill), pp. 413–63.

Smith, Richard (1990). 'Ritual in Ch'ing culture', in Liu Kwang-Ching (ed.), *Orthodoxy in Late Imperial China* (Berkeley, University of California Press), pp. 281–310.

—— (1991). *Fortune-tellers and Philosophers: Divination in Traditional Chinese Society* (Boulder CO, Westwood).

Spence, Jonathan (1996). *God's Chinese Son: The Taiping Heavenly Kingdom of Hong Xiuquan* (New York, W.W. Norton).

Sun Xiaochun and Jacob Kistermaker (1997). *The Chinese Sky During the Han* (Leiden, E.J. Brill).

Tang Xianzu (2002) *The Peony Pavilion*, trans. Cyril Birch (Bloomington, Indiana University Press).

Thompson, Lydia (2001). 'The Empress' New Clothes: A Daoist Ordination Scroll and Female Authority in the Ming Period'. Accessed on March 1, 2005. www.foxthompson.net/ldt/

aaszhang/

Toshiaki, Yamada (2004). 'The Lingbao School', in Livia Kohn (ed.), *Daoism Handbook* (Boston, Brill), pp. 225–55.

Vankeerberghen, Griet (2001). *The Huainanzi and Liu An's Claim to Moral Authority* (Albany, State University of New York Press).

Verellen, Franciscus (1995). 'The Beyond Within: Grotto-Heavens (*dongtian*) in Taoist Ritual and Cosmology', *Cahiers d'Extreme-Asie* 8, pp. 265–90.

Von Glahn, Richard (2004). *The Sinister Way: The Divine and the Demonic in Chinese Religious Culture* (Berkeley, University of California Press).

Watson, Burton (trans.) (1968). *The Complete Works of Chuang-tzu* (New York, Columbia University Press).

Wiggins, Sally (2004). *The Silk Road Journey with Xuanzang* (Boulder CO, Westview).

Wong, Eva (trans.) (2003). *Lao-Tzu's Treatise on the Response of the Tao: A Contemporary Translation of the Most Popular Taoist Book in China* (Walnut Creek CA, Alta Mira Press).

Wu Hung (2000). 'Mapping Early Taoist Art: The Visual Culture of Wudoumi Dao', in Stephen Little, *Taoism and the Arts of China* (Chicago, The Art Institute of Chicago), pp. 77–111.

Yao, Tao-Chung (2004). 'Quanzhen – Complete Perfection', in Livia Kohn (ed.), *Daoism Handbook* (Boston, Brill), pp. 567–93.

Yu, Anthony (trans.) (1977–83). *The Journey to the West*, 4 vols (Chicago, University of Chicago Press).

Yu Yingshi (1964). 'Life and Immortality in the Mind of Han China', *Harvard Journal of Asiatic Studies* 25, pp. 80–122.

Index